THE COMPLETE VEGETABLE COOKBOOK

THE
COMPLETE
VEGETABLE
COOKBOOK

MARY NORWAK

BISON BOOKS

Published by Bison Books Ltd
4 Cromwell Place, London SW7

CONTENTS

Vegetables are universal. All over the world they are enjoyed as part of a meal or as a complete meal, and the variety of vegetable recipes seems almost endless. For many people, vegetables have been the staple diet for centuries. Once meat was only for rich people and special occasions, but as countries became more affluent, vegetables often became no more than an accompaniment to a dish of meat or fish. In today's more stringent economic climate, vegetables are again replacing meat or fish as main meals, and many people feel that it is morally preferable to live on a vegetable diet rather than using land for cultivating grain crops for feeding cattle.

The Ancient Greeks counseled moderation in all things, and perhaps this is a wise rule for the kitchen. Those who are not dedicated vegetarians can enjoy delicious vegetables on their own or accompanied by meat or fish, and may enhance their dishes with a knob of butter, a little chicken or beef stock, or perhaps some chopped crisp bacon. Aromatic seasonings, spices and herbs all add to the pleasure of vegetables and will appeal to everyone who cooks and eats for pleasure.

Whether vegetables are home-grown or bought from markets, they must always be young and fresh for maximum flavor and perfect texture. Always pick or buy them in small quantities and rush them to the kitchen for immediate cooking – no vegetable is improved by hanging around in a warm place. Treat each vegetable as a beautiful thing, eat it raw or cook it with loving care, and you will enjoy my harvest of international recipes.

HOW TO COOK VEGETABLES

Vegetables are beautiful. Most of them are delicious raw, but when they are cooked, they deserve star treatment. Vegetables suffer sadly from over-cooking, drowning in gallons of water, and elaborate dressing. In all the recipes in this book, light cooking is recommended and careful timing is essential to produce the best results – many vegetables are best served when still *al dente* or slightly crisp when bitten. Try a variety of ways of cooking each vegetable to see which suits individual palates best.

Boiling

Use a large pan for cooking vegetables to avoid spillage, but do not make this an excuse for drowning the vegetables. Only just cover them in lightly salted boiling water, and never add the old-fashioned baking soda (this used to be done to keep a good green color, but it also destroys the nutritive value of vegetables). Cook until just tender, drain very thoroughly and serve hot with a knob of butter or other dressing.

Steaming

If you do not like the idea of losing valuable nutrients in cooking water, steam vegetables instead. Do this by putting them in a steamer, a colander standing in simmering water, or a double boiler, always ensuring that the lid is tightly on to catch the steam. Again, just cook the vegetables until they are tender and they will be full of flavor.

Braising

This method of cooking conserves the flavor, and saves fuel if the vegetables are put into an oven at the same time as meat or a sweet dish. Put the vegetables into a tightly lidded ovenproof dish and just cover with water or stock, well-seasoned with salt and pepper. Cook at 180°C/350°F/Gas Mark 4 for 20–25 minutes. The vegetables may be served in the cooking juices, or the liquid can be reduced by fast boiling in a clean pan to produce a glaze. Add a knob of butter to this glaze and pour over the vegetables.

Roasting

Root vegetables are extremely good when cooking around a roasting joint in the pan juices. Try boiling potatoes, parsnips, Jerusalem artichokes, turnips or rutabagas for 5 minutes first, then draining them well and putting them round the meat for 45 minutes –1 hour, basting occasionally with the hot fat from the joint.

Frying

Root vegetables are also good fried, and Jerusalem artichokes and celeriac for instance make excellent chips in the same way as potatoes. Always use plenty of clean hot fat, and fry quickly until the vegetable is soft and pale. Lift out of the fat for a few seconds to allow the fat temperature to rise again and then plunge back the vegetables into the very hot fat to become golden and crisp.

Stir-Frying

Eastern cooks specialize in cooking vegetables very quickly by the stir-fry method, so that they remain slightly crisp and full of flavor. For this method of frying use a large shallow heavy pan and hot oil. Usually 2 tablespoons/30 ml oil will be enough for a 1 lb/500 g batch of vegetables. Cut the vegetables into very thin slices or into small diagonal chunks or matchsticks. Add to the hot fat and stir quickly over high heat for 1–2 minutes. Add a little stock, dry wine, or sauce thickened with cornstarch (cornflour), together with any seasoning, and continue cooking and stirring quickly for 2 minutes before serving at once.

Casseroling

Very small young vegetables such as green peas, baby carrots, tiny onions or broad beans may be cooked in a casserole in the oven. Put the vegetables into an ovenware casserole with a tight-fitting lid. For 1 lb/500 g vegetables add 3 tablespoons/45 ml water and $\frac{1}{4}$ cup/2 oz/50 g butter with seasoning. Cover and cook at 180°C/350°F/Gas Mark 4 for 25–30 minutes until the vegetables are tender. Adjust seasoning, sprinkle with fresh herbs and serve with the cooking liquid.

Stuffing

Many vegetables can be stuffed to make a complete meal. Squash, zucchini, cucumber, peppers, eggplants, tomatoes and mushrooms are all suitable for hollowing out and filling with a meat, cheese, breadcrumb or rice stuffing, with plenty of seasoning and herbs. A homemade tomato or mushroom sauce or brown gravy may be added before or after baking the stuffed vegetables.

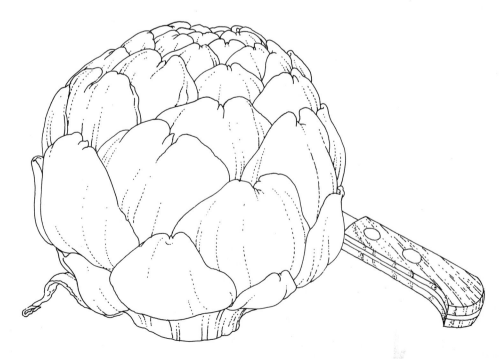

How to Make Salads

Salads may be made from many traditional salad vegetables such as lettuce, radishes, cucumber and tomatoes, but they may also be made from a wide variety of other raw vegetables, and from lightly cooked ones.

Salad Vegetables

Prepare the individual salad vegetables and serve them individually rather than in a mixed bowl. Serve each vegetable in its own dressing with an appropriate topping of herbs. Each person can assemble his own choice of salads, and each bowl remains fresh and attractive.

Raw Vegetables

Try carrots, celeriac, cabbage, celery, peppers, cauliflower flowerets, mushrooms, green peas and broad beans. Keep peas and beans and very small mushrooms whole, but cut the other kinds in thin slices, or in chunks or matchstick pieces, or grate them coarsely. Make the vegetables very crisp by leaving them to stand for 30 minutes in chilled salted water before draining and serving with coarse sea salt, or with lemon juice, French dressing, Mayonnaise or Aioli (recipes on pages 11–12).

Cooked Vegetables

Cooked young leeks, asparagus and globe artichokes may be served slightly warm and dressed with French dressing. Other vegetables, either freshly cooked or leftover, may be mixed or left in individual bowls dressed with French dressing or with Mayonnaise. A more substantial salad can be made by mixing beans, peas or cauliflower with a root vegetable such as potatoes or celeriac.

The Art of Seasoning

All good cooks keep a range of seasonings and herbs by the kitchen stove so that they can flavor each dish individually. Each vegetable has its complementary herb (see Herbs pages 174–79), but the correct seasoning is just as important.

Salt is essential to bring out the flavor of vegetables and the best salt to use is sea salt. This may be in fine flakes or of a coarser texture which needs grinding in a mill before use. Garlic salt, celery salt and onion salt are useful, but beware of adding extra salt to the recipe.

Pepper should always be freshly ground in a mill as the ready-ground variety quickly loses flavor. Black peppercorns are most commonly used and have a fine flavor, but the specks of dark powder can spoil the appearance of dishes and of sauces in particular. It is worth keeping a special mill full of white peppercorns.

Mustard is available in powder and made up in jars. A pinch of mustard powder is

Below : Left, globe artichoke and right, a steamer full of fresh vegetables.

useful in some dishes, but it is a good idea to keep a range of 'made' mustards to give variety to seasoning. A small spoonful of mustard made with wine or lemon juice for instance can enhance dressings beyond recognition.

Spices should be fresh, but they tend to get musty once opened, or if stored for any length of time. Buy only small packs of ground spice, or grind whole spices in a small mill so that the flavor is fresh every time.

Oil can make a great difference to the flavor of both cooked vegetables and salads. Olive oil has a strong distinctive flavor which some people do not care for, and sesame, peanut or sunflower oils can be substituted. Commercial frying oils will give a crisp texture to food, but should be tried in small quantities first in case the flavor is not liked. Walnut oil is particularly delicious for salads.

Vinegar can be vicious stuff and should be chosen with care. Ordinary malt vinegar will color and flavor strongly. If the flavor is liked, but brown coloring is not needed, use white vinegar. Cider vinegar, white and red wine vinegar have a better flavor. Herb-flavored vinegars add an extra savor, and tarragon, garlic and fennel are the most useful to keep available.

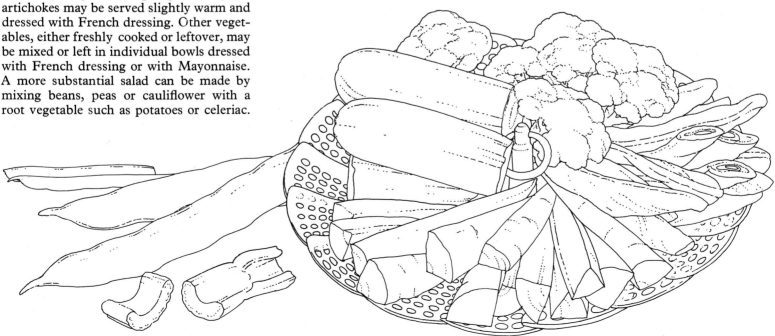

Basic Recipes

Although many of the recipes in this book are complete in themselves, some of them need a basic starting point such as ordinary pastry, white sauce or French dressing. To avoid tedious repetition, here are the most important basic recipes which will be needed.

Basic White Sauce

2⅔ cups/ 1 pint/ 500 ml milk
1 small onion
Sprig of parsley
Sprig of thyme
1 bay leaf
6 peppercorns (½ teaspoon pepper)
Pinch of salt
3 tablespoons/ 1½ oz/ 40 g butter
6 tablespoons/ 1½ oz/ 40 g flour

Put the milk into a pan with the onion, parsley, thyme, bay leaf, peppercorns and salt, and heat gently for 10 minutes without boiling. Strain the milk. Melt the butter in a heavy saucepan and stir in the flour. Cook for 1 minute and then work in the milk a little at a time, stirring all the time to make the sauce smooth. Keep stirring when all the milk has been added, until the sauce comes to the boil. Check seasoning and use as required. This sauce may be used to coat such vegetables as cauliflower and squash. Cheese, chopped herbs, hard-boiled eggs and other flavorings may be added at the end of cooking. The sauce is also a useful base for vegetable soups.

Herb Butters

⅜ cup/ 3 oz/ 75 g butter
Fresh herbs

Suitable herbs to use include mint, parsley, chives, fennel and dill which should be finely chopped. Garlic should be crushed and fresh horseradish finely grated. Soften the butter without melting it. Cream the butter with the chosen herb and then cool until the butter is just firm. A squeeze of lemon juice may be added. Shape the butter into a cylinder about 1½ in (3.75 cm) across,

and cut with a sharp knife into circular pats. These pieces of butter may be made up in advance and refrigerated until needed. Serve pats of herb-flavored butter on portions of vegetables, or in bowls of vegetable soup.

French Dressing (Vinaigrette)

3 parts olive or salad oil
1 part wine vinegar or lemon juice
Pinch of salt
Pinch of mustard powder

Mix the vinegar or lemon juice in a bowl with the salt and mustard. Stir well and slowly beat in the oil until mixed. The oil will float to the top if the dressing stands, but can be beaten again before serving. It is worth making up a large quantity of this dressing, storing it in a screwtop jar in a cold place; the jar only needs shaking just before some of the dressing is needed. A little pepper, a pinch of sugar and some chopped fresh herbs may be added. This dressing is useful for salads and also for pouring over just warm leeks, asparagus and globe artichokes.

Easy Mayonnaise

1 egg
1 tablespoon/ 15 ml vinegar or lemon juice
½ teaspoon/ 2.5 g salt
1 teaspoon/ 5 g sugar
Pinch of mustard powder
Pinch of pepper
1⅓ cups/ ½ pint/ 250 ml olive oil

Put the whole egg, vinegar or lemon juice and seasonings in a bowl and work together with a spoon to make a paste. Slowly beat in the oil, drop by drop until the mayonnaise is thick. This mayonnaise has a creamy texture which is very suitable for serving with vegetable salads, and it can be made very quickly and easily in a blender running on low speed. Salad oil may be substituted for olive oil.

Aioli (Garlic Sauce)

3 garlic cloves
2 egg yolks
Salt and pepper
1 teaspoon/ 5 g mustard powder
¾ cup/ 7 fl oz/ 175 ml olive oil
1 teaspoon/ 5 ml lemon juice

Crush the garlic cloves and work in the egg yolks, salt, pepper and mustard. Mix thoroughly and then add the olive oil gradually drop by drop, beating with a wooden spoon or wire whisk. When all the oil has been incorporated and the mixture is thick, stir in the lemon juice. This garlic mayonnaise sometimes has a few breadcrumbs added. It is excellent served with plainly cooked vegetables such as beans, onions, fennel and globe artichokes.

Hollandaise Sauce

1½ tablespoons/ 23 ml lemon juice
1 tablespoon/ 15 ml cold water
1 egg yolk
Salt and white pepper
⅝ cup/ 5 oz/ 125 g butter

The butter should be soft, but not melted, before starting this recipe. Put the lemon juice, water, egg yolk, salt, pepper and one-third butter into a bowl over hot water. Beat thoroughly until the butter has melted. Add the rest of the butter in small pieces gradually, beating until the sauce thickens like mayonnaise. The water beneath the bowl should be hot but not boiling as it will spoil the sauce if it splashes into the mixture. This sauce is particularly good served with rather delicately flavored vegetables such as asparagus and globe artichokes.

Basic Batter

1 cup/ 4 oz/ 100 g flour
¼ teaspoon/ 1.25 g salt
1 egg
⅔ cup/ ¼ pint/ 125 ml milk

Sift the flour and salt into a bowl. Make a well in the center and drop in the beaten egg. Gradually add half the milk, drawing the flour into the center. Beat thoroughly, until the mixture is smooth and bubbly. Cover the bowl and leave in a cool place for 30 minutes. Stir in the remaining milk just before cooking. Beer may be substituted for milk and will make a very crisp batter. This batter is useful for coating vegetables such as cauliflower flowerets, small pieces of celeriac, tiny Jerusalem artichokes and frying them until crisp and golden to make an appetizing first course.

Basic Pancakes

1 cup/ 4 oz/ 100 g flour
¼ teaspoon/ 1.25 g salt
1 egg
1⅓ cups/ ½ pint/ 250 ml milk

Sift the flour and salt into a bowl. Make a well in the center and drop in the beaten egg. Gradually add half the milk, drawing the flour into the center. Beat thoroughly, until the mixture is smooth and bubbly. Cover the bowl and leave in a cool place for 30 minutes. Stir in the remaining milk just before cooking. This will make eight 8-in (20 cm) pancakes. Pancakes can be filled with freshly cooked or leftover vegetables, and make a complete meal if coated with cheese sauce, mushroom sauce or tomato sauce.

Basic Pastry

Note: This recipe makes 2 cups/ 8 oz/ 225 g of pastry.

2 cups/ 8 oz/ 225 g flour
½ teaspoon/ 2.5 g salt
¼ cup/ 2 oz/ 50 g margarine
¼ cup/ 2 oz/ 50 g lard
2–3 tablespoons/ 30–45 ml cold water

Sift the flour and salt into a bowl and cut in the fat in pieces. Rub into the flour until the mixture is like fine breadcrumbs. Add the water and mix to a soft dough. Turn out on to a floured board and knead lightly until smooth. Roll out to required thickness to line a pie plate or to cover a pie dish. This pastry is useful for making savory pies with fresh vegetables in an egg custard, or leftover vegetables in white sauce or cheese sauce. The pastry may be made more savory if ½ cup/ 4 oz/ 100 g grated hard cheese is added with a little pepper, and the pastry is mixed with 1 egg yolk and 2 teaspoons/ 10 ml cold water.

A-Z
OF VEGETABLES

Where a recipe is asterisked, it
indicates that there is a color
illustration for that recipe.

All recipes are prepared for 4-6 servings

Acorn Squash

see Squash

Afou

see Yam

Ai-kwa

see Eggplant

All-Good

see Good King Henry

American Cress

see Cress

Artichoke, Globe

The globe artichoke is a kind of thistle of which the budding head is eaten. The heart or 'fond' at the base of the heart is surrounded by small prickly leafy bracts which enclose the fluffy embryonic flower or 'choke' which is discarded. Artichokes may be eaten with melted butter, Hollandaise sauce or French dressing, but the hole left by the discarded 'choke' may be stuffed. The hearts alone are used for dishes, particularly in France, Italy and Spain.

To prepare globe artichokes, strip off the large outside leaves, cut off the stalks and trim the bases neatly, rubbing with lemon to prevent blackening. Snip across the end of each leaf to within 2 in (5 cm) of the base. Remove the inner 'choke' with a sharp knife. Cook head down in boiling salted water with a squeeze of lemon juice and simmer for 20–25 minutes until an outside leaf will pull out easily. Drain very thoroughly and serve with butter or chosen sauce. To eat the artichoke, pull off leaves one at a time, dip into sauce and nibble off the tender base of the leaf, discarding the rest. At the base of

Right : Globe Artichoke

the artichoke, the heart is finished by cutting into pieces and dipping in the sauce.

To prepare artichoke hearts for dishes, cook the whole artichokes and then take off the leaves to expose the hearts.

Stuffed Artichokes

4 globe artichokes
1⅓ cups/ ½ pint/ 250 ml stock or white wine
⅔ cup/ 4 oz/ 100 g minced cooked ham
⅓ cup/ 2 oz/ 50 g mushrooms
1 small onion
1 garlic clove
¼ cup/ 2 oz/ 50 g butter
Salt and pepper

Cook artichokes until just tender. Mix together the ham, finely chopped mushrooms and onions, and crushed garlic and put this stuffing inside the artichokes. Put the stock or white wine into an ovenware dish and put in the artichokes close together. Cover and cook at 180°C/350°F/Gas Mark 4 for 25 minutes. Lift them on to hot serving plates. Add the butter to the liquid left in the cooking pan and heat until the butter has melted. Season to taste and use as a sauce.

Artichokes in White Wine

6 large globe artichokes
⅓ cup/ 2 oz/ 50 g lean pork
7 slices of bacon
1 small onion
2–3 tablespoons/ 30 ml olive oil
1⅓ cups/ 8 oz/ 225 g mushrooms
Salt and pepper
⅔ cup/ ¼ pint/ 125 ml white wine
⅔ cup/ ¼ pint/ 125 ml chicken stock

Trim the bases of the artichokes and cut off half the tops. Boil in salted water for 10 minutes, drop into cold water and drain thoroughly. Scrape out the 'choke' from each artichoke. Mince the pork with 1 slice of bacon and mix with finely chopped onion. Cook gently in a thick pan until just turning color and then add oil, chopped mushrooms and seasoning. Cook for 5 minutes, stirring well. Drain off fat and reserve it. Fill the artichokes with the meat mixture. Tie a slice of bacon round each artichoke and fry lightly in the reserved fat. Add the wine and stock, cover and cook at 170°C/325°F/Gas Mark 3 for 1 hour. Remove the string from the artichokes before serving.

Fried Artichokes

12 small young globe artichokes
6 tablespoons/ 1½ oz/ 40 g flour
1 egg yolk
1 tablespoon/ 15 ml olive oil
Salt and pepper
½ cup/ 4 fl oz/ 120 ml water
Oil for frying
1 lemon

Very small young artichokes are essential for this dish. Trim the bases and cut off one-third of the tops. Pull off outer leaves and cut each artichoke into four pieces. Put the artichokes into ice-cold water while the batter is prepared. Put flour, egg yolk, oil and seasoning into a bowl. Mix well and gradually add the water to make a thick creamy batter. Whisk the egg white to stiff peaks and fold into the batter. Dip the artichoke pieces into the batter and fry in deep hot oil until golden. Serve with quarters of lemon.

Tartare Artichokes

6 large globe artichokes
2 anchovy fillets
1 shallot
3 sprigs of tarragon

Below : Jerusalem Artichoke

1 tablespoon/ 15 g capers
1 tablespoon/ 15 ml wine vinegar
2 egg yolks
⅜ cup/ 3 fl oz/ 90 ml olive oil

Trim the bases and tops of the artichokes and boil in salted water for 20 minutes until the bases are tender. Drain very well. Meanwhile, make the sauce by chopping very finely the anchovies, shallot, tarragon and capers. Work in the vinegar and then the egg yolks, then the oil drop by drop until the mixture is like mayonnaise (the sauce is most easily made in a blender). Serve over the artichokes.

Artichoke Salad

8 small globe artichokes
1 tablespoon/ 15 ml lemon juice
Salt and pepper
4–5 tablespoons/ 60 ml olive oil
2–3 tablespoons/ 30 ml wine vinegar
1 teaspoon/ 5 g chopped chervil
1 teaspoon/ 5 g chopped chives
Cooked prawns (or shrimps)
Stuffed olives

Wash and trim the artichokes and cut them into quarters. Scoop out the 'chokes' and rub the cut sides of the artichokes with lemon juice. Boil in salted water with a squeeze of lemon juice for 10 minutes. Drain well and put into a buttered pan over very low heat. Season well and simmer gently until tender, then leave until cold. Just before serving, mix the oil, vinegar and herbs. Put the artichokes into a serving bowl, pour over the dressing, and add plenty of prawns and olives. Anchovies may be used as well if liked.

Italian Artichokes

4 globe artichokes
4 garlic cloves
½ cup/ 4 fl oz/ 120 ml olive oil
4 anchovy fillets
1⅓ cups/ ½ pint/ 250 ml white wine
1 tablespoon/ 15 ml capers
2 tablespoons/ 1 oz/ 25 g grated
   Parmesan cheese

Cook the artichokes until just tender. Drain them well and put them into an ovenware dish. Crush the garlic cloves and chop the anchovy fillets. Mix the garlic, half the oil

and the anchovy fillets, and stuff the artichokes with the mixture. Put the remaining oil and the wine into the dish. Cover tightly and cook at 180°C/350°F/Gas Mark 4 for 25 minutes. Lift the artichokes on to hot serving plates. Add the capers to the cooking liquid and use as sauce. Sprinkle cheese on the artichokes just before serving.

Artichoke, Japanese or Chinese

The Japanese or Chinese artichoke is a small knotted tuber 2–3 in (5–7.5 cm) long. It is white and crisp when dug, but quickly turns brown and softens. The flavor is sweet and nutty, more like a sweet potato than an artichoke. Japanese artichokes may be scrubbed, sliced and eaten raw with salt or an oil-and-vinegar dressing. For cooking, it is best to wash them well, put into boiling water for a minute and then rub off skins with a clean cloth. These tubers may be boiled and served with butter, a cream sauce or cheese sauce, or put round a roasting joint to absorb the meat juices.

Artichoke, Jerusalem

The Jerusalem artichoke is a member of the sunflower family, and is said to derive its name from the Italian *girasole* or sunflower, which became corrupted to 'Jerusalem' by the British.

It is more likely that the name was a corruption of Artischokappeln van Ter Neusen, this being the name of the Dutch town where they were cultivated by Pastor Petrus Hondius who sent tubers to friends in London, and they were known in England before the name of *girasole* was applied to them in Italy. The French name of *topinambour* derives from the fact that they arrived in France at the same time as some odd-looking savages from the Topinambous tribe were brought to Paris from Brazil and exhibited by the Seigneur de Razilly — the tubers were also considered to be curious-looking.

Artichokes with Cheese*

1½ lb/ 750 g Jerusalem artichokes
1⅓ cups/ ½ pint/ 250 ml white sauce
Salt and pepper
Pinch of nutmeg
6 tablespoons/ 3 oz/ 75 g grated cheese

Peel the artichokes thinly and boil them in just enough water to cover for about 20 minutes until tender. Drain, but keep ⅔ cup/ ¼ pint/ 125 ml cooking liquid. Cut the artichokes in slices and arrange in a shallow ovenware dish. Mix the sauce with the cooking liquid, season well with salt, pepper and nutmeg, and pour over the vegetables. Sprinkle on the cheese and grill (broil) until golden-brown.

Artichoke and Scallop Soup

1 medium onion
¼ cup/ 2 oz/ 50 g butter
1½ lb/ 750 g Jerusalem artichokes
2⅔ cups/ 1 pint/ 500 ml chicken stock
Salt and pepper
2 scallops
5–6 tablespoons/ 75 ml white wine
5–6 tablespoons/ 75 ml water
⅔ cup/ ¼ pint/ 125 ml milk
2–3 tablespoons/ 30 ml cream
1 tablespoon chopped parsley

Peel the onion and chop it finely. Soften in the butter until golden. Peel the artichokes and chop them, and add to the onion. Cover and cook over low heat for 5 minutes. Stir in the stock and seasoning and simmer very gently for 25 minutes until the artichokes are tender. Take off the heat, cool and liquidize in a blender or sieve. Clean the scallops and poach them in the wine and water for 4 minutes until just tender. Slice them thinly and add to the artichoke purée together with the cooking liquid. Reheat gently and stir in the milk. When hot, stir in the cream and parsley and serve at once.

Braised Artichokes

1 lb/ 500 g Jerusalem artichokes
1⅓ cups/ 8 oz/ 225 g button onions
¼ cup/ 2 oz/ 50 g butter
2 tablespoons/ 1 oz/ 25 g sugar
Salt and pepper

Peel the artichokes and onions and leave them whole. Melt the butter in a heavy flameproof casserole and stir in the sugar. Add the artichokes and onions and toss in the butter mixture. Season with salt and pepper, cover and cook at 170°C/325°F/Gas Mark 3 for 1 hour. Serve hot with meat or fish.

Cream of Artichoke Soup

2 lb/ 1 kg Jerusalem artichokes
¼ cup/ 2 oz/ 50 g butter
1 medium onion
2 celery sticks
2 bay leaves
Salt and pepper
2⅔ cups/ 1 pint/ 500 ml creamy milk
1 tablespoon/ 15 g chopped parsley

Peel the artichokes and chop them. Melt the butter and cook the sliced onion until soft and golden. Add the artichokes, chopped celery, bay leaves and seasoning. Cover and cook very gently for 20 minutes until the vegetables are soft. Remove the bay leaves. Put through a sieve, or liquidize in a blender. Add the milk and reheat, adjusting the seasoning. Serve very hot, sprinkled with parsley.

Artichoke Pancakes

1 lb/ 500 g Jerusalem artichokes
1 small onion
1 egg
Salt and pepper
4 tablespoons/ 1 oz/ 25 g flour

Peel the artichokes thinly, grate them, and drain off surplus juice. Grate the onion and mix with the artichokes, beaten egg, seasoning and flour. Do not leave the mixture to stand, or surplus liquid will run out. Fry spoonfuls of the mixture in hot oil until golden, and serve hot with broiled or grilled meat or fish, or with bacon.

Asparagus

Asparagus is said to be a native plant from Asia, whence it spread to the tables of Ancient Rome, but it also grows wild in the sandy soils of the Rhône and Loire valleys of France. Asparagus was a popular vegetable in England from the middle of the eighteenth century, when it was known as sparrow-grass by the street sellers.

There are three basic types of asparagus – the white, the violet and the green. The thick white Argenteuil asparagus with a pale purple tip is prized for its size but does not have the fine flavor of the thinner green English asparagus. The Italian or Genoa asparagus, violet in color, is free-growing but the flavor is not so good.

Asparagus stems should be prepared by snapping off or cutting the tough bottoms of the stalks, removing any scales and washing the stalks well. Asparagus is spoiled by overcooking, and the Emperor Augustus, when he wanted anything to be done quickly, said 'Let this be done quicker than you would cook asparagus,' since it was traditionally cooked very slowly. It is an art to cook the asparagus stems until just tender, but still slightly firm to the bite and yet retain the green tips which should only be steamed until tender and not mushy. Asparagus should be cooked 'standing,' so that the stems are in water but the tips are above. The stems should be put into small bundles of equal length, and the stems should be of equal thickness, not a mixture of thick and thin which take different cooking times. If an asparagus boiler is not available, use a narrow, very deep pan, and in it bring the water to boiling point. Put in the asparagus bundles so that the tips are above the water, and put on a lid so that a little steam can escape. Cook for 15–20 minutes and drain well. Cold water should never be used, or the flavor will be ruined. Serve hot with melted butter or Hollandaise sauce, or cold in a French dressing or with mayonnaise.

The thin hard green stems of asparagus known as sprue which are either the wild variety or thinnings from an asparagus bed, have a good flavor and are excellent for soup or to add to egg dishes. Cooked asparagus tips are often used as a garnish for dishes or are added to salads.

Below : Asparagus

Dutch Asparagus

2 lb/ 1 kg asparagus
½ cup/ 4 oz/ 100 g butter
2 tablespoons/ ½ oz/ 15 g flour
1⅓ cups/ ½ pint/ 250 ml chicken stock
2 bay leaves
1 tablespoon/ 15 g chopped parsley
1 shallot
Salt and pepper
3 egg yolks
Juice of ½ lemon

Prepare the asparagus and cook until tender. Drain and put on to a serving dish. Melt the butter and work in the flour. Cook for 1 minute, then stir in chicken stock, bay leaves, parsley, finely chopped shallot, salt and pepper. Bring to the boil and simmer for 5 minutes. Take off the heat. Put the egg yolks and lemon juice in a bowl and beat into the sauce. Pour over the asparagus and serve at once.

Japanese Asparagus

2 lb/ 1 kg asparagus
3–4 tablespoons/ 45 ml peanut oil
1 tablespoon/ 15 g sea salt

Clean the asparagus and cut in extreme diagonal slices about 2 in (5 cm) long. Cook in boiling water for 10 minutes and drain very well. Heat the oil in a heavy pan and stir-fry the asparagus pieces over high heat for about 2 minutes until they are almost crisp. Drain with a slotted spoon, dust liberally with salt and serve at once.

Asparagus Soup

2 lb/ 1 kg asparagus
8 cups/ 3 pints/ 1.5 liters chicken stock
2 tablespoons/ 1 oz/ 25 g butter
2 tablespoons/ ½ oz/ 15 g flour
Salt and pepper
Pinch of ground nutmeg
⅔ cup/ ¼ pint/ 125 ml cream
2 egg yolks

Trim about 2-in (5 cm) tips from the asparagus and keep in reserve. Cut the stalks in 1-in (2.5 cm) lengths and put into a saucepan with the stock. Simmer gently for 1 hour, crushing the asparagus into the stock as it softens. Put through a strainer, pressing the asparagus well, but discarding the pulp. Melt the butter and work in the flour. Cook for 2 minutes and work in a little of the soup. Continue cooking and stirring and gradually add the remaining soup. Add the salt and pepper, a pinch of nutmeg and the asparagus tips and simmer for 15 minutes. Heat the cream gently but do not boil. Remove from the heat and mix in the egg yolks. Put into a soup tureen, and pour in the hot soup, mixing well. Serve with fried or toasted bread cubes.

Asparagus in Lemon Butter

1 lb/ 500 g asparagus
⅜ cup/ 3 oz/ 75 g unsalted butter
1 teaspoon/ 5 ml lemon juice
Salt and pepper

Cook the asparagus and drain very thoroughly. Melt the butter, stir in the lemon juice and season to taste. Pour over the asparagus and serve hot.

Asparagus Pie

2 cups/ 8 oz/ 225 g basic pastry (see
   page 12)
1 lb/ 500 g asparagus
1⅓ cups/ ½ pint/ 250 ml milk
3 eggs
½ cup/ 3 oz/ 75 g Cheddar cheese

Roll out the pastry and line a pie plate. Prick all over with a fork, line with foil and baking beads and bake at 200°C/400°F/Gas Mark 6 for 10 minutes. Remove the beads and foil. Cook the asparagus until just tender and then cut into 2-in (5 cm) lengths. Mix together the milk, eggs, salt, pepper and grated cheese. Arrange the asparagus in the pastry shell, putting the green tips at the top. Pour on the milk mixture. Bake at 180°C/350°F/Gas Mark 4 for 30 minutes. Serve hot or cold.

Asparagus in Almond Cream Sauce

1 lb/ 500 g asparagus
½ cup/ 4 oz/ 100 g butter
2–3 tablespoons/ 30 ml cream
Juice of ½ lemon
Pepper
½ cup/ 3 oz/ 75 g split toasted almonds

Prepare and cook the asparagus until tender. Drain and put on to a serving dish. Melt the butter gently and add the cream. Stir until bubbling, then stir in the lemon juice, pepper and almonds, and pour over the asparagus.

Asparagus Broccoli

see Calabrese

Asparagus Peas

see Peas, Asparagus

Aubergine

see Eggplant

Autumn Cabbage

see Cabbage

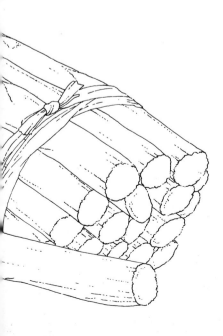

Italian Asparagus*

2 lb/ 1 kg asparagus
¼ cup/ 2 fl oz/ 60 ml olive oil
2 garlic cloves
Salt and pepper
2 teaspoons/ 10 ml lemon juice
Grated Parmesan cheese

Cook the asparagus and drain it well. Put it onto a warm serving dish. Heat the oil with the crushed garlic cloves, and season with salt, pepper and lemon juice. Pour over the asparagus, and sprinkle on grated cheese.

Bamboo Shoots

The young ivory-colored sprouts of several kinds of bamboo are used a great deal in Oriental cooking. They are cut just as they push above the soil, and when young and tender may be cooked with the same recipes as asparagus. Bamboo shoots are most commonly bought canned, and only a small quantity is usually necessary in a recipe. Once a can has been opened, unused shoots should be placed in cold water, covered and stored in the refrigerator. The water should be changed daily and it is best to use them quickly as they soon lose their nutty flavor and texture. Bamboo shoots are usually sliced thinly or cubed and added to a recipe at the last minute so that they are not over-cooked. They may also be added to seafood or chicken salads, or to clear soup.

Bamboo Shoots and Prawns*

½ lb/ 225 g drained bamboo shoots
1 lb/ 500 g cooked prawns (or shrimps)
2 tablespoons/ ½ oz/ 15 g cornstarch
1 tablespoon/ 15 ml soy sauce
1 tablespoon/ 15 ml dry sherry
½ teaspoon/ 2.5 g ground ginger
2–3 tablespoons/ 30 ml peanut oil
12 scallions
⅓ cup/ 2 oz/ 50 g cooked green peas

Cut the bamboo shoots in cubes. Cut the prawns in half and put into a bowl. Mix the cornstarch, soy sauce, sherry and ginger. Pour over the prawns and leave for 30 minutes. Heat the oil in a large shallow thick pan and stir in the prawns. Stir-fry for 1 minute, then add the bamboo shoots and thinly sliced scallions and stir fry for 2 minutes. Add the peas, stir well and serve at once with rice.

Banana Squash

see Squash

Batata

see Sweet Potato

Batinjan

see Eggplant

Beans, Broad†

Broad beans, also known as Windsor beans and horse beans were well known in the ancient world, but considered unlucky, and they were consecrated to the dead. The little black spot on the bean was looked on as a sign of death, and although the bean was offered as a sacrifice to Apollo, the priests were strictly forbidden to eat or touch it, or even mention its name. It is in fact one of the most delicious beans and high in protein, but like so many vegetables is best eaten when very young. The very young pods may also be eaten, but usually the beans are shelled and cooked in boiling salted water. As the beans become older, their skins become tough and may be removed after cooking so that the beans are easier and more pleasant to eat. Skinned broad beans make an excellent purée and are also good in salads. Traditional accompaniments to broad beans are bacon and parsley sauce, and they may also be cooked with the herb, savory.

†Note: Lima beans may be substituted for broad beans in most of the following recipes.

Broad Bean Soup

1½ lb/ 750 g shelled broad beans
8 cups/ 3 pints/ 1.5 liters water
2 slices of bacon
1 small onion
2 tablespoons/ 1 oz/ 25 g butter
4 tablespoons/ 1 oz/ 25 g flour
Salt and pepper
Chopped parsley

Put the beans into boiling water and cook for 10 minutes. Drain and keep the cooking liquid. Slip the skins off the beans. Chop the bacon and onion finely and cook in the butter until soft and golden. Mix in the flour and then gradually add the cooking liquid. Heat gently, stirring well, until the mixture is smooth. Add the cooked beans and heat through. Press through a sieve, or liquidize in a blender. Season with salt and pepper, reheat and serve garnished with parsley.

Broad Beans in their Pods

1 lb/ 500 g broad beans in pods
Salt and pepper
Squeeze of lemon juice
Chopped parsley
¼ cup/ 2 oz/ 50 g butter
3–4 tablespoons/ 45 ml whipping
  cream

Use very young beans and keep them in their pods. Top and tail the pods and pare thinly down the sides. Cook whole in unsalted boiling water for 15 minutes. Drain

Above : An opened broad bean pod

well. Add salt and pepper, lemon juice, parsley, butter and cream and heat through gently before serving.

Broad Beans in White Wine

1 lb/ 500 g shelled broad beans
2 tablespoons/ 1 oz/ 25 g butter
1 small onion
4 tablespoons/ 1 oz/ 25 g flour
$\frac{2}{3}$ cup/ $\frac{1}{4}$ pint/ 125 ml dry white wine
$\frac{2}{3}$ cup/ $\frac{1}{4}$ pint/ 125 ml chicken stock
Sprig of marjoram
Salt and pepper
1 teaspoon/ 5 g sugar

Melt the butter and cook the finely chopped onion until soft but not colored. Stir in the flour and cook for 1 minute. Add the wine and stock, chopped marjoram, seasoning and sugar. Add the beans. Bring to the boil and cook for 10 minutes.

Roman Broad Beans

1 lb/ 500 g shelled broad beans
1 medium onion
2–3 tablespoons/ 30 ml olive oil
1 tablespoon/ 15 g chopped sage
2 teaspoons/ 10 g concentrated tomato purée
Salt and pepper

Chop the onion and cook in the oil until soft and golden. Add the sage, tomato purée,

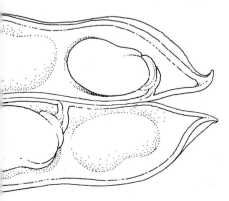

seasoning and beans and just cover with boiling water. Stir well and boil for 10 minutes until the liquid has reduced and just covers the beans. Serve hot or cold. This is particularly good with a thick slice of grilled ham.

Broad Beans with Lamb*

1 lb/ 500 g shelled broad beans
1 lb/ 500 g shoulder lamb
3–4 tablespoons/ 45 ml butter
1 tablespoon/ 15 ml olive oil
1 medium onion
1 garlic clove
$\frac{2}{3}$ cup/ $\frac{1}{4}$ pint/ 125 ml water
Salt and pepper
Chopped parsley

Cut the lamb into cubes and brown in the butter and oil, stirring often so that they are evenly cooked. Chop the onion and crush the garlic, and add to the lamb. Pour in the water and simmer for 10 minutes. Add the beans and water, cover the saucepan and simmer for 10 minutes. Serve hot, sprinkled with chopped parsley.

Broad Bean Salad

1 lb/ 500 g shelled broad beans
1 teaspoon/ 5 g paprika
1 teaspoon/ 5 g mustard
1 garlic clove
Salt and pepper
1 tablespoon/ 15 g chopped parsley
1 tablespoon/15 ml wine vinegar
3–4 tablespoons/ 45 ml olive oil

Cook the beans in boiling water until tender. Slip them from their skins while still hot. Mix the mustard, paprika, crushed garlic, salt, pepper, parsley, vinegar and oil. Add the beans and toss them in the mustard dressing.

Beans, Dried

see Pulses pages 162–73
(Dried beans included in the Pulse Chapter are Adzuki, black, black-eyed, boriotti, broad, brown Dutch, butter, Egyptian brown, flageolets, haricot, lima, navy, pearl, red kidney, soya, white haricot)

Beans, French, String or Dwarf

There are many varieties of the low-growing dwarf bean, including some which can be dried to use as pulses. They probably originated in a sub-tropical climate and are certainly much favored in Mediterranean countries. Dwarf beans must be cooked when young, small and tender and are best cooked whole, with only the ends snipped off. Larger beans may be cut in chunks, but they should never be shredded, and they are excellent simply dressed with butter and seasoning.

French Bean and Almond Soup

$\frac{3}{4}$ lb/ 350 g French beans
5 cups/ 2 pints/ 1 liter chicken stock
$\frac{1}{3}$ cup/ 2 oz/ 50 g almonds
2 tablespoons/ 1 oz/ 25 g butter
1 teaspoon/ 5 ml lemon juice
Salt and pepper

Cut the beans in $\frac{1}{2}$-in (1.25 cm) lengths and cook in the chicken stock. Dip the almonds in hot water and then cold, and remove the skins. Melt the butter, brown the almonds and chop them roughly. Season the beans with lemon juice, salt and pepper and stir in the almonds. Serve hot.

Creamed Beans

1 lb/ 500 g French beans
1 small onion
1 small green pepper
2 slices of bacon
Salt and pepper
3–4 tablespoons/ 45 ml cream

Cut the beans in chunks and cook until tender. Chop the onion, green pepper and bacon finely. Put the bacon into a pan and heat until the fat begins to run. Add the onion and pepper and cook gently for 5 minutes. Add the beans with $\frac{2}{3}$ cup/ $\frac{1}{4}$ pint/ 125 ml water and cover tightly. Simmer for 15 minutes, watching carefully so that the beans do not burn. Season well with salt and pepper. Remove from the heat and stir in the cream.

Bamboo Shoots and Prawns

see page 22

bamboo shoots
cooked prawns (or shrimps)
cornstarch
soy sauce
dry sherry
ground ginger
peanut oil
scallions
cooked peas

Broad Beans
with Lamb

see page 23

broad beans (or lima beans)
shoulder of lamb
butter
olive oil
onion
garlic
water
salt and pepper
parsley

Bean Salad

1 lb/ 500 g French beans
French dressing
½ cup/ 3 oz/ 75 g anchovy fillets
2 hard-boiled eggs

Cut the beans into chunks and cook until tender. Cool slightly, then toss in French dressing. Arrange in a serving dish and garnish with drained anchovies and finely chopped eggs.

Beans, Mung or Chinese

see Bean Sprouts

Bean Sprouts

The mung or Chinese bean is used for producing bean sprouts which are widely used in Oriental cooking. Adzuki beans and soya beans may be sprouted in the same way. To grow the beans, put about 1 tablespoon/ ½ oz/ 15 g seeds into a clean jam jar and cut a piece of cheesecloth which will fit over the opening, securing with an elastic band. Fill with tepid water through the cheesecloth and shake vigorously. Drain and repeat the process three times. Put the container on its side where a warm temperature 20–31°C/68–86°F can be maintained. Every morning and evening, fill the jar with tepid

Right : Bean sprouts can be grown from mung (or Chinese) beans.

water and drain it off. The sprouts will be ready to harvest in four days, and should be rinsed well before using. The sprouts may be eaten raw or stir-fried in recipes.

Bean Sprout Salad*

1 cup/ 8 oz/ 225 g bean sprouts
3 celery sticks
2 large carrots
⅓ cup/ 2 oz/ 50 g cashew nuts
1 tablespoon/ 15 g sesame seeds
French dressing
Lettuce

Mix together the bean sprouts, finely chopped celery and grated carrots. Add chopped nuts and sesame seeds and toss lightly in French dressing. Serve on a bed of lettuce.

Bean Sprout Eggs

¼ cup/ 2 oz/ 50 g butter
4 eggs
1 cup/ 8 oz/ 250 g bean sprouts

Melt the butter and stir in the beaten eggs. Cook gently, stirring until eggs begin to set. Season and stir in bean sprouts.

Beans, Runner or String

Runner beans or green beans are grown for the eating value of their seed pods, not for the seeds themselves. They are best eaten when young and tender, and small ones need only have the side strings removed before cooking in boiling salted water. Larger beans may be cut in chunks before cooking, but the beans should never be allowed to grow long, strong and tough. It is a great mistake to shred the beans in the traditional way as the flavor is lost in the cooking water and the texture becomes mushy. A little of the herb, savory, enhances the flavor of runner beans if added to the cooking water. Hot runner beans are delicious with a dressing of butter and seasoning, and are good with poultry, and with boiled ham. They pair well with mushrooms, almonds and chestnuts in hot dishes, and make a good salad with tomatoes.

Bean Salad

1 lb/ 500 g French or runner beans
1 small onion
1 tablespoon/ 15 ml wine vinegar
3 tablespoons/ 45 ml oil
Squeeze of lemon juice
Salt and pepper
Pinch of sugar
1 tablespoon/ 15 g chopped parsley

Cook the beans in boiling salted water until just tender. Drain and put into a serving dish. Peel the onion and chop very finely.

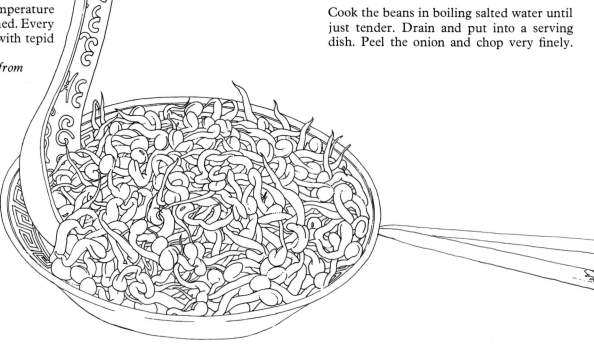

Sprinkle on the beans. Beat together the vinegar, oil, lemon juice, salt, pepper and sugar and pour over the beans. Sprinkle with parsley. This salad is particularly good when paired with a tomato salad.

Salt Pickle for Beans

1 lb/ 500 g block cooking salt
3 lb/ 1.5 kg runner beans

It is important to use block or bag cooking salt, and not table salt which contains chemicals which make it unsuitable for preservation. Use glass or stoneware jars for storing the beans. Wash and dry young, fresh, tender beans and remove any strings. Put a layer of salt in the jar and then a layer of beans. Continue with alternate layers, pressing down each layer well, and finishing with a layer of salt. Cover and leave for a few days until the beans have shrunk and the jar needs topping up. Put in more layers of beans and salt, finishing with a layer of salt. The salt will draw moisture from the beans and become a strong brine. Cover with a moisture-proof lid such as cork or plastic material tied down tightly. If using stoneware jars, do not stand them on stone, brick or concrete floors as they will draw up moisture. If the beans do not keep and become slimy, it is because insufficient salt has been added, or the beans have not been pressed down enough and air pockets have formed allowing bacteria and molds to develop.

To use the beans, remove the quantity needed from the jar and wash thoroughly in several waters. Soak for 2 hours in warm water, but do not soak overnight or the beans will toughen. Cook in boiling water without salt until the beans are tender.

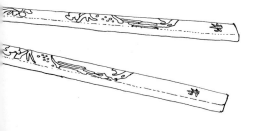

Beans with Mushrooms

1 lb/ 500 g runner beans
1 small onion
1 small green pepper
2 slices of bacon
1½ cups/ 9 oz/ 250 g mushrooms
⅜ cup/ 3 oz/ 75 g butter
Pinch of nutmeg
¼ cup/ 2 fl oz/ 60 ml cream

Remove the tips from the beans and cut them in half if they are large. Chop the onion, pepper and bacon in small pieces. Put the bacon in a thick pan and heat gently until the fat runs. Add the onion and pepper and cook until soft and golden. Add the beans and ⅔ cup/ ¼ pint/ 125 ml water, cover tightly and cook gently for 15 minutes until the beans are tender. Meanwhile wipe the mushrooms and cook them in the butter for 5 minutes. Drain off liquid from the beans and mix them with the mushrooms. Season with nutmeg and stir in the cream.

Beets

Beets were used frequently in ancient Greece and Rome, and Apicius who wrote an early cookbook gave several recipes for the vegetable, often combining them with leeks. One favorite recipe was for cooking beets in gravy and raisin wine with salt, pepper, coriander and cumin.

While beets are often only used these days for salads and pickles, they are one of the most delicious vegetables to eat hot as an accompaniment to meat, or as an important soup ingredient. Because of their sweetness, they blend well with fruit like apples, oranges, and lemons, but can also combine with other root or green vegetables. Chives and caraway are the herbs to enhance the flavor of beets.

Beets are commonly boiled, but the flavor is better if they are baked.

To boil beets, cut off the leaves and wash the beets, but do not scratch or cut any roots or fibers, or the juice will run out during cooking and leave the beets pale. Put into boiling salted water, cover and simmer gently until tender. Small beets will take about 1½ to 2 hours. Take from the water, cut off the roots and rub off the skin and fibers.

To bake beets cut off the leaves and wash thoroughly without damage. Put into a baking tin and bake at 180°C/350°F/Gas Mark 4 for 1½ to 2 hours until tender. Rub off the skins.

Beet Soup (1)

8 medium beets
1 small onion
2 cups/ ¾ pint/ 375 ml chicken stock
Salt and pepper
Juice of 1 lemon
1 tablespoon/ 15 ml clear honey
Pinch of ground cloves
⅔ cup/ ¼ pint/ 125 ml soured cream
Chopped chives

Wash the beets without breaking the skin and simmer until tender. Drain the beets, reserving the cooking liquid. Peel them and put through a sieve with 1⅓ cups/ ½ pint/ 250 ml cooking water. Mix with finely chopped onion, stock, and seasonings, and simmer for 10 minutes. Serve with a garnish of soured cream and chopped chives.

Beet Soup (2)

1 lb/ 500 g lean stewing beef
13 cups/ 5 pints/ 8 liters water
1½ lb/ 750 g beets
2 teaspoons/ 10 g salt
⅔ cup/ 4 oz/ 100 g shredded carrots
2 large onions
1 tablespoon/ 15 ml tomato purée
1 tablespoon/15 ml wine vinegar
Salt and pepper
Soured cream

Cut the beef into small pieces and simmer in the water with a lid on until the meat is falling apart. Chop the beets finely and add them to the beef, together with shredded carrots, chopped onion, tomato paste and vinegar. Cover and simmer until the vegetables are tender and the soup is thick. Season to taste and serve hot with spoonfuls of sour cream in each bowl.

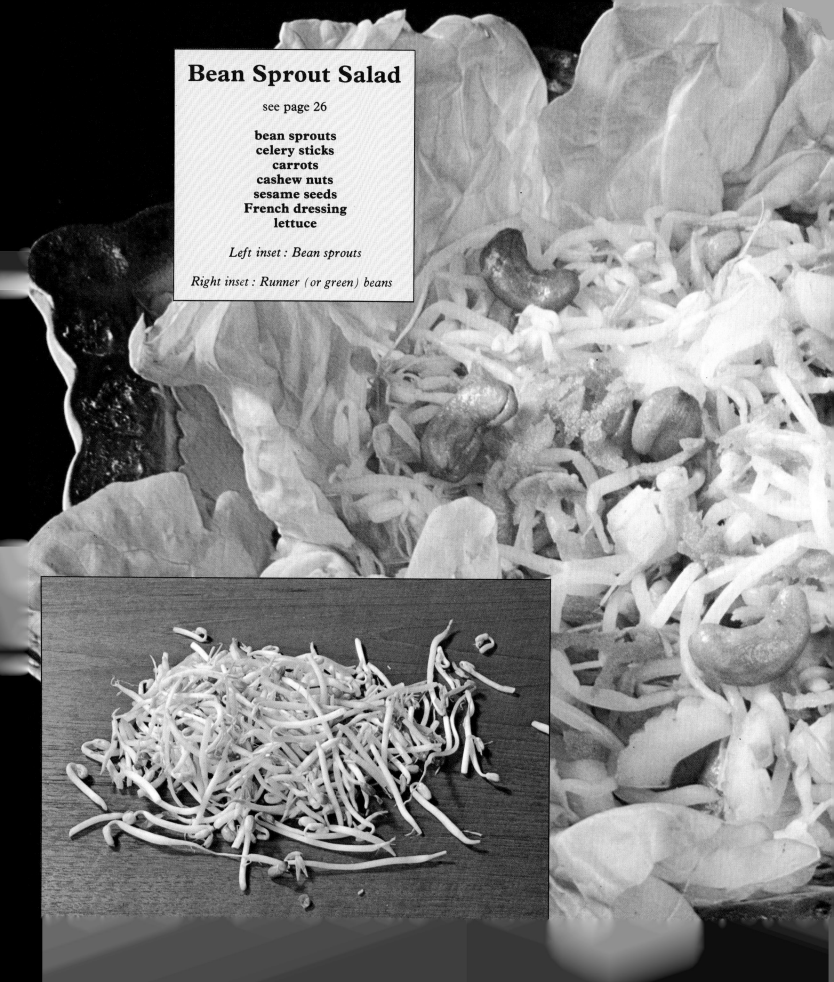

Bean Sprout Salad

see page 26

bean sprouts
celery sticks
carrots
cashew nuts
sesame seeds
French dressing
lettuce

Left inset : Bean sprouts

Right inset : Runner (or green) beans

Beet Soup (3)

10 cups/ 4 pints/ 2.5 liters stock
½ lb/ 8 oz/ 225 g beets
½ lb/ 8 oz/ 225 g potatoes
½ lb/ 8 oz/ 225 g cooking apples
½ lb/ 8 oz/ 225 g cabbage
Salt and pepper
2 teaspoons/ 10 g sugar
1 teaspoon/ 5 ml lemon juice

Put the stock into a saucepan and add grated cooked beets, grated raw potatoes and apples, and finely shredded cabbage. Add salt, pepper and sugar and simmer for 30 minutes. Stir in lemon juice and serve very hot. This is one of the many variations of *Borsch* which comes from Poland and Russia. Soured cream is a traditional accompaniment, and a few caraway seeds may be added. A very rich soup can be made with stock from beef, bacon and a duck simmered together – the meat is cut up to add to the soup, together with crisp thin sausages fried in goose fat.

Sweet and Sour Beets

1 lb/ 500 g beets
2 tablespoons/ 1 oz/ 25 g sugar
2 tablespoons/ ½ oz/ 15 g flour
2–3 tablespoons/ 30 ml water
⅔ cup/ ¼ pint/ 125 ml vinegar
½ teaspoon/ 2.5 g chopped dill
Salt and pepper
2 tablespoons/ 1 oz/ 25 g butter

Cook the beets, peel and cut in slices. Mix the sugar, flour, water and vinegar in a small thick saucepan and bring to the boil, stirring well. Simmer until thick and creamy. Add the beets, dill, salt and pepper and stir until coated with the sauce. Cover and simmer very gently for 10 minutes. Put into a serving dish and top with the butter.

Beets in Cream Sauce

6 medium beets
1 tablespoon/ ½ oz/ 15 g butter
2 tablespoons/ ½ oz/ 15 g flour
1⅓ cups/ ½ pint/ 250 ml cream
Salt and pepper
1 tablespoon/ 15 g chopped chives

Boil the beets, peel and cut into small dice. Keep warm while the sauce is prepared. Melt the butter, stir in the flour and cook for 1 minute. Stir in the cream, seasoning and chives and bring to the boil. Simmer for 4 minutes, pour over the beets and serve at once.

Beets in Soured Cream*

1 lb/ 500 g cooked beets
Scant 1⅓ cups/ ½ pint/ 250 ml soured cream
2–3 tablespoons/ 30 g chopped chives
Crisp lettuce leaves

Cut the beets into matchstick shapes or small cubes, and arrange on a bed of lettuce leaves. In winter, chicory (American endive) may be used instead. Top with soured cream and a sprinkling of chives. Serve very cold.

Beets in Orange Sauce

6 small cooked beets
¼ cup/ 2 oz/ 50 g butter
½ cup/ 2 oz/ 50 g flour
2 cups/ ¾ pint/ 375 ml water
2 cups/ ¾ pint/ 375 ml orange juice
Rind of 2 oranges
2 teaspoons/ 10 g soft brown sugar
Salt and pepper

Slice the beets thinly Melt the butter in a thick saucepan and stir in the flour. Cook for 2 minutes, stirring well and then work in the water and orange juice. Simmer and stir well until the sauce begins to thicken. Add the orange rind, sugar, salt and pepper and simmer for 3 minutes. Stir in the slices of beet and serve hot. This is very good with ham.

Dutch Beets

2 large beets
1 large onion
¼ cup/ 2 oz/ 50 g butter
4 cooking apples
Salt and pepper
Ground nutmeg
Chopped chives

Cook the beets, peel and chop roughly. Chop the onion finely and cook in the butter, with a lid on, until the onion is soft but not colored. Add the beets. Peel, core and chop the apple, and add to the mixture. Simmer for about 30 minutes until a thick purée is formed. Season well with salt, pepper and nutmeg and sprinkle with chopped chives. Serve with rich meat such as duck, ham, pork or sausages.

Baked Beets with Parmesan

18 small beets
1⅓ cups/ ½ pint/ 250 ml cream
Salt and pepper
1 tablespoon/ 15 g chopped chives
¼ cup/ 2 oz/ 50 g grated Parmesan cheese
2 tablespoons/ 1 oz/ 25 g butter

Boil the beets, peel and keep whole. Put into a greased ovenware dish. Mix the cream with seasoning, chives and cheese and pour over the beets. Dot with flakes of butter. Bake at 180°C/350°F/Gas Mark 4 for 20 minutes and serve hot.

Beet Salad

5 medium cooked beets
2–3 tablespoons/ 30 ml oil
1 tablespoon/ 15 ml red wine vinegar
1 garlic clove
Salt and pepper
1 teaspoon/ 5 g caraway seeds
1 tablespoon/ 15 g chopped parsley

Slice the beets thinly into a serving dish. Mix the oil and vinegar, crushed garlic, salt and pepper and stir in the caraway seeds. Pour over the beets and sprinkle with parsley.

Beet Chutney

2 lb/ 1 kg beets
2 medium onions
1 lb/ 500 g apples
1 cup/ 8 oz/ 225 g sugar
2⅔ cups/ 1 pint/ 500 ml vinegar
¼ teaspoon/ 1.25 g ground ginger
½ teaspoon/ 2.5 g salt
1 tablespoon/ 15 ml lemon juice

Below : Beet

Wash the beets well without breaking the roots, and then boil them in water until tender. Cool and peel, and dice the beets quite finely. Peel the onions and apples and cut them in cubes. Put the onions and apples into a saucepan with the sugar, vinegar, ginger, salt and lemon juice, and boil for 30 minutes. Add the beet cubes and simmer for 15 minutes. Pour into clean jars, cool and cover tightly with vinegar-proof lids.

Beet Pickle

8 medium beets
2 teaspoons/ 8 g black peppercorns
2 teaspoons/ 8 g whole allspice
1 teaspoon/ 5 g salt
2 tablespoons/ 1 oz/ 25 g grated horseradish
5 cups/ 2 pints/ 1 liter vinegar

Wash the beets well without breaking the skin or breaking off the roots. Cook until tender. Cool the beets, skin and cut into slices or dice. Put into clean jars. Put the peppercorns, allspice, salt, horseradish and vinegar into a saucepan and bring to the boil. Boil for 2 minutes and cool. Pour over the beets and cover tightly with vinegar-proof lids.

Beet Relish

1 lb/ 500 g cooked beets
½ lb/ 8 oz/ 225 g horseradish root
½ cup/ 4 oz/ 125 g sugar
Pinch of salt
1⅓ cup/ ½ pint/ 250 ml white wine vinegar
3–4 tablespoons/ 45 g chopped dill

Grate the beets and horseradish coarsely. Mix in all the other ingredients until well blended. Put into screwtop jars with vinegar-proof lids and store in a cool place.

Khrain

1 medium beet
¼ lb/ 4 oz/ 100 g horseradish root
2 teaspoons/ 10 g brown sugar
Juice of 1 lemon

Do not cook the beet, but peel it and grate finely. Peel and grate the horseradish finely. Mix together with the sugar and lemon juice and put into a screwtop jar. Store in the refrigerator.

Belgian Endive

see Chicory, English

Bell-isle

see Cress

Berenjena

see Eggplant

Berinjela

see Eggplant

Black Salsify

see Scorzonera

Blett/Blite

see Good King Henry

Blewit

see Mushroom

Bok-Choi

see Pak-Choi

Borecole Kale

see Kale

Brinjal

see Eggplant

Inset top: Purple-sprouting broccoli is sown later in spring and can be harvested throughout the winter and into spring.

Inset above: Brussels sprouts can be grown so that they can be cropped from autumn through winter into late spring.

Green broccoli or calabrese can be grown in any well-drained and sunny position in the spring and can be harvested in late summer.

Broad Beans

see Beans, Broad

Broccoli

This member of the cabbage family is a variety of cauliflower with small white or purple heads, or with green heads known as calabrese. The plant is a native of southern Europe, and although it was enjoyed by the Romans some two thousand years ago, was not introduced to France and England until the eighteenth century, and did not reach America until the 1920s.

Broccoli heads should be used very fresh with close heads which are not breaking into flower, and there should be no yellowing stems or leaves. Cook in boiling water without a lid and drain very carefully so that the heads do not break. Serve with melted butter and seasoning, or with Hollandaise sauce, or chill and serve in an oil and vinegar dressing or mayonnaise. Broccoli takes well to many garnishes, such as crisp bacon, nuts, coriander and nutmeg.

Creamed Broccoli

1 lb/ 500 g broccoli
1 cup/ 8 fl oz/ 225 ml soured cream
2 tablespoons/ ½ oz/ 15 g flour
1 tablespoon/ ½ oz/ 15 g grated
  horseradish
1 teaspoon/ 5 ml wine vinegar
Salt and pepper

Clean and wash the broccoli and cook in boiling water for 15 minutes. Drain well. See that the soured cream is at room temperature, or it may curdle when heated. Mix the cream and flour together and put into a bowl over boiling water, or the top of a double boiler. Cook until warm and smooth, stirring all the time. Add the remaining ingredients and pour over the hot broccoli. A few oven-browned almonds may be scattered on top of the sauce. Serve with ham, pork or veal.

Italian Broccoli

1 lb/ 500 g broccoli
2 garlic cloves
¼ cup/ 2 fl oz/ 50 ml olive oil
¼ cup/ 2 oz/ 50 g cooked ham
Salt and pepper
2 tablespoons/ 1 oz/ 25 g grated
  Parmesan cheese

Clean and wash the broccoli and cook in boiling water for 15 minutes. Drain well. Crush the garlic cloves and warm in the olive oil. Stir in the finely chopped ham and season well. Pour over the broccoli and sprinkle grated cheese on top.

Broccoli Hollandaise

2 lb/ 1 kg broccoli
⅜ cup/ 3 oz/ 75 g butter
2 egg yolks
Juice of ½ lemon
Pinch of white pepper

Clean and wash the broccoli and cook in boiling water for 25 minutes. Drain well and put on a serving dish. Meanwhile, melt the butter gently but do not boil. Put the egg yolks in a bowl over hot water and beat with the lemon juice and pepper until creamy. Take off the heat and stir in the butter until well mixed. Pour over broccoli.

Brussels Sprouts

Sprouts are members of the cabbage family, the little green knobs growing up the thick stem topped with a tuft of leaves. They are best cooked when very fresh, small and hard, rather than when large and leafy. They should be bright green in color and very firm. Sprouts lose their texture and special flavor very quickly, and overcooking is a serious fault when dealing with them. They should be steamed or cooked rapidly in only a little boiling water before being dressed with plenty of butter and seasoning. A pinch of cayenne pepper, paprika or ground nutmeg enhances the flavor of sprouts, and they pair well with both almonds and chestnuts, and also with a sprinkling of strongly-flavored cheese such as Parmesan.

Sprout Soup

2 lb/ 1 kg Brussels sprouts
6½ cups/ 2½ pints/ 1.5 liters chicken stock
2 tablespoons/ 1 oz/ 25 g butter
4 tablespoons/ 1 oz/ 25 g flour
1 tablespoon/ 15 ml lemon juice
Pinch of nutmeg
Salt and pepper
Grated cheese

Clean the sprouts and simmer them in stock for 10 minutes. Reserve 10 small sprouts, and put the rest through a sieve with the cooking liquid. Melt the butter and work in the flour. Add the puréed sprouts gradually and heat gently, stirring well until the mixture is creamy and smooth. Add the lemon juice, nutmeg, salt and pepper and simmer for 5 minutes. Serve hot garnished with sprouts.

Italian Sprouts

2 lb/ 1 kg small Brussels sprouts
2 tablespoons/ 1 oz/ 25 g butter
2–3 tablespoons/ 30 ml olive oil
2 tablespoons/ 1 oz/ 25 g fresh
  breadcrumbs
2 tablespoons/ 1 oz/ 25 g grated
  Parmesan cheese

Prepare the sprouts and cook them in boiling salted water for 10 minutes. Drain very thoroughly. Melt the butter and oil and fry quickly, tossing them well, until they begin to turn golden brown. Sprinkle on the breadcrumbs and cheese and stir well until the crumbs are golden. Serve very hot.

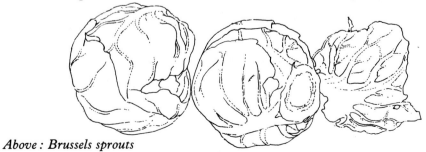

Above : Brussels sprouts

Brussels Sprouts with Chestnuts

see page 36

Brussels sprouts
butter
peeled chestnuts
sugar
beef stock
salt and pepper
cayenne pepper

Brussels Sprouts with Cheese

1 lb/ 500 g Brussels sprouts
2 tablespoons/ 1 oz/ 25 g butter
Salt and pepper
Ground nutmeg
2–3 tablespoons/ 30 ml cream
2 tablespoons/ 1 oz/ 25 g grated hard
  cheese

Cook the sprouts until just tender and drain very thoroughly. Put them into an ovenware dish and dot with the butter. Season with salt, pepper and a little nutmeg, and pour on the cream. Sprinkle with grated cheese and put under a hot grill (broiler) until the cheese is golden brown.

Sprouts in Lemon Sauce

2 lb/ 1 kg Brussels sprouts
½ cup/ 4 oz/ 100 g butter
4 tablespoons/1 oz/ 25 g flour
1¼ cups/ ½ pint/ 250 ml chicken stock
Salt and pepper
Pinch of paprika
Juice of 2 lemons

Cook the sprouts in boiling salted water until tender, drain them well and put into a deep serving dish. While they are cooking, make the sauce. Do this by melting the butter and stirring in the flour and stock, then cooking gently until it boils. Take off the heat, season with salt, pepper and paprika, and stir in the lemon juice. Pour over the sprouts and serve hot. This is particularly good with chicken.

Brussels Sprouts with Chestnuts*

2 lb/ 1 kg Brussels sprouts
½ cup/ 4 oz/ 100 g butter
1⅓ cups/ ½ lb/ 225 g peeled chestnuts
2 teaspoons/ 10 g sugar
⅔ cup/ ¼ pint/ 125 ml beef stock
Salt and pepper
Pinch of cayenne pepper

Cook the sprouts until just tender, then drain and toss them in half the butter over low heat until just golden. Meanwhile, pre-pare the chestnuts. Blanch them in boiling water to remove all the brown skin. Put into fresh water with a pinch of salt and boil until tender but not broken. Melt the sugar in the remaining butter and add the drained chestnuts. Stir over heat until they are golden brown. Add the chestnuts, stock and seasoning, and stir well together. Serve very hot.

Cabbage

There is a cabbage for every month of the year, for this ancient vegetable has been developed so that there are different varieties available according to the weather. *Spring cabbages* have less heart than the other kinds, but are young, tender and succulent, and need the minimum of cooking. *Summer* and *autumn cabbages* have more heart and should be firm, solid and fresh-looking. In *winter cabbage*, the heart is covered with darker, tough outer leaves, but even these can be used for soups to add flavor. *White cabbage* grown from Dutch and Danish strains, is particularly solid and therefore very popular for shredding and eating raw. The *Savoy cabbage* has particularly good keeping qualities, and has hard, dark-green heads with crimped outer leaves – this kind of cabbage is particularly good for stuffing. *Red cabbage* is a versatile vegetable, equally delicious cooked or pickled when raw. This is the only cabbage which actually benefits from long cooking and is the basis of many favorite European dishes which include vinegar, spice apples and onions.

Too often the cabbage is despised because it has been badly cooked, yet it has an honorable history as one of man's favorite vegetables. The Egyptians actually worshipped the cabbage at altars, giving special honor to the red cabbage, and it was served as the first dish at banquets. The Romans believed it would save them from drunkenness, and it was given as a remedy for colic and paralysis. Cato said that it had kept his family free from the plague. The old Saxon name of colewort given to the cabbage family is said by some, to have been the namesake of the favorite American salad, cole slaw. However, *Webster's Dictionary* says that cole slaw is derived from the Dutch 'kool sla,' meaning cabbage salad.

Raw crisp cabbage is delicious, and plainly cooked cabbage should always retain the slightly crisp nutty texture of the raw vegetable. It may be steamed or only lightly boiled in salted water before thorough draining and tossing in butter, salt and pepper.

Below: Winter cabbage

Cabbage Soup

½ small green cabbage
2 medium onions
1 garlic clove
4 tablespoons/ 2 oz/ 50 g butter
1 tablespoon/ 15 ml oil
2 potatoes
Salt and pepper
4 cups/ 1½ pints/ 750 ml stock
Crisp bacon

Shred the cabbage finely. Slice the onion and crush the garlic. Melt the butter with the oil and cook the onions and garlic for 5 minutes. Add the cabbage and stir over gentle heat until coated with fat. Peel and slice the potatoes. Add to the cabbage with the salt, pepper and stock, and bring to the boil. Reduce the heat, cover, and simmer for 30 minutes. Serve hot garnished with small pieces of crisp bacon.

Creamed Cabbage

1 small green cabbage
⅔ cup/ ¼ pint stock
3 tablespoons/ 1½ oz/ 40 g butter
Salt and pepper
⅔ cup/ ¼ pint/ 125 ml whipping cream
Ground nutmeg

Cut the cabbage into quarters and then cut each quarter in half lengthwise. Remove any tough stalk and put the cabbage in the stock, butter, salt and pepper. Cover and bring to the boil, then reduce the heat and simmer until the cabbage is just tender and most of the liquid has evaporated. Stir in the cream and a pinch of nutmeg and heat gently. A little grated horseradish is good stirred in at the last minute.

Braised Cabbage and Sausages*

1 large white cabbage
1⅓ cups/ ½ pint/ 250 ml stock
Salt and pepper
1 lb/ 500 g pork sausages
½ cup/ 4 oz/ 100 g butter

Cut the cabbage into eight segments and remove any tough stalk. Wash well and cook in boiling water for 10 minutes. Drain and rinse in cold water, then drain well again. Put into a buttered shallow ovenware dish and pour on the stock and season to taste. Cook the sausages until golden brown and arrange round the cabbage. Dot the surface with butter. Cover and cook at 200°C/400°F/ Gas Mark 6 for 30 minutes. If liked, cubes of ham or salt pork may be added as well.

Cabbage Braised in Beer

1 small green cabbage
1 medium onion
¼ cup/ 2 oz/ 50 g butter
3 slices of bacon
1 bay leaf
Salt and pepper
½ pint brown ale (or beer)

Cut the cabbage into eight sections and remove tough stalk. Chop the onion and put half into a greased ovenware dish. Put the cabbage on top and add the butter cut in small pieces. Cover with the chopped bacon, bay leaf, seasoning, remaining onion and the beer. Cover with a lid and cook at 180°C/350°F/Gas Mark 4 for 45 minutes.

Stuffed Cabbage

1 firm cabbage
4 tablespoons/ 2 oz/ 50 g long grain rice
1 small onion
1 tablespoon/ 15 g chopped parsley
1 lb/ 400 g pork sausage meat

Put the cabbage into a bowl and remove any discolored or bruised leaves. Pour on boiling water and leave to stand for 15 minutes. Drain, cover with boiling water and leave again for 15 minutes. Drain thoroughly. Meanwhile, cook the rice in boiling water for 12 minutes and drain well. Mix the rice, chopped onion, parsley and sausage meat together and season well. Cut the stalk out of the cabbage and put in some mixture. Fold over 2 or 3 leaves, cover with more mixture. Continue until each layer is stuffed. Tie in a cloth, put in a pan of beef or chicken stock and simmer for 1½ hours. Put cabbage in a dish and serve with butter. If liked, the cabbage may be cooked in a casserole at 180°C/350°F/Gas Mark 4.

Above: White cabbage is the most popular cabbage.

Cabbage Provençal

1 small green cabbage
1 medium onion
⅔ cup/ ¼ pint/ 125 ml red wine
Salt and pepper
1 garlic clove
2 slices of bacon
1 tablespoon/ 15 ml oil
4 tomatoes
1 tablespoon/ 15 ml concentrated tomato purée
⅓ cup/ 2 oz/ 50 g black olives

Shred the cabbage coarsely and put into a saucepan with the chopped onion, wine, salt and pepper. Cover and bring to the boil, then reduce the heat and simmer until the cabbage is just tender. Drain the cabbage well, reserving the liquid. Crush the garlic and chop the bacon and fry in oil for 3 minutes. Add the chopped tomatoes, tomato purée and the cooking liquid from the cabbage. Bring to the boil, add the olives and pour over the cabbage. This is particularly good with pork sausages.

Braised Cabbage and Sausages

see page 37

white cabbage
stock
salt and pepper
pork sausages
butter

Inset left : Red cabbage is attractive and appetizing.

Inset right : Winter cabbage

Oriental Cabbage

1 medium white cabbage
4–5 tablespoons/ 2 fl oz/ 60 ml peanut
    oil
2 scallions
1 small green pepper
1 small garlic clove
3–4 tablespoons/ 45 ml cider vinegar
2–3 tablespoons/ 30 ml dry sherry
2–3 tablespoons/ 30 ml soy sauce
1/4 cup/ 2 oz/ 50 g sugar
1/4 teaspoon/ 1.25 g chili powder
1/2 teaspoon/ 2.5 g salt
2 tablespoons/ 1/2 oz/ 15 g cornstarch
1 tablespoon/ 15 ml water

Cut the cabbage into 12 wedges and remove any coarse ribs and stalk. Put the oil into a thick pan and stir the chopped onions, green pepper and garlic over high heat until they begin to brown. Add the cabbage pieces and cook for 2 minutes. Add all the other ingredients except the cornstarch and water, cover and simmer for 3 minutes. Add the cornstarch mixed with water, blend in well and cook until the sauce thickens slightly. Serve hot.

Spiced Stuffed Cabbage Leaves

8 large cabbage leaves
1 tablespoon/ 15 ml oil
1 medium onion
1 lb/ 500 g raw ground beef
1 lb/ 450 g canned tomatoes
4 teaspoons/ 10 g cornstarch
2–3 tablespoons/ 30 ml Worcestershire
    sauce
1/4 teaspoon/ 15 g chopped parsley
Salt and pepper

Sauce
1 tablespoon/ 15 ml concentrated
    tomato purée
4 teaspoons/ 10 g cornstarch
1 teaspoon/ 5 ml Worcestershire sauce
1/2 teaspoon/ 2.5 g sugar
Salt and pepper

Wash the cabbage leaves and cook them in boiling water for 2 minutes. Drain very thoroughly. Heat the oil and fry the chopped onion until soft and golden. Add the beef and fry until browned, stirring well. Drain the tomatoes and reserve the liquid. Add the tomatoes to the meat mixture. Mix the corn-starch and Worcestershire sauce and stir into the meat with the herbs, chopped parsley and seasoning. Cover and simmer for 20 minutes, stirring occasionally. Divide the stuffing between the cabbage leaves and roll up each one, folding the edges to enclose the stuffing completely. Put into a greased shallow ovenware dish, cover and bake at 190°C/375°F/Gas Mark 5 for 20 minutes. Make the sauce by blending the liquid from the tomatoes with the tomato purée, making the mixture up to 1 1/3 cups/ 1/2 pint/ 250 ml with water. Mix the cornstarch with a little of this liquid. Put into a pan, bring to the boil and stir, adding the Worcestershire sauce, sugar, salt and pepper. Simmer for 3 minutes and pour over the cabbage parcels. Serve hot with rice.

Spiced Red Cabbage

1 medium red cabbage
1/2 cup/ 4 oz/ 100 g butter
1 medium onion
1/3 cup/ 2 oz/ 50 g lean bacon
2 cloves
1 bay leaf
Salt and pepper

Cut the cabbage in eight segments and remove any tough stalk. Shred the cabbage coarsely. Cook in boiling salted water for 5 minutes. Drain well and put in a pan with the butter, very finely chopped onion, chopped bacon, cloves, bay leaf and seasoning. Cover and cook gently for 30 minutes. Take out the bay leaf and cloves, and serve hot. This is very good with sausages.

Hot Cole Slaw

1 small white cabbage
1 1/3 cups/ 1/2 pint/ 250 ml water
2 small onions
1 clove
1 bay leaf
Salt and pepper
1/4 cup/ 2 oz/ 50 g butter
1 tablespoon/ 15 ml oil
1 eating apple
1/3 cup/ 2 oz/ 50 g seedless raisins

Shred the cabbage finely and put into a saucepan with the water. Stick the clove into one of the onions and add to the cabbage with the bay leaf, salt and pepper. Bring to the boil, cover and simmer for 15 minutes. Drain thoroughly and remove the onion and bay leaf. Heat the butter and oil. Peel and slice the second onion finely. Fry for 5 minutes in the fat over gentle heat. Add the cabbage and stir well. Do not peel the apple but cut in quarters, remove the core, and cut the apple in thin slices. Add to the cabbage with the raisins and toss over low heat for 5 minutes. This is particularly good with pork or ham.

Cole Slaw

1 large white cabbage
1 teaspoon/ 5 g salt
3/4 cup/ 6 fl oz/ 150 ml mayonnaise
1 tablespoon/ 15 ml wine vinegar
1/2 teaspoon/ 2.5 g mustard powder
1/2 teaspoon/ 2.5 g grated onion
Pinch of sugar

Cut the cabbage in quarters and take out the stalk. Shred the cabbage very thinly and put in a bowl of iced water with the salt. Leave in the refrigerator for 1 hour. Mix the mayonnaise, vinegar, mustard powder, onion and sugar, and chill. Drain the cabbage very thoroughly and toss in the dressing just before serving.

Caraway seeds or celery seeds may be added for extra flavor. Finely chopped green pepper, grated raw carrot, finely chopped celery, finely chopped eating apple, sliced stuffed olives, drained crushed pineapple, raisins or nuts, may be added according to taste. Other creamy salad dressings may be used instead of mayonnaise, but it is important that the dressing should have the addition of mustard. The cabbage must be very well-hearted and shred thinly, and it must be thoroughly chilled and drained before mixing with the dressing.

Red Cabbage Casserole

1 small red cabbage
2 tablespoons/ 1 oz/ 25 g cooking fat
1 medium onion
1 apple
Salt and pepper
2 teaspoons/ 10 g flour
2 cups/ 3/4 pint/ 375 ml stock
3–4 tablespoons/ 45 ml vinegar
Pinch of ground cinnamon
1 teaspoon/ 5 g sugar

Shred the cabbage finely. Melt the fat and add the chopped onion and apple. Season with salt and pepper and stir in the flour. Cook for 2 minutes. Add the cabbage, stock and vinegar, cover and cook at 180°C/350°F/Gas Mark 4 for 2 hours. Stir in cinnamon and sugar and serve hot. This is particularly good with rich meat such as pork, ham or goose.

Normandy Red Cabbage

1 medium red cabbage
½ cup/ 4 oz/ 100 g butter
1 large onion
4 large cooking apples
2 garlic cloves
¼ teaspoon/ 1.25 g ground nutmeg
¼ teaspoon/ 1.25 g ground allspice
¼ teaspoon/ 1.25 g caraway seed
Salt and pepper
1 teaspoon/ 5 g grated orange rind
2 tablespoons/ 1 oz/ 25 g soft brown sugar
2 cups/ ¾ pint/ 375 ml red wine
2–3 tablespoons/ 30 ml wine vinegar
3–4 tablespoons/ 45 ml water

Cut the cabbage in quarters and take out the heavy ribs and stalk. Shred coarsely and cook with the butter in a heavy pan with the lid on. Stir once while the cabbage cooks for 5 minutes. Put a layer of cabbage into an ovenware casserole. Top with a layer of sliced onions and of peeled apples cut in quarters. Sprinkle with half the crushed garlic and half the spices, salt, pepper and orange rind. Put in the remaining cabbage, then onions and apples. Sprinkle on the brown sugar and add the wine, vinegar and water. Cover and cook at 190°C/375°F/Gas Mark 5 for 1 hour, adding a little more wine if necessary. Serve very hot with sausages or other rich meat.

Red Cabbage Pickle

1 large red cabbage
Block cooking salt
Cayenne pepper
Vinegar

Cut the cabbage into quarters and remove the thick central stalk. Slice the cabbage into very thin shreds and spread out on a large flat dish. Sprinkle with salt. Leave overnight and then stir the salt and liquid to mix them. Drain the cabbage very thoroughly and pack into clean jars. Put ¼ teaspoon of cayenne pepper into each jar. Cover with cold vinegar and cover tightly with vinegar-proof lids.

Sauerkraut

6 large white cabbages
Salt
Cooking apples

Trim the outer leaves from the cabbages and cut them into quarters. Take out the hard stalks and shred the cabbage finely. Pack the cabbage into a large barrel or crock with salt and apples. Do this by putting in a layer of cabbage about 4-in (10 cm) deep and sprinkling with ⅜ cup/ 3 oz/ 75 g salt and 1 finely chopped apple. Press down the layers and continue, pressing and pounding very thoroughly so that the moisture is released and the cabbage becomes covered with brine. Fill the crock, but leave enough space for the cabbage to swell and ferment without overflowing. Cover with a layer of whole cabbage leaves and a thick layer of salt. Place on a clean cloth and a piece of wood which fits into the top of the crock, and put a heavy weight on top. Keep in a warm place to ferment. After two weeks, skim off scum and replace with a clean cloth. Wash the lid and sides of the crock and replace the lid and weight. Put in a cool place for storage. Each week, put on a clean cloth, and wash the lid and crock. The sauerkraut can be used 3–4 weeks after fermentation has ceased.

To keep sauerkraut for a longer period, drain off the juice when it is ready and bring to boiling point. Add the cabbage and bring to simmering point, then pack into heated preserving jars. Screw on the lids and then turn back one-half turn. Put into boiling water to cover the lids and keep at the same temperature for 25 minutes. Take out the jars, tighten the lids and cool before storage.

To serve sauerkraut, drain 2 lb/ 1 kg and rinse in cold water. Drain again and squeeze out most of the moisture but do not crush the cabbage. Put some thin slices of salt pork on the bottom of a heavy pan and arrange half the sauerkraut on top with a little minced garlic and some freshly ground black pepper. Top with remaining sauerkraut, more garlic and pepper and add equal quantities of dry white wine and rich chicken stock just to cover the sauerkraut. Add 2 medium onions stuck with cloves. Cover and cook on low heat, or at 170°C/325°F/Gas Mark 3 for 2 hours so that the liquid has been absorbed. Drain and serve with hot boiled potatoes, some rye bread or pumpernickel, a selection of meats, and plenty of mustard. Any good Continental sausages may be eaten with sauerkraut, as well as spare ribs, roast pork, baked ham, pork chops, roast goose, duck, or pheasant.

Below : A cross-section of a white cabbage

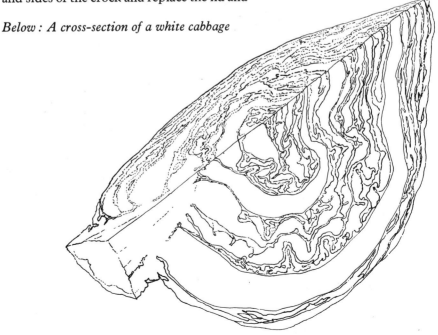

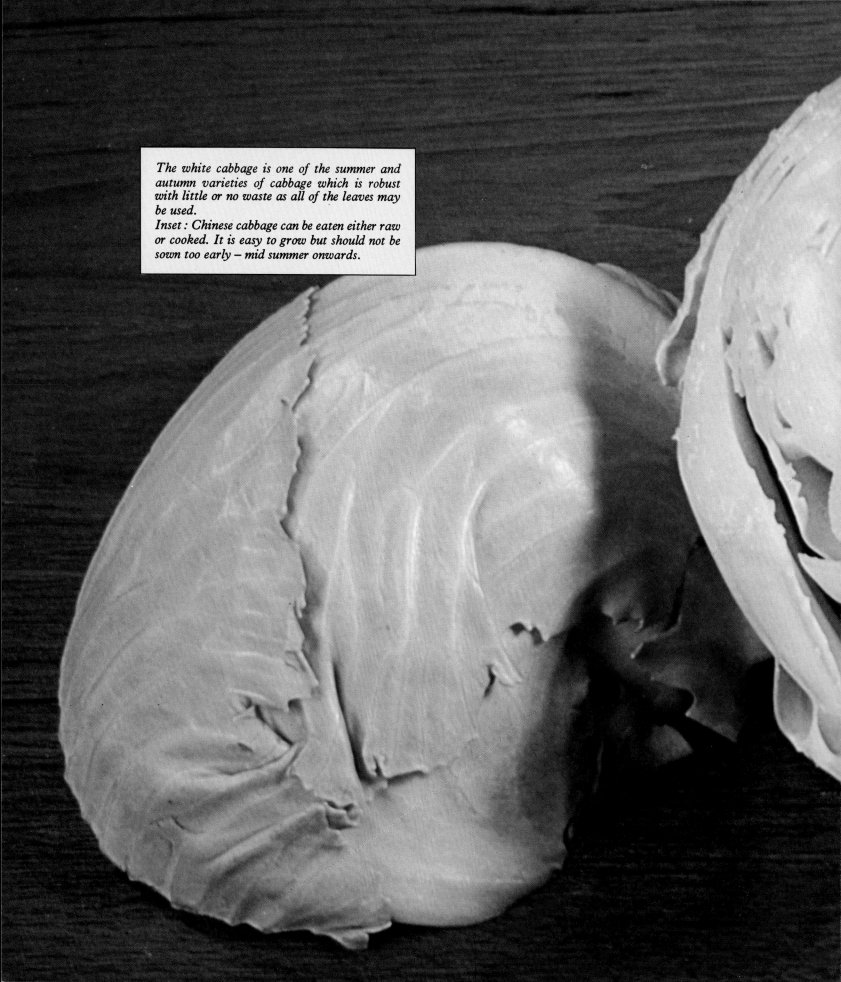

The white cabbage is one of the summer and autumn varieties of cabbage which is robust with little or no waste as all of the leaves may be used.

Inset : Chinese cabbage can be eaten either raw or cooked. It is easy to grow but should not be sown too early – mid summer onwards.

550g (1¼ lb) carrots
White of 1 large leek
1 stick of celery
1 onion, chopped
2 cloves of garlic, chopped
45g (1½ oz) butter
2 sprigs of thyme
2 sprigs of parsley
1 bay leaf
55g (2 oz) pudding rice
1-1.2 litres (1¾-2 pints)
  chicken or
  vegetable stock
Lemon juice
Salt and pepper

To serve:
4 tbsp yoghurt, crème
  fraîche or whipped cream
Chives, chervil or dill

Carrot and rice soup

Serves 4

● Slice the carrots, leek and celery thickly. Put them, along with the chopped onion and garlic, into a pan with the butter. Tie the thyme, parsley and bay leaf together with string to make a bouquet garni and add it to the pan. Cook, covered, over a low heat for 10 minutes, stirring occasionally.

● Add the rice. Stir to coat with the pan juices.

● Pour in 1 litre (1¾ pints) of the stock. Season with salt and pepper. Bring to the boil and simmer gently for 15-20 minutes until the vegetables and rice are tender.

● Cool slightly and discard the bouquet garni. Process until smooth, adding extra stock if the soup is too thick for your liking.

● To finish, stir in a squeeze or two of lemon juice to heighten the flavour, then adjust the seasoning.

● Spoon into bowls. Top each one with a tablespoon of yoghurt, crème fraîche or whipped cream (the cream is prettiest, as it floats perfectly, melting gently). Scatter with chopped chives, chervil or dill. Serve straight away.

Sophie's notes:

You can substitute a medium-sized potato (peeled and diced) for the rice, putting it in the pan with the vegetables.

Joanna Simon's wine choice

A lively white wine with soft citrus overtones is needed with the sweetness of the carrots in this recipe. You could try the well-priced Estorila, an aromatic Portuguese blend with a hint of orange (£2.79, Somerfield) or Marks & Spencer's 1994 Pinot Grigio della Toscana Le Rime (£4.99).

PHOTOGRAPH BY SIMON WHEELER/STYLING BY JOY DAVIES

- 3 stalks of lemon grass
- 900ml (generous 1½ pints) light chicken stock
- 2 kaffir lime leaves, roughly torn up, or 4 wide strips of lime zest
- 2-3 red chillies, thinly sliced
- 8 stems of coriander with leaves, chopped roughly
- 2cm (¾in) piece of galingale or root ginger, thinly sliced
- 340g (12 oz) raw, peeled prawns, thawed if frozen, and deveined
- 3-4 tbsp freshly squeezed lime juice
- 3 tbsp oriental fish sauce

Thai prawn soup Tom yam goong

Serves 4

● Cut off the top, thin, end of the lemon grass stalks and discard, leaving about 12.5cm (5in) of the plumper end. Slice diagonally into pieces about 3mm (⅛in) thick.

● Bring the stock up to the boil. Add the lemon grass, lime leaves (or zest), chillies, coriander and galingale (or ginger). Bring back to the boil. Simmer for 1 minute.

● Add the prawns, lime juice and oriental fish sauce. Bring back to the boil and simmer for 2-3 minutes until the prawns are just cooked through.

● Adjust the seasoning: the flavour should be fairly sour. Serve immediately.

Sophie's notes:

Most large supermarkets now sell lemon grass and oriental fish sauce. Some also have kaffir lime leaves; otherwise use lime zest. Fresh root ginger can be substituted for the closely related galingale. As a general rule, the smaller the chilli the hotter it is, so if you use the tiny, thin Eastern chillis, add them with caution.

Joanna Simon's wine choice

Although a hot and sour liquid might sound the perfect enemy of wine, lemon grass, chilli and ginger are not the problems you might expect; but you must match sourness with sourness and choose a wine with a good acid tang. Dry sparkling wines can work well, as do Sancerre and Pouilly Fumé. Try Sainsbury's 1993 Sancerre, Domaine Henry Pellé (£7.35). A cheaper alternative is a 1994 Vin de Pays des Côtes de Gascogne, such as Marks & Spencer's (£3.25).

1 red pepper, deseeded and
  cut into strips
1 green pepper, deseeded
  and cut into strips
1 onion, chopped
4 tbsp olive oil
2 cloves of garlic, chopped
450 g (1 lb) tomatoes,
  skinned and roughly
  chopped
1 tbsp tomato purée
½ tsp sugar
Salt and pepper
2 tbsp chopped parsley
4 eggs, lightly beaten
4 slices Bayonne ham or
  high-quality cooked ham

Basque eggs with tomato and pepper

Piperade

Serves 4 generously

- Fry the peppers and onion gently in 3 tablespoons of the oil until tender without browning. Add the garlic and cook for a minute or so longer. Now add the tomatoes, tomato purée, sugar, salt and pepper and boil hard until reduced to a thick, pulpy sauce.
- Stir in the beaten eggs and the parsley. Stir for a few minutes until creamy and very lightly set. Adjust seasoning. Divide between four plates.
- Meanwhile, heat the remaining oil in a large frying pan over a high heat. Warm the ham slices quickly in the oil and lay one on top of each plate of piperade. Serve immediately.

Sophie's notes:
Cured Bayonne ham is the proper choice for this Basque dish but, failing that, slices of cooked ham with no added water, cut from the bone, will make for a more than creditable meal. The tomato and pepper base can be cooked in advance, but don't stir in the eggs or heat the ham until the last moment. Butter can be used instead of olive oil.

Joanna Simon's wine choice

I've yet to find a marriage made in heaven for piperade, but there are few out-and-out disasters either. Aim to complement the peppers' sweetness and the salt of the ham with a crisp, fruity white or rosé that has good acidity and little or no oak, or a young, fruity beaujolais-type red. Try 1995 Fairview Dry Rosé from South Africa (£3.49, Asda), or an Australian riesling from the Clare Valley, such as 1994 Bridgewater Mill (£4.99, Thresher, Wine Rack and Bottoms Up).

PHOTOGRAPH BY SIMON WHEELER/STYLING BY JOY DAVIES

280 g (10 oz) shortcrust pastry
Filling:
110 g (4 oz) shallots, sliced
60 g (2 oz) butter
3 egg yolks
240 ml (8 fl oz) crème fraîche or double cream mixed with soured cream
1 tbsp chopped fresh dill
Finely grated zest of 1 lemon
Salt and pepper
110 g (4 oz) smoked salmon, cut into thin strips

Smoked salmon and shallot quiche

Serves 8

● Line a deep 20cm (8in) tart tin with pastry and rest in the fridge for 30 minutes. Prick the base with a fork, line with greaseproof paper or foil and fill with baking beans. Bake blind at 200C (400F, gas mark 6) for 10 minutes. Remove beans and paper and return to the oven for 5 minutes or so to dry out. Cool at least until tepid before filling.

● Cook the shallots gently in the butter until translucent without browning. Beat the eggs with the cream, dill, lemon zest, salt and pepper.

● Distribute the shallots and strips of salmon evenly over the base of the pastry case. Pour in the cream mixture. Bake at 180C (350F, gas mark 4) for about 30-40 minutes until just set. Serve warm or cold.

Sophie's notes:

This is definitely a quiche for a special occasion, so don't try to cut corners. You could just about get away with using whipping cream instead of crème fraîche, but please don't ruin it by using milk. Make something else instead.

Joanna Simon's wine choice

There is no point in cutting corners on the wine here, and if you need an excuse to drink champagne, this quiche is it. Majestic's pink Oeil de Perdrix is as pretty as a picture and very good value (£14.49 before quantity discounts). If you don't run to champagne, Tesco's Robertson Sparkling Wine (£6.99) is soft, dry and stylish; otherwise, go for as good a dry white as you can afford.

PHOTOGRAPH BY SIMON WHEELER/STYLING BY JOY DAVIES

450 g (1 lb) spaghetti
1½ tbsp olive oil
Freshly grated Parmesan
to serve

Meatball sauce:
1 thick slice of white bread
4 tbsp milk
340g (12 oz) lean minced
beef
3 tbsp chopped parsley
3 cloves of garlic, crushed
Salt and pepper
1 egg, beaten
3 tbsp olive oil
1½ x 400 g (14 oz) tins
chopped tomatoes
2 tbsp tomato purée
½-1 tsp sugar
1 glass of red wine or water
1 tsp dried oregano

Spaghetti with meatballs and tomato sauce

Serves 4 generously
● First make the sauce. Remove crust from the bread and tear into small pieces. Soak in the milk for 10 minutes, then add the minced beef, half the parsley and half the garlic, salt and pepper. Mix well, kneading with your hands to break up the bread. Add just enough egg to bind. Roll heaped teaspoonfuls of the mixture into small balls.
● Heat the oil over a medium heat in a frying pan large enough to take the meatballs in a single layer. Fry the meatballs briskly until browned all over. Add all the remaining ingredients, including the

rest of the parsley and garlic. Stir gently to mix without breaking up the meatballs. Heat until simmering, then reduce heat to low and cover. Simmer for 30 minutes.
● Adjust seasoning, adding a hint more sugar if the sauce seems on the sharp side. Reheat when needed, adding a splash of water if the sauce is too thick.
● Bring a large pan of salted water to the boil and add the spaghetti. Boil until al dente then drain. Return to the pan and toss with a tablespoonful of olive oil. Divide between four large bowls or plates and top with meatballs in their sauce.

Joanna Simon's wine choice

You need a medium to full-bodied red that will stand up to both the meatballs and the sweet-acid aspect of the tomato sauce. Cheap chianti and valpolicella are usually too gutless (the same applies with a decent spaghetti bolognaise), but Montepulciano d'Abruzzo has what it takes: try Marks & Spencer's 1994 (£3.29). Better still, try 1994 Torre del Falco, a splendid, rich, warmly fruity red from the far south of Italy (£4.99, Oddbins).

PHOTOGRAPH BY SIMON WHEELER/STYLING BY JOY DAVIES

220 g (8 oz) Basmati or
other high-quality long-
grain rice
1 tbsp oil or butter
5 cm (2 in) cinnamon stick
1 bay leaf
550 ml (18 fl oz) water
Salt
15-30g ($\frac{1}{2}$-1 oz) butter
to finish

Plain pilau rice

Serves 4-6

● Tip the rice into a sieve and rinse thoroughly. Leave to drain and dry for at least 20 minutes.

● Heat the oil or butter over a medium heat and add the rice, cinnamon stick and bay leaf. Stir for 1 minute. Pour in the water and season with salt.

● Bring up to the boil, then reduce heat as low as possible. Cover the pan, and leave to cook for 10 minutes without disturbing. Test a few grains of rice — they should be just al dente, ie still slightly firm to the bite. The liquid should all have been absorbed. If necessary, uncover and cook off any excess quickly.

● Spoon the rice (with the cinnamon stick and bay leaf) into a shallow dish, dot with the extra butter, then cover loosely with foil. Place in a low to medium oven (it should not be too hot) and leave for 5-10 minutes to steam-finish. Fluff up with a fork and serve.

Sophie's notes:

This method may seem long-winded but it produces perfect, separate grains, glistening, light and delicately flavoured — an ideal accompaniment to a hundred and one dishes. It can be adapted to any quantity: just measure the rice in a measuring jug, then add twice the volume of liquid. If you wish, add a shake of turmeric as the rice cooks to colour it yellow.

Joanna Simon's wine choice

You are unlikely to be eating plain pilau rice unaccompanied, and so you will be matching the wine to the main dish, but if you were eating it alone, or with something very light and simple, a wine like 1994 Lugana Sanroseda Boscaini, a zesty, floral, dry white from the Valpolicella region (Asda, £3.99), would be ideal.

PHOTOGRAPH BY SIMON WHEELER/STYLING BY JOY DAVIES

450 g (1 lb) shelled broad
   beans, thawed if frozen
450 g (1 lb) tagliatelle
5 tbsp olive oil
2 cloves of garlic, sliced
175 g (6 oz) pancetta or
   streaky bacon, cut into
   thin strips
45 g (1½ oz) freshly grated
   Parmesan
2 tbsp chopped fresh
   parsley
Salt and pepper

Tagliatelle with broad beans and pancetta

Serves 4 generously

● If using frozen broad beans, let them thaw (or dunk into boiling water for 1 minute), then slit open the pale grey-green outer skins and squeeze out the bright green inner beanlet. With fresh broad beans, blanch in boiling water for 1 minute, drain then skin. Either way, cook the skinned beanlets in fresh water until just done.

● Cook the tagliatelle in boiling salted water in the usual way until just al dente.

● As soon as the tagliatelle is in the pan, put the olive oil and garlic in a frying pan over a moderate heat. When the garlic begins to colour, add the pancetta and broad beans. Fry over a low heat, stirring occasionally, until the tagliatelle is done.

● Drain the tagliatelle, pile into a warm serving bowl and pour over the contents of the frying pan. Add Parmesan, parsley, salt and pepper and toss. Serve immediately.

Sophie's notes:

This is a marvellous but unusual pasta dish that we first ate in Sicily. It's only worth making if you can be bothered to skin the broad beans. Pancetta is an Italian form of bacon available from delicatessens and some good supermarkets.

Joanna Simon's wine choice

Don't overwhelm this dish with a pungent sauvignon or a thumping New World chardonnay: Italy has many gentle, crisp, dry whites that support rather than compete with food. Sainsbury's 1994 Bianco di Custoza (£3.49) is one. Or 1994 Laperouse Blanc, from the south of France, offers subtlety, but with more weight and depth (£4.49, very widely available).

PHOTOGRAPH BY SIMON WHEELER/STYLING BY JOY DAVIES

1 onion, chopped
2 cloves of garlic, chopped
1 chilli, deseeded and finely chopped
2 tbsp olive oil
220 g (8 oz) long-grain rice, rinsed
340 g (12 oz) tomatoes, skinned, deseeded and chopped
$\frac{1}{4}$ tsp ground saffron
2 tbsp chopped parsley
45 g (1$\frac{1}{2}$ oz) currants
350 g (12 oz) cooked turkey, torn into small pieces
570 ml (1 pint) stock
Salt

Turkey and saffron rice

Serves 4-6

● Heat the oven to 150C (300F, gas mark 2).

● Cook the onion, garlic and chilli gently in the oil until tender without browning. Mix in the rice, stirring to coat evenly.

● Draw off the heat and mix with all the remaining ingredients except the stock in a shallow ovenproof dish (eg a medium-sized roasting tin or a gratin dish), to give a layer about 2.5-4 cm (1-1$\frac{1}{2}$ in) deep.

● Pour over the stock. Cover with foil, and transfer to the oven. Bake for 40-50 minutes, or until rice is tender. Taste and adjust seasoning, and serve.

Sophie's notes:

This is a tremendous way to use up left-over turkey (or, of course, chicken, if that's what you happen to have to hand), producing a moist, filling dish packed with flavour and pretty to look at, too. Most good supermarkets sell powdered saffron. To make your own, dry-fry saffron threads briefly over a high heat to crisp, then grind to a powder using a mortar and pestle. The chilli adds a gentle tingle of heat, but you can omit it, adding plenty of freshly ground black pepper instead.

Joanna Simon's wine choice

This adaptable dish takes well to both red and white wines. Choose medium to full-bodied, characterful whites (but nothing too sharp or pungent) and reds of a similar weight (but not too tannic). Chardonnays work very well — even the big, fruity, oaky Australian styles like 1994 Penfolds Koonunga Hill (£4.99, very widely available) — and reds such as the full, plummy, smooth 1993 Penfolds Organic Red (£6.99, Safeway).

45 g (1½ oz) slightly stale
   breadcrumbs
200 g (7 oz) caster sugar
100 g (3½ oz) ground
   almonds
1½ tsp baking powder
200 ml (7 fl oz) sunflower or
   vegetable oil
4 eggs
Finely grated zest of 1 large
   orange
Finely grated zest of ½ a
   lemon

Syrup:
Juice of 1 orange
Juice of ½ lemon
85 g (3 oz) sugar
2 cloves
1 cinnamon stick

Tunisian almond and orange cake

Serves 8

● Mix the breadcrumbs with the sugar, almonds and baking powder. Add the oil and eggs and beat well. Stir in the orange and lemon zest. Pour the mixture into a greased 20cm (8in) cake tin.

● Put into a cold oven and set to heat to 190C (375F, gas mark 5). Bake for 40-50 minutes until the cake is a rich brown and a skewer inserted into the centre comes out clean.

● Cool for 5 minutes in the tin then turn out onto a plate.

● While the cake cooks, make the syrup. Bring all the ingredients gently to the boil in a pan, stirring until the sugar has dissolved.

Simmer for 3 minutes.

● Pierce holes in the cake with a skewer while still warm and pour the syrup over it. Leave to cool, spooning the syrup over the cake every now and then until it is all soaked up. Serve with whipped cream or thick Greek yoghurt.

Sophie's notes:

If you are in a hurry, you can leave out the syrup. You'll still end up with a fine, moist cake, but it won't be as gooey, rich and fragrant. The syrup also improves the keeping quality. Syrup-soaked cake tastes best a day after it is made and will keep in the fridge, covered in foil, for 3 or 4 days.

Joanna Simon's wine choice

Devotees of muscat de beaumes de venise, and similar sweet muscats (rivesaltes, st jean de minervois, frontignan etc), should make this cake. Tesco's Muscat de Rivesaltes Les Abeilles is always reliable, with a spicy, demerara sugar flavour (£5.99). Victoria Wine's Moscatel de Valencia is just as reliable, in a slightly lighter, zestier style (£3.79, or £2.19 a half).

600 ml (1 pint) freshly
squeezed orange juice
30 ml (1 fl oz) Grand
Marnier or Cointreau
(optional)
1 sachet (12 g or 0.4 oz) of
powdered gelatine
4-6 tbsp single cream

Orange jellies

Serves 6

● Mix the orange juice with the Grand Marnier or Cointreau, if using. Sprinkle the gelatine over 4 tablespoons of hot water in a small pan. Leave for 3 minutes to soften, then stir to dissolve. If necessary, warm gently without boiling, stirring until the liquid is quite clear and speck-free.

● Now mix in one tablespoon of the orange juice, then a second, then a third. Tip the whole lot back into the rest of the orange juice and stir to mix.

● Pour into 6 wine glasses, then leave to set in the fridge for at least 4 hours.

● Just before serving, spoon a little cream over each jelly.

Sophie's notes:

You can use the same method to make apple jellies from apple juice (use the best you can get, pressed from apples, not reconstituted from apple concentrate), or other fruit jellies. For a black coffee jelly, make real coffee, sweeten very lightly while still hot, and sprinkle the gelatine directly over the hot coffee. When it is set, top with a swirl of whipped cream.

Joanna Simon's wine choice

This is a difficult pudding to match because it is not really sweet, or at least only as sweet as the oranges you use. Traditional sweet wines don't work, but asti does, despite being very sweet, because its refreshing fizz and acidity balance its sweetness; it is also sufficiently light-bodied for the jelly. When buying asti, it is important to go to a shop with a rapid turnover (eg a big supermarket), so that your bottle is young and fresh. Asti Martini is a good brand (£5.99-£6.59, widely available). A moscato spumante, such as Safeway's (£3.99), works equally well.

Cabbage, Chinese

Chinese cabbage is also known as Chinese leaf, shantung cabbage, wong bok, chihli cabbage, pe-tsai, celery cabbage and *brassica pekinensis*, and is a special kind of cabbage from Eastern Asia. It is a long crisp heavy cabbage which can weigh up to 5 lb (2.5 kg), with solidly packed pale green leaves striped with white ribs. The texture is crunchy and the flavor more delicate than other types of cabbage, and it may be eaten raw or lightly cooked, and can be used in any favorite cabbage recipe.

This cabbage is best stir-fried in the Chinese way. Slice the cabbage across and wash quickly in cold water. Put a thin layer of lard or corn oil in a large frying pan and heat it. Add the cabbage slices from the stalk end and stir in the oil for about 3 minutes. Sprinkle on a little salt and add the remaining cabbage. Continue stirring for 4 minutes so that the cabbage is cooked but crisp.

Chinese Cabbage Salad

1 Chinese cabbage
1 red pepper
1 small onion
1 medium cucumber
$\frac{3}{8}$ cup/ 3 fl oz/ 90 ml corn oil
3–4 tablespoons/ 45 ml wine vinegar

Slice the cabbage finely, wash and drain well. Mix with sliced pepper, finely chopped onion and thinly sliced cucumber. Mix oil and vinegar and toss the salad in this dressing just before serving.

Sweet and Sour Cabbage

1 Chinese cabbage
$\frac{1}{4}$ cup/ 2 oz/ 50 g sugar
2 tablespoons/ 30 ml wine vinegar
3 tablespoons/ 1 oz/ 25 g cornstarch
$\frac{2}{3}$ cup/ $\frac{1}{4}$ pint/ 125 ml water

Slice the cabbage across and wash in cold water. Put a thin layer of lard or corn oil into a large frying pan, heat it, and tip in the slices from the stalk. Cook for 3 minutes, stirring well. Sprinkle on a little salt. Mix the sugar, vinegar, cornstarch and water until smooth, and stir into the cabbage. Add the remaining cabbage and cook, stirring well, until the cabbage is cooked but still crisp and coated with sauce.

Chinese Cabbage Rolls

1 Chinese cabbage
2–3 tablespoons/ 30 ml peanut oil
2 green peppers
2–3 tablespoons/ 30 ml soy sauce
2 teaspoons/ 10 g salt
$\frac{1}{4}$ teaspoon chili powder
2–3 tablespoons/ 30 ml cider vinegar
2 tablespoons/ 1 oz/ 25 g sugar
Pinch of monosodium glutamate

Separate the cabbage into leaves and boil them in lightly salted water for 5 minutes. Drain carefully and rinse in cold water. Cut each leaf crosswise into two pieces. Roll each piece up tight, and cut each roll into 1-in (2.5 cm) lengths. Put into a shallow serving dish. Remove seeds and membranes from the peppers and cut the flesh into strips. Heat the oil and cook the peppers over high heat for 3 minutes, stirring well. Add the rest of the ingredients and continue cooking for 2 minutes. Pour over the cabbage rolls. Chill and serve as an appetizer.

Calabrese

An improved variety of broccoli, sometimes known as asparagus broccoli or green sprouting broccoli. It has an abundance of small flowerets (which suffer during the first frosts) and these heads remain green, with a fine flavor. Broccoli and cauliflower recipes may be used for cooking calabrese.

Capsicum

see Peppers

Cardoon

The cardoon is a thistle-like plant which is similar to the globe artichoke, but the flower heads are not used. The edible portion is the thickened stalk and midrib of the prickly young leaves, and the best cardoons are blanched during growing like celery. To prepare the cardoons, the fleshy leaf ribs are cleaned and all stringy and fibrous parts removed, and the stems are then cut into short lengths. They may be simply cooked until crisply tender in boiling salted water with a squeeze of lemon juice to prevent darkening, and can then be served with butter and seasoning, a cream sauce or cheese sauce. Cardoons may be chilled and served with an oil and vinegar dressing and can be par-boiled until just tender, then drained and dipped in batter before frying until golden.

Cardoons with Melted Butter

1 lb/ 500 g cardoons
$\frac{1}{4}$ cup/ 2 oz/ 50 g butter
Squeeze of lemon juice
Salt and pepper

Peel the cardoons and cut them in two lengthwise, putting the pieces into cold water as they are prepared so that they remain white. Put into boiling salted water and boil for 10 minutes. Meanwhile, melt the butter over low heat, add lemon juice, salt and pepper. Drain the cardoons thoroughly and put into a serving dish. Pour on the butter and serve at once.

Fried Cardoons

1 lb/ 500 g cardoons
4 tablespoons/ 1 oz/ 25 g flour
½ cup/ 4 fl oz/ 120 ml olive oil
2 teaspoons lemon juice
2 tablespoons/ 1 oz/ 25 g grated
   Parmesan cheese

Peel the cardoons, cut them in 2-in (5 cm) lengths and drop in cold water until they are all prepared. Cook in boiling salted water for 5 minutes, drain very thoroughly and toss in the flour. Heat the oil and fry the cardoons until golden brown. Put into a serving dish, sprinkle on the lemon juice, and then the grated cheese.

Carrots

Carrots were enjoyed in the early civilization of Egypt, and later by the Greeks and Romans. In common with many other edible plants, they came into general use in the sixteenth century, first being popular in Flanders and France. Carrots are at their best when young and tender, simmered in a little water, or in butter. Older carrots give a good flavor to meat casseroles, but it may be necessary to cut away the hard center core which can be unpleasant and stringy to eat. Raw carrots make a pleasant and simple salad if coarsely grated and dressed with lemon juice. Because carrots are rather sweet, they used to be used frequently in steamed puddings and in cakes, and are still often used in rich plum pudding for Christmas.

Below: The ever-popular, raw or cooked, carrot

Carrot Soup

1 lb/ 500 g carrots
3 large tomatoes
2⅔ cups/ 1 pint/ 500 ml water
2 tablespoons/ 1 oz/ 25 g butter
2⅔ cups/ 1 pint/ 500 ml milk
Chopped parsley

Scrape the carrots and cook for 30 minutes in the water. Dip in the tomatoes and skin them. Drain the carrots, reserving liquid. Grate the carrots. Melt the butter and lightly cook the skinned tomatoes. Add the grated carrot and cook until all the butter is absorbed. In a double boiler, bring the milk to the boil, add carrot and tomato, and liquid from carrots. Simmer for 45 minutes, seasoning lightly with salt and pepper. Serve hot sprinkled with parsley.

Carrot and Orange Soup

1 lb/ 500 g carrots
2⅔ cups/ 1 pint/ 500 ml chicken stock
2 oranges
Salt and pepper
1 medium onion
1 teaspoon/ 5 g soft brown sugar
⅔ cup/ ¼ pint/ 125 ml cream

Grate the carrots and cook with the chicken stock, some grated orange rind, salt, pepper, chopped onion and sugar. Simmer for 30 minutes in a covered pan until carrots are soft. Blend or liquidize until smooth. Stir in the cream and reheat gently. Peel the oranges and cut across in slices. Serve the soup garnished with orange slices. The soup may be chilled for 2 hours to serve cold.

Braised Carrots

1 lb/ 500 g medium carrots
1⅓ cups/ ½ pint/ 250 ml stock
Salt and pepper
Pinch of thyme
¼ cup/ 2 oz/ 50 g butter

Scrape or peel the carrots according to age, put into cold water and boil for 10 minutes. Drain well and put into a greased ovenware dish. Put in stock, seasoning, thyme and flakes of butter. Cover and cook at 190°C/ 375°F/Gas Mark 5 for 25 minutes.

Carrots in Vermouth*

6 large carrots
¼ cup/ 2 oz/ 50 g butter
Salt and pepper
Pinch of sugar
⅜ cup/ 3 fl oz/ 75 ml white vermouth
1 tablespoon/ 15 g chopped parsley

Peel the carrots, quarter them lengthwise and remove the center core. Dice the carrot flesh and put in a thick saucepan with the butter, salt, pepper and sugar. Cook gently for 3 minutes and add the vermouth. Cover and cook very gently shaking the pan occasionally for 25 minutes. Add a little water if necessary to prevent the carrots drying out. Take off the cover and continue cooking until the liquid thickens to a syrup. Serve sprinkled with chopped parsley.

Carrots and Celery in Cider

2⅔ cups/ 1 pint/ 500 ml cider
1 lb/ 500 g carrots
1 small head of celery
Salt and pepper
Chopped parsley

Bring the cider to the boil. Cut the vegetables into 2-in (5 cm) pieces. Put the carrots into the cider and cook gently for 15 minutes. Add the celery, salt and pepper and cook for 30 minutes. Drain the vegetables and keep them hot. Boil up the cider until it has been reduced to about 4 tablespoonsful. Pour over the vegetables and sprinkle with parsley. This is particularly good with beef and with boiled ham.

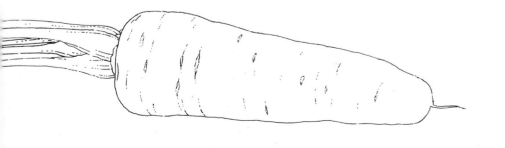

Carrots in Vermouth

see page 45

carrots
butter
salt and pepper
sugar
white vermouth
parsley

Inset: Carrots are easy to grow and their foliage is most attractive. (In earlier times, ladies used to wear the leaves as part of a corsage.) They prefer a sandy soil but can and will grow in almost any soil.

Carrot-Stuffed Onions

4 large onions
4 large carrots
1⅓ cups/ ½ pint/ 250 ml white sauce (see
    page 10)
1 cup/ 3 oz/ 75 g fine white
    breadcrumbs
1 tablespoon/ ½ oz/ 15 g butter
Salt and pepper

Boil the onions until they are tender and
scoop out the centers carefully. Cook the
carrots and cut them into small pieces. Dip
them into melted butter, season with salt
and pepper, and mix them with the scraped-
out onion pieces. Put the whole onions into
a buttered dish, fill with the mixture of
carrots and onions, and pour on the white
sauce. Sprinkle with the breadcrumbs and
dot with a few bits of butter. Grate on a
little nutmeg if liked. Put in the oven at
180°C/350°F/Gas Mark 4 until the breadcrumbs are just brown and serve very hot.
A little grated cheese and chopped parsley
may be added if liked.

Carrots Lyonnaise

1 lb/ 500 g carrots
1 large onion
1⅓ cups/ ½ pint/ 250 ml white wine or
    dry cider
¼ cup/ 2 oz/ 50 g butter
Salt and pepper
Juice of ½ lemon

Slice the carrots and put into a shallow pan
with the sliced onion, wine or cider, butter,
salt, pepper and lemon juice. Cover and
bring to the boil. Reduce the heat and simmer for 40 minutes until the carrots are just
tender.

Carrots Vichy

1 lb/ 500 g small young carrots
⅜ cup/ 3 oz/ 75 g butter
Pinch of salt
2 teaspoons/ 10 g sugar
Chopped parsley

Scrape the carrots and cut them across into
thin slices. Melt half the butter and add the

salt, sugar and carrots. Stir well and add just
enough water to cover. Bring to the boil and
simmer uncovered until the water has
evaporated and the carrots are tender. Add
the remaining butter, and sprinkle with
chopped parsley.

Carrots Braised in Beer

1 medium onion
1 lb/ 500 g carrots
1 bay leaf
2–3 tablespoons/ 30 g chopped parsley
Salt and pepper
1 teaspoon/ 5 g sugar
⅔ cup/ ¼ pint/ 125 ml chicken stock
⅔ cup/ ¼ pint/ 125 ml brown ale or beer

Peel and slice the onion and put into an
ovenware dish. Cut the carrots in lengthwise slices and put into the casserole with
the bay leaf, parsley, salt, pepper, sugar,
stock and ale. Cover and cook at 180°C/
350°F/Gas Mark 4 for 45 minutes.

Carrot Salad

4 large carrots
2 eating apples
1 teaspoon/ 5 ml lemon juice
4 lettuce leaves
2 tablespoons/ 1 oz/ 25 g chopped nuts
Salt and pepper
⅔ cup/ ¼ pint/ 125 ml mayonnaise

Grate the carrots coarsely. Do not peel the
apples but cut them in quarters, remove
cores, and cut the flesh in dice. Sprinkle the
apple pieces with lemon juice. Shred the
lettuce leaves finely. Mix the carrots, apples,
lettuce, nuts, salt and pepper and bind with
the mayonnaise.

Carrot and Orange Marmalade

2 sweet oranges
1 lemon
2 lb/ 1 kg carrots
2⅔ cup/ 1 pint/ 500 ml water
4 cups/ 2 lb/ 1 kg sugar

Squeeze the juice from the oranges and the
lemon. Shred the peel finely and soak in the
water overnight. Cut the carrots into matchstick pieces. Put carrots and peel into a pan,
with the pips suspended in a cheesecloth or
muslin bag. Simmer 1 hour until the peel
is tender. Take out the bag of pips and
squeeze out the liquid. Stir in the sugar and
lemon juice until the sugar has dissolved.
Boil rapidly to setting point. Cool slightly,
stir well, pour into hot jars and cover. Use
with toast or as a tart or pie filling.

Swedish Carrots

12 large carrots
½ cup/ 4 oz/ 100 g butter
½ cup/ 4 oz/ 100 g sugar
Pinch of ground nutmeg
Pinch of salt
1⅓ cups/ ½ pint/ 250 ml white wine
    vinegar
Pinch of paprika

Shred the carrots in rather long thick pieces
and put into a thick saucepan with butter,
sugar, nutmeg, salt and vinegar. Cover and
simmer gently for 1 hour, stirring occasionally. When the liquid has nearly evaporated,
strain it off. Reheat the carrots with a little
extra butter, stir in the paprika and serve
hot.

Sweet Carrot Pudding

1½ lb/ 750 g carrots
2½ cups/ 8 oz/ 225 g fine breadcrumbs
¾ cup/ 6 oz/ 150 g shredded suet
⅔ cup/ 4 oz/ 100 g currants
⅔ cup/ 4 oz/ 100 g seedless raisins
½ cup/ 4 oz/ 100 g soft brown sugar
Pinch of ground nutmeg
Pinch of salt
3 eggs
1⅓ cups/ ½ pint/ 250 ml milk

Cook the carrots until tender and then sieve
them to make 1 lb/ 500 g purée. Mix with the
breadcrumbs, suet, currants, raisins, sugar,
nutmeg and salt. Add the eggs and enough
milk to make a thick batter. The pudding
may be baked in an ovenware dish at 180°C/
350°F/Gas Mark 4 for 1½ hours, or it may be
steamed in a pan of boiling water for 3 hours.
Serve with a sweet sauce or egg custard.

Cauliflower

This variety of the cabbage family is grown for its undeveloped flowers or curds which are best when thick and white, and it is important not to use cauliflowers which have bruised or discolored patches. The flavor is delicate and is excellent when the vegetable is only lightly cooked. Overcooking will spoil both flavor and texture, and the ideal cauliflower should retain a firm texture when cooked for only a short time in boiling water – the head may be cooked whole or broken into individual flowerets. A teaspoon (5 ml) of lemon juice in the cooking water will help to keep the whiteness of the head. A simple dressing of melted butter, salt and pepper and a pinch of ground nutmeg is enough for a cauliflower, but it may also be served with white sauce or cheese sauce. Lightly cooked or raw cauliflower may be used for salad dressed with mayonnaise or French dressing.

Fried Cauliflower Sprigs

1 cauliflower
¼ cup/ 1 oz/ 25 g flour
1 egg
⅔ cup/ 2 oz/ 50 g fine dry breadcrumbs
¼ cup/ 2 oz/ 50 g butter
4–5 tablespoons/ 60 ml olive oil
2 tablespoons/ 1 oz/ 25 g grated
    Parmesan cheese

Trim the leaves from the cauliflower and cut off each sprig from the stem. Put into boiling water and cook for 8 minutes. Drain very thoroughly. Dip first in flour, then beaten egg, then breadcrumbs. Heat the butter and oil together, and fry the cauliflower sprigs until golden and crisp on the surface. Serve hot sprinkled with cheese. If liked, hot tomato or mushroom sauce may be served with the sprigs.

Cauliflower Polonaise*

1 cauliflower
¼ cup/ 2 oz/ 50 g butter
⅓ cup/ 1 oz/ 25 g fresh white bread-
    crumbs
1 hard-boiled egg
2 slices of bacon
Chopped parsley

Trim the cauliflower but keep the curd whole. Cook in boiling salted water until tender. Drain very thoroughly and put into a serving dish. Melt the butter and stir in the breadcrumbs. Stir them over low heat until golden. Chop the hard-boiled egg finely. Broil (grill) the bacon crisply and chop finely. Pour the butter and crumbs over the cauliflower. Sprinkle thickly with egg, bacon and parsley.

Cauliflower Salad

1 lb/ 500 g cauliflower sprigs
½ cup/ 3 oz/ 75 g anchovy fillets
⅓ cup/ 2 oz/ 50 g stuffed olives
⅓ cup/ 2 oz/ 50 g red pepper
1 medium onion
4 tablespoons/ 60 ml olive oil
Salt and pepper

Cook the cauliflower sprigs until just tender and drain them well. Cool and put into a

serving bowl. Drain and chop the anchovies. Slice the olives and red peppers and chop the onion. Mix them all with the oil, vinegar and seasoning, and pour on the cauliflower. Toss gently and chill for 2 hours before serving.

Cauliflower Soup

1 large onion
¼ cup/ 2 oz/ 50 g butter
1 medium cauliflower
4 cups/ 1½ pints/ 750 ml chicken stock
Pinch of ground mace
Salt and pepper
1⅓ cups/ ½ pint/ 250 ml milk
⅔ cup/ ¼ pint/ 125 ml cream
1 tablespoon/ 15 g chopped parsley
¼ cup/ 2 oz/ 50 g cooked shrimps
Fried bread or toast cubes

Peel and chop the onion finely and cook in the butter until soft and golden. Cut the cauliflower into sprigs, add stock and seasoning. Bring to the boil, stir well, then cover and simmer for 25 minutes. Cool and then liquidize in a blender until smooth, or put through a sieve. Stir in the milk and reheat. Stir in the cream and adjust seasoning. Serve hot, sprinkled with parsley, shrimps and cubes of fried or toasted bread.

Special Cauliflower Cheese

1 lb/ 500 g cauliflower sprigs
2 cups/ ¾ pint/ 375 ml cheese sauce (see
    page 10)
2 medium onions
2 tablespoons/ 1 oz/ 25 g toasted
    almonds
Pinch of paprika
1 tablespoon/ 15 g chopped parsley

Cook the cauliflower sprigs and drain them well. Put them in a buttered ovenware dish. Cut the onions into very thin rings, dip them in a little flour and fry until crisp and golden. Stir half the onions into the hot cheese sauce. Cut the almonds into thin slivers and add these to the sauce also. Pour over the cauliflower, sprinkle with paprika, cover and bake at 200°C/400°F/Gas Mark 6 for 15 minutes. Take off the cover, sprinkle with the remaining onions and parsley and bake for 5 minutes. Serve very hot.

Curried Cauliflower

1 medium onion
4 garlic cloves
2 tablespoons/ 1 oz/ 25 g root ginger
4–5 tablespoons/ 60 ml water
4–5 tablespoons/ 60 ml oil
½ teaspoon/ 2.5 g ground turmeric
2 medium tomatoes
¼ teaspoon/ 1.25 g cayenne pepper
2 teaspoons/ 10 g ground coriander
1 teaspoon/ 5 g ground cumin
2 teaspoons/ 10 g salt
Pinch of pepper
Pinch of ground cinnamon
1 cardamon pod (split)
Juice of ½ lemon
1 cauliflower

Peel and chop the onion and garlic cloves. Put into a blender with the ginger and water and blend until smooth. Heat the oil in a thick shallow pan and add the blended mixture and all the remaining ingredients except the cauliflower. Cook gently for 5 minutes, adding a little water if the mixture sticks. Wash the cauliflower and divide it into sprigs. Add to the curry sauce and stir well. Cover and cook very gently for 20 minutes, until the cauliflower is just tender. Serve hot with a side dish of yogurt.

Celeriac

Celeriac, sometimes known as celery root, celery knob or turnip-rooted celery is cultivated for its large root, similar in shape to a turnip, rather than for stalks or foliage. It has a rich celery flavor and nutty texture. The best roots to use are small or mediumsized as the larger ones sometimes become hollow and woody. Celeriac has to be peeled before cooking, and needs to be cut in pieces as it takes some time to soften when cooked in boiling salted water, or in stock. Plainly cooked celeriac is delicious in melted butter, or with a Hollandaise or Béchamel sauce, and it also makes excellent soup or can be added to casseroles as it has a better texture than celery.

Raw celeriac has a very good flavor, and may be simply cut in cubes and eaten with sea salt. Matchstick pieces are often chilled and added to mayonnaise or French dressing – a little lemon juice will keep the color of the raw pieces.

Below : Celeriac and florets of cauliflower

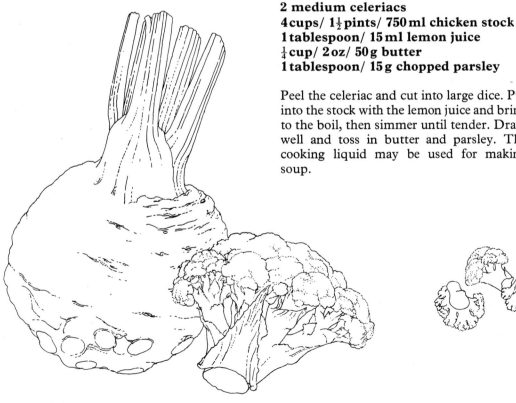

Celeriac Casserole

1½ lb/ 750 g celeriac
½ lb/ 8 oz/ 225 g onions
½ lb/ 8 oz/ 225 g tomatoes
1 carrot
⅜ cup/ 3 oz/ 75 g butter
1 garlic clove
Salt and pepper
2 slices of bread

Peel the celeriac and cut it into slices. Simmer in stock or water for 10 minutes. Peel and slice the onions. Peel the tomatoes, take out the pips, and cut the flesh into pieces. Peel and slice the carrot. Melt the butter and fry the onions, tomatoes and carrot lightly until the onion pieces are soft and golden. Add the drained celeriac pieces and the garlic. Season with salt and pepper, and add enough of the liquid used in cooking the celeriac to cover the vegetables. Cover and simmer until the vegetables are tender. Just before serving, cut the bread into triangles and fry in oil until golden, and garnish the casserole.

Braised Celeriac

2 medium celeriacs
4 cups/ 1½ pints/ 750 ml chicken stock
1 tablespoon/ 15 ml lemon juice
¼ cup/ 2 oz/ 50 g butter
1 tablespoon/ 15 g chopped parsley

Peel the celeriac and cut into large dice. Put into the stock with the lemon juice and bring to the boil, then simmer until tender. Drain well and toss in butter and parsley. The cooking liquid may be used for making soup.

Celeriac Rémoulade

1 medium celeriac
1 tablespoon/ 15 ml lemon juice
2 egg yolks
1 tablespoon/ 15 ml tarragon vinegar
2 tablespoons/ 30 ml French mustard
Salt and pepper
2–3 tablespoons/ 30 ml olive oil
2–3 tablespoons/ 30 ml whipping cream
2 teaspoons/ 10 g chopped parsley
2 teaspoons/ 10 g chopped chives

Peel the celeriac root and cut into thin slices, then cut the slices into long matchstick pieces. Sprinkle with lemon juice. Mix together the egg yolks, vinegar, mustard, salt and pepper, and gradually work in the oil and cream. Mix the celeriac pieces into the sauce and garnish with parsley and chives.

Celeriac Purée

1 lb/ 500 g celeriac
⅔ cup/ ¼ pint/ 125 ml stock
2 medium potatoes
¼ cup/ 2 oz/ 50 g butter
Salt and pepper
2 tablespoons/ 30 ml whipping cream
1 tablespoon/ 15 g chopped parsley

Peel the celeriac and cut in slices. Put into boiling salted water and cook for 5 minutes. Drain well and then put into the stock. Cover and simmer for 10 minutes. Add the potatoes, cover and cook for 15 minutes until the liquid has been absorbed. Take off the heat and mash with the butter and seasoning until smooth. Stir in the cream and parsley and serve hot. This is very good with poultry or game.

Celery

Celery is cultivated for its leaf-stalks or ribs which are bleached during growing and may be eaten raw or cooked. The flavor is supposedly improved after the first frost has touched the stems. The plant is a cultivated variety of a common weed called smallage, which Italian gardeners improved during the seventeenth century, followed by French gardeners who continued the improvement. Dutch farmers introduced the plant to Kalamazoo, Michigan in 1874, and this is commemorated by the name of the Kalamazoo variety which grows naturally white without blanching.

In Imperial Rome, Maecenas fed the asses he intended for consumption at banquets on celery, and also gave it to all kinds of domestic poultry. Roman epicures wore celery leaves in wreaths on their heads to counteract the effect of too much wine at their vast feasts. Today we appreciate this versatile vegetable for its refreshing flavor and crisp texture. Raw celery is a traditional accompaniment to the cheeseboard and gives texture to salads, and for this purpose it is best cleaned and then chilled in iced water until serving time. The leaves need not be wasted as they can be dried in a very slow oven and then rubbed through a sieve to make a strongly flavored powder for flavoring fish, meat, vegetables or soup.

Celery is spoiled if cooked in boiling salted water, except for a few minutes to blanch and tenderize it. Cooking should then be completed in stock for really good flavor. Small celery heads may be cooked whole, but larger ones should be split into stalks and then chopped.

Far left: Celeriac is sometimes called the turnip-rooted celery. It is very hardy and easy to grow.
Left: Celery is popular both raw and cooked.

Celery Soup

1 large head of celery
1 large onion
¼ cup/ 2 oz/ 50 g butter
1 carrot
1 large potato
1 teaspoon/ 5 g brown sugar
Salt and pepper
1⅓ cups/ ½ pint/ 250 ml chicken stock
2⅔ cups/ 1 pint/ 500 ml creamy milk
Chopped fresh herbs

Clean the celery and cut into small pieces. Chop the onion. Melt the butter, add the celery and onion, and stir over gentle heat for 4 minutes. Add the diced carrot and potato and cook for 2 minutes. Add sugar, salt and pepper, and 1⅓ cups/ ½ pint/ 250 ml water and simmer until the vegetables are tender. Put through a sieve, or liquidize. Add stock and milk and simmer for 10 minutes. Serve hot sprinkled with chopped herbs.

Celery Sauce (for Chicken or Turkey)

1 large head of celery
2 cups/ ¾ pint/ 375 ml stock
2 tablespoons/ 1 oz/ 25 g butter
4 tablespoons/ 1 oz/ 25 g flour
Salt and pepper
½ cup/ 4 fl oz/ 100 ml soured cream

Chop the celery very finely and simmer in the stock until tender. Heat the butter and stir in the flour. Cook gently for 3 minutes, then blend in the liquid from the celery. Simmer for 5 minutes until the sauce thickens, and season well. If a smooth sauce is preferred, put the sauce and celery into a blender and liquidize until creamy. Otherwise, stir the celery into the sauce and heat. Just before serving, stir in the soured cream.

North American Celery Salad

1 medium head of celery
1 large green or red pepper
6 scallions
⅜ cup/ 3 fl oz/ 90 ml mayonnaise
Salt and pepper
1 tablespoon/ 15 g chopped parsley
Crisp lettuce leaves

Clean the celery and chop the stalks. Remove seeds and membrane from the pepper and chop the flesh coarsely. Slice the scallions finely. Mix together and fold into mayonnaise with salt and pepper to taste. Chill thoroughly. Just before serving, arrange portions on lettuce leaves and sprinkle with parsley.

Stuffed Celery

1 medium head of celery
Variety of fillings

Clean the celery and crisp the stalks in iced water for 30 minutes. Drain well and cut into 2-in (5 cm) lengths. Stuff with one of the following fillings and serve as an appetizer with drinks:
(a) Chopped shrimps, prawns or crab mixed with well-seasoned mayonnaise
(b) Cream cheese softened and mixed with finely chopped olives, crumbled crisp bacon or finely chopped peppers
(c) Blue cheese creamed with a little cream cheese and a sprinkling of chopped parsley or finely chopped onion
(d) Minced ham or chicken with finely chopped peppers, olives and mayonnaise

Braised Celery and Mushrooms

1 head of celery
2⅔ cups/ 1 pint/ 500 ml chicken stock
⅔ cup/ 4 oz/ 100 g mushrooms
¼ cup/ 2 oz/ 50 g butter
4 tablespoons/ 1 oz/ 25 g flour
⅔ cup/ ¼ pint/ 125 ml milk
2 tablespoons/ 1 oz/ 25 g grated hard cheese

Break the celery into sticks and cut in 2-in (5 cm) lengths. Boil the stock and add the celery. Simmer for 20 minutes until tender. Drain the celery, reserving the cooking liquid. Slice the mushrooms and fry until just soft in half the butter. Drain well and arrange the mushrooms on the celery. Melt the remaining butter and work in the flour. Cook gently for 2 minutes and add the milk and ⅔ cup/ ¼ pint/ 125 ml reserved cooking liquid. Bring to the boil, stirring well, and simmer for 3 minutes. Pour over the vegetables and sprinkle with cheese. Put under a hot broiler or grill until golden and bubbling. Serve very hot on its own, or with meat or fish.

Italian Celery

1 large head of celery
⅔ cup/ ¼ pint/ 125 ml olive oil
1 medium onion
1⅓ cups/ ½ pint/ 250 ml tomato juice
Salt and pepper
1 teaspoon/ 5 g chopped thyme

Trim the outer stalks from the celery and cut off leaves. Cut the other stalks into 1-in (2.5 cm) lengths and wash thoroughly, then drain well. Heat the oil and fry the finely chopped onion until golden. Add the celery and continue cooking until the celery is golden. Add the tomato juice, salt, pepper and thyme and simmer together for 10 minutes.

Grecian Celery

1 large head of celery
1⅓ cups/ ½ pint/ 250 ml stock
Juice of 1 lemon
4–5 tablespoons/ 60 ml olive oil
3 bay leaves
1 tablespoon/ 15 g coriander seeds
Salt and pepper

Trim the outer stalks from the celery and cut off leaves. Cut the other stalks into 2-in (5 cm) lengths and wash thoroughly, then drain well. Put into boiling salted water and cook for 10 minutes. Drain well and put the celery into a saucepan with all the remaining ingredients. Bring to the boil and then simmer until the celery is tender and the stock has reduced to the consistency of cream. Serve hot or cold. This is very good with poultry or lamb.

Braised Celery with Bacon

1 large head of celery
1 cup/ 6 oz/ 150 g lean bacon
Pepper
2⅔ cups/ 1 pint/ 500 ml stock
3 bay leaves
2 tablespoons/ 1 oz/ 25 g butter

Below : Chard is very easy to grow and is so attractive that it can be used for decoration in the garden.

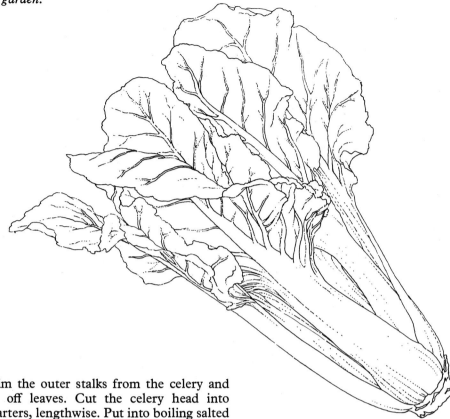

Trim the outer stalks from the celery and cut off leaves. Cut the celery head into quarters, lengthwise. Put into boiling salted water and cook for 10 minutes. Drain well and put the celery in a greased ovenware dish. Cover with chopped bacon and season with pepper. Add the stock and arrange the bay leaves and small pieces of butter on top. Cook at 190°C/375°F/Gas Mark 5 for 30 minutes. A little grated Parmesan cheese may be sprinkled on top if liked.

Celery and Herb Yogurt Scones

2 cups/ 8 oz/ 225 g wholewheat flour
1 teaspoon/ 5 g baking powder
½ teaspoon/ 2.5 g baking soda
½ teaspoon/ 2.5 g salt
¼ cup/ 2 oz/ 50 g butter
1 teaspoon/ 5 ml basil
3 celery sticks
⅔ cup/ ¼ pint/ 125 ml natural yogurt

Sift together flour, baking powder, baking soda and salt. Rub in the butter until the mixture is like fine breadcrumbs. Add the basil and finely chopped celery and mix well. Using a knife, bind the mixture with yogurt to form a soft dough. Pat out to a rectangle about 1-in (2.5 cm) thick on a floured board. Cut out into 1½-in (3.75 cm) scones. Place on greased and floured baking sheet and bake at 200°C/400°F/Gas Mark 6 for 12–15 minutes. Cool on a wire rack and serve with butter.

Celery with Cheese

1 lb/ 500 g celery
Juice of ½ lemon
1 bay leaf
1 sprig of parsley
3⅓ cups/ 1¼ pints/ 675 ml beef stock
⅔ cup/ ¼ pint/ 125 ml cream
2–3 tablespoons/ 30 ml sherry
½ cup/ 4 oz/ 100 g grated cheese
1 cup/ 3 oz/ 75 g coarse breadcrumbs
2 tablespoons/ 1 oz/ 25 g butter

Put the celery into a pan with the lemon juice, bay leaf, parsley and stock. Simmer until just tender. Drain off the liquid and reduce the liquid over heat to about ⅔ cup/ ¼ pint/ 125 ml. Stir in the cream, season to taste, and add the sherry. Put half the celery into a shallow greased ovenware dish. Pour on half the creamy sauce and sprinkle with half the cheese. Put on the rest of the celery and the remaining sauce. Sprinkle with the remaining cheese and crumbs mixed together. Melt the butter and sprinkle it on top of the dish. Bake at 220°C/425°F/Gas Mark 7 for 10 minutes. Serve very hot with poultry, game, veal or pork.

Celery Root

see Celeriac

Celtuce

see Lettuce

Cetriolini

see Gherkin

Chard

Chard is a variety of beet with tufts of vivid green foliage, of which the midribs and stalks are much enlarged. Variously known as leaf-chard, leaf-beet, swiss chard, seakale-beet, silver beet and white leaf-beet, the chard has midribs which are tender when young, but stringy when old, and has a slight asparagus flavor. The outer green of the leaves can be cooked like spinach, while the white midribs can be cooked in any way suitable for seakale or cardoon. In large leaves, the midrib may be 3–4 in (7.5–10 cm) wide, and should be cut in small pieces for serving. To retain the faint flavor of the chard, it is usually better to steam the midribs (large ones will require an hour's cooking), and to cut them up after cooking. The midribs may be served simply with butter and seasoning.

Chick Peas

see Pulses pages 162–71

Chicory, American

see Endive, English

Chicory, English

Chicory (*cichorium intybus*) is a member of the same family as endive, and the names are often interchanged. It is known as endive in France and the USA, but in England the plant chicory is sometimes known as succory or Belgian endive or Witloof. The compact heads which are blanched during growing have a rather bitter flavor but can be used both raw and cooked. The leaves may be pulled off and used whole in salads, or the chicory heads cut across in rings, but they will quickly darken and discolor when cut this way. Chicory may be simply dressed in oil and vinegar dressing, and a mixture of chicory and orange slices is very good served like this, with an additional pinch of sugar. When cooked, chicory is best braised in stock and should not be overcooked or it becomes slimy in texture. Celery recipes may be used for cooking chicory.

English chicory is known as endive *in the United States.*
Inset: Small green chilies make colorful additions to spicy dishes but must be used in moderation as they are very hot.

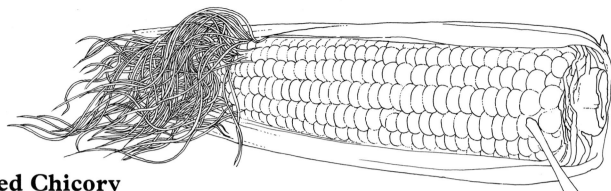

Braised Chicory

1 lb/ 500 g chicory heads
¼ cup/ 2 oz/ 50 g butter
1⅓ cups/ ½ pint/ 250 ml chicken stock
Salt and pepper
Juice of ½ lemon
1 teaspoon/ 5 g sugar
1 tablespoon/ 15 g chopped parsley

Wash the chicory and put into a flat greased ovenware dish. If any of the heads are very thick, split them lengthwise into two or three pieces. Put the butter on top in small flakes. Boil the stock, season with salt, pepper, lemon juice and sugar and pour over the chicory. Cover and cook at 190°C/ 375°F/Gas Mark 5 for 20 minutes. Remove the lid and continue cooking for 10 minutes. Sprinkle with chopped parsley just before serving.

Chicory and Ham Rolls

8 chicory heads
A little lemon juice
8 thin slices cooked ham
¼ cup/ 2 oz/ 50 g Cheddar cheese
2⅔ cups/ 1 pint/ 500 ml white sauce (see page 10)
Salt and pepper
2 tablespoons/ 1 oz/ 25 g fresh white breadcrumbs
2 tablespoons/ 1 oz/ 25 g butter

Clean the chicory and cook in water with a little lemon juice for 15 minutes. Drain very thoroughly. Roll each piece of chicory in a slice of ham and put into a greased shallow ovenware dish. Grate the cheese and mix it with the white sauce. Season well with salt and pepper and pour over the ham rolls. Sprinkle with breadcrumbs and top with flakes of butter. Bake at 190°C/375°F/Gas Mark 5 for 30 minutes.

Chihli Cabbage

see Cabbage, Chinese

Chilies

The name applies to very small hot peppers which may be bright red, vivid yellow, emerald green, chocolate or black-purple in color. These very hot peppers are used as seasoning for the hot dishes of South America, Mexico, Africa, Indonesia and Korea and should be used with great care. Hands should be scrubbed after handling them, and unwashed hands should never be put near the eyes or mouth as the chilies are very fiery indeed. Hot chili pepper is made from these peppers and is used for spicing a number of dishes; dried chilies are included in pickling spices.

Chinese Beans

see Bean Sprouts

Chinese Peas

see Peas, Edible-Pod

Chinese Potato

see Yam

Ciboule

see Onions, Welsh

Above: A cob or ear of corn and a pair of hot green chilies

Cinnamon Vine

see Yam

Cole or Colewort

see Kale or Cabbage

Corn

Sweetcorn is known variously as Indian corn, maize and corn-on-the-cob, and is thought to derive from a Mexican plant. Columbus found sweetcorn in Cuba and took it back to Europe where it was originally used for the preparation of cornmeal used under the name of hominy or polenta.

Corn should be cooked and eaten as soon as gathered as the grains quickly become starchy and unappetizing after exposure to air. The unhusked ears may be roasted in the oven or on a barbecue until lightly browned and eaten straight away from the cob with melted butter and a pinch of salt. The husked corn may be boiled for 7–15 minutes (depending on freshness) in unsalted water and eaten in the same way. The kernels may be stripped from the cobs to use in a variety of dishes.

Baked Corn

Strip the husks and remove the silk from the cobs. Put them in an ovenware dish and cover with milk. Bake at 180°C/350°F/Gas Mark 4 for 45 minutes. Drain and soak in melted butter until shiny. Season with salt and pepper and grill quickly until golden. Serve very hot.

Fried Corn

1⅓ cup/ 8oz/ 225g corn kernels
2 tablespoons/ 1oz/ 25g butter
¼ cup/ 2oz/ 50g onion
2 tablespoons/ 1oz/ 25g green pepper
Salt and pepper
3–4 tablespoons/ 45ml cream

Melt the butter and add the corn, chopped onion and pepper and plenty of seasoning. Toss over a high heat until the corn is lightly browned. Stir in the cream and serve hot. A little hot sauce, such as Tabasco, is good with this mixture.

Corn Chowder*

4 slices of bacon
1 large onion
1lb/ 500g potatoes
4 cups/ 1½ pints/ 750ml milk
2 cups/ 12oz/ 300g cooked corn kernels
Salt and pepper
Pinch of rosemary
1 teaspoon/ 5g sugar

Cut the bacon into thin strips and heat gently in a thick pan until the fat runs. Continue frying until the bacon is crisp. Drain off the fat and keep the bacon pieces on one side. Slice the onion thinly and cut the potatoes in cubes. Cook in the bacon fat, stirring gently for 3 minutes, then cover and cook until tender. Bring the milk to the boil, add the onions, potatoes and corn and seasonings. Simmer for 5 minutes, then re-move from heat and leave to stand for 1 hour. Just before serving, reheat and garnish with bacon pieces.

Corn Fritters

1⅓ cups/ 8oz/ 225g corn kernels
1 cup/ 4oz/ 100g flour
1 teaspoon/ 5g baking powder
½ teaspoon/ 2.5g salt
2 eggs
4–5 tablespoons/ 60ml milk
1 tablespoon/ 15ml melted butter

Sift together the flour, baking powder and salt. Combine the eggs and milk and add to the flour mixture. Add the corn kernels and butter and mix thoroughly. Fry a tablespoonful in hot fat until golden on both sides. Drain thoroughly and serve very hot with chicken, ham or fish.

Virginia Corn Pudding

6 large cobs of corn
2 eggs
4 tablespoons/ 1oz/ 25g flour
Salt and pepper
2⅔ cups/ 1 pint/ 500ml milk
⅜ cup/ 3oz/ 75g butter

Scrape the kernels from the uncooked ears and mix with the eggs. Mix the flour with plenty of seasoning and a little of the milk and stir into the egg mixture. Add the remaining milk and put into a buttered pie plate. Dot with pieces of butter. Bake at 190°C/375°F/Gas Mark 5 for 1 hour and serve hot.

Corn Relish

18 cobs of corn
1 small white cabbage
1 head of celery
4 medium onions
2 green peppers
11 cups/ 4 pints/ 2 liters vinegar
2 cups/ 1lb/ 500g sugar
1 cup/ 4oz/ 100g flour
¼ cup/ 2oz/ 50g salt
½ teaspoon/ 2.5g mustard powder
½ teaspoon/ 2.5g turmeric
¼ teaspoon/ 1.25g cayenne pepper

Cut the corn kernels from the cobs with a sharp pointed knife. Chop the cabbage, celery, onions and peppers finely. Put all the vegetables into a saucepan with half the vinegar. Mix the sugar, flour and seasonings with the remaining vinegar and stir into the saucepan. Bring to the boil and then simmer for 45 minutes. Put into clean jars and cover tightly with vinegar-proof lids.

Cornichon

see Gherkin

Corn Salad

One of the most popular winter salad vegetables in Europe, the French version has round leaves, while the Italian corn salad has lighter, longer leaves with slightly toothed edges. The leaves are best when eaten while still quite small. Corn salad may be used as lettuce for salads, but is not usually dressed with herbs. A favorite French salad is a combination of corn salad, thin slices of cooked beet and thinly-sliced celery, dressed with an oil and vinegar dressing. The leaves may be quickly cooked like spinach.

Courgette

see Zucchini

Cress, American

Sometimes known as land cress, belle-isle cress or upland cress, this is a plant which looks and tastes like watercress but can be grown on land. The leaves and stems have a peppery flavor and can be used in all watercress recipes.

Cress, Marine

see Samphire

Lebanese Cucumber Soup

see page 62

tomato juice
yogurt
chicken stock
cream
garlic
salt and pepper
cucumber
mint

Cress, Salad

This Persian native plant grows quickly and easily, and is commonly cultivated in seed pans or on wet cotton. The tiny stems and leaves are widely used in England for garnishing, for salads, and for sandwiches. It is often grown and used with white mustard.

Crooknecks

(including Canada and Winter)

see Squash

Cucumber

The cucumber is one of our oldest vegetables, once a common and cheap food under the Egyptian Pharaohs, craved for by the Israelites in the wilderness, a culinary treasure in Ancient Rome, and a cultivated plant in China many thousands of years ago. The plant originally comes from southern Asia and comes in a number of varieties, with special kinds being raised in large quantities for pickling.

In the seventeenth century, John Evelyn wrote that the cucumber was considered poisonous, and it has a reputation for being unwholesome and causing indigestion. Ude, the great chef to Louis XVI, who also cooked in a London club, said that 'the cucumber is of very easy digestion and must be recommended as very healthy food.' It is suggested that raw cucumber is better peeled but André Simon recommended it should be sliced thickly enough to ensure careful chewing and better digestion, and the skin should be retained because it holds rich salts as well as good flavor, and also holds a small quantity of a pepsin-like substance which helps to digest the cellulose part of the pulp with the aid of the ptyalin brought out during eating.

Many recipes also recommend draining off all the liquid from cucumbers during preparation. Urbain Dubois, a great French authority on the science of gastronomy, said however that 'cucumbers eaten with their water are less heavy on the stomach.'

Lebanese Cucumber Soup*

⅔ cup/ ¼ pint/ 125 ml tomato juice
1⅓ cups/ ½ pint/ 250 ml natural yogurt
2 cups/ ¾ pint/ 375 ml chicken stock
⅔ cup/ ¼ pint/ 125 ml cream
1 garlic clove
Salt and pepper
1 small cucumber
1 tablespoon/ 15 g chopped mint

Put the tomato juice, yogurt, stock, cream, chopped garlic and seasoning into a blender and liquidize until smooth. Chill for 30 minutes. Peel the cucumber and cut in quarters lengthwise. Scoop out the seeds and cut the flesh into dice. Stir the cucumber and mint into the soup just before serving.

Italian Cucumber Salad

1 cucumber
1 small onion
1 tablespoon/ 15 ml tarragon vinegar
2–3 tablespoons/ 30 ml olive oil
Salt and pepper

Wipe the cucumber but do not peel. Slice very thinly and put into a serving dish. Sprinkle with very finely chopped onion, vinegar and oil, and season with salt and pepper.

Danish Cucumber Salad

1 large cucumber
1 tablespoon/ 15 ml salt
1 cup/ 8 fl oz/ 250 ml cider vinegar
½ cup/ 4 oz/ 100 g sugar
½ teaspoon/ 2.5 ml black pepper
1 tablespoon/ 15 ml chopped parsley

Peel the cucumber and cut it into very thin slices. Spread out on a plate and sprinkle with salt. Leave to stand for 1 hour and drain off all the liquid. Put the vinegar, sugar and pepper into a saucepan and bring to the boil. Leave to cool and pour over the drained cucumber slices. Leave to stand at room temperature for 2 hours, and then chill. Drain befor serving and sprinkle with chopped parsley.

Brazilian Cucumber Salad

1 large cucumber
2 teaspoons/ 10 ml lemon juice
Salt and pepper

Peel the cucumber and cut the flesh into small dice. Put into a serving bowl and sprinkle with lemon juice, salt and pepper. Chill for 1 hour and drain before serving.

Cucumber Raita

1 large cucumber
1⅓ cup/ ½ pint/ 250 ml natural yogurt
1 small onion
½ teaspoon/ 2.5 ml salt
Pinch of cayenne pepper
Pinch of ground cinnamon
Pinch of ground cloves

Peel the cucumber and slice wafer-thin. Stir into the yogurt and add the grated onion and seasonings. Chill and serve with curry, roast lamb or shish kebab.

Cucumber in Cream Sauce

1 cucumber
2 oz/ 50 g butter
½ cup/ 4 fl oz/ 100 ml water
Salt and pepper
⅔ cup/ ¼ pint/ 125 ml whipping cream
⅔ cup/ ¼ teaspoon ground nutmeg
Pinch of paprika

Wipe the cucumber and peel it. Cut into thick slices and put in a heavy saucepan with the butter, water, salt and pepper. Simmer until the cucumber slices are tender. Stir in the cream and nutmeg and cook very gently, shaking the pan, until the cream thickens. Put into a serving dish and sprinkle with paprika. This is very good with ham or chicken.

Stuffed Cucumbers

2 cucumbers
1 cup/ 8 oz/ 225 g cooked ham
1 cup/ 8 oz/ 225 g cooked chicken
Salt and pepper

Pinch of ground nutmeg
Pinch of chopped thyme
1 egg
2 medium onions
3 medium carrots
3–4 tablespoons/ 45 ml oil
6 medium tomatoes

Wipe the cucumbers but do not peel them. Cut each cucumber in half across, then in half lengthwise and scoop out the seeds. Mince the ham and chicken. Season with salt, pepper, nutmeg and thyme, and bind with the egg. Fill the cucumber pieces with this mixture and put two pieces together, tying them to keep the filling inside. Peel and slice the onions and chop the carrots. Heat the oil and fry the onions and carrots until golden and soft. Lift out with a slotted spoon and keep on one side. Fry the cucumbers in the oil until golden, then add the onions and carrots. Put into a casserole and top with the tomatoes cut in half. Cover and cook at 180°C/350°F/Gas Mark 4 for 30 minutes. Lift the cucumbers on to a serving dish. Purée the remaining vegetables and cooking liquid. Reheat and pour over the cucumbers. Sprinkle with a little extra chopped thyme.

Sweet Cucumber Pickle

3 lb/ 1.5 kg cucumbers
1 tablespoon/ ½ oz/ 15 g powdered alum
5 cups/ 2 pints/ 1 liter water
2 lb/ 1 kg sugar
⅓ cup/ 2 oz/ 50 g whole cloves
2-in/ 5 cm cinnamon stick
2⅔ cups/ 1 pint/ 500 ml vinegar

Peel the cucumbers as thinly as possible. Cut them in 3-in (7.5 cm) pieces and then cut each piece into quarters. Stir the alum into the water and add the cucumber pieces. Bring slowly to the boil and then drain. Cover the cucumber in iced water until it is chilled. Put the sugar, spices and vinegar into a saucepan, bring to the boil and continue boiling for 5 minutes. Take out the spices. Drain the cucumber, add to the vinegar syrup, and simmer for 10 minutes. Take off the heat and leave the cucumber in the syrup overnight. Next day, drain off the syrup and boil it hard for 1 minute. Pour over the cucumbers and leave overnight. Repeat this process twice more. Take the cucumber pieces from the syrup and pack them into clean jars. Boil the syrup and pour over the cucumber pieces. Cool and cover tightly with vinegar-proof lids.

Cucumber Conserve

4 large cucumbers
4 lb/ 2 kg sugar
4 tablespoons/ 2 oz/ 50 g root ginger

Peel the cucumbers and slice thinly. Cover with the sugar and leave for 24 hours. Strain the juice and sugar into a pan, and simmer gently until the sugar dissolves. Tie the root ginger into a muslin bag and crush it with a heavy weight. Put the bag into the syrup and boil for 45 minutes. Add the cucumber slices and boil for 10 minutes. Leave to stand for 12 hours. Boil for 15 minutes, remove ginger, pour into hot jars and cover.

Baked Cucumber

1 large cucumber
Salt and pepper
Pinch of sugar
½ teaspoon/ 2.5 ml wine vinegar
1 tablespoon/ 15 g fresh herbs
¼ cup/ 2 oz/ 50 g butter

Wipe the cucumber and cut into quarters lengthwise. Scoop away the seeds and cut the flesh into ½-in (1.25 cm) lengths. Put into a bowl and sprinkle well with salt, adding the sugar and vinegar. Leave for 30 minutes and then drain away the liquid. Put into a greased ovenware dish and add the herbs, a little pepper and the butter cut in flakes. Bake at 220°C/425°F/Gas Mark 7 for 30 minutes. This is excellent with both meat and fish.

Cucumber Sauce (for Fish)

1 cucumber
2 tablespoons/ 1 oz/ 25 g butter
2 egg yolks
⅔ cup/ ¼ pint/ 125 ml cream
Salt and pepper
1 teaspoon/ 5 ml French mustard
Squeeze of lemon juice
Chopped chives
Chopped parsley
Chopped tarragon

Do not peel the cucumber, but cut into chunks, discarding the seeds. Melt the butter in a heavy saucepan and toss the cucumber pieces so they are coated in butter. Beat the egg yolks and cream and add the salt, pepper and mustard. Add to the cucumber and stir over very low heat to thicken. Add lemon juice and herbs before serving. The sauce may be served hot or cold.

Cushaw Squash

see Squash

Daikon

see Radish

Dandelion

While the dandelion is usually considered to be a weed, it is cultivated in many countries as a salad vegetable. The plants may be successfully blanched like celery to give pale, crisp leaves which have a slight and refreshing bitterness. The youngest leaves are the best to eat because as the older leaves mature, they become very fibrous. The leaves must be washed very thoroughly and dried and can be eaten with a simple oil and vinegar dressing. The leaves may also be boiled or steamed to use in soups, omelettes and savory pies, in the same way as sorrel or spinach.

Yankee Style Dandelions

1 large bunch young dandelion leaves
⅔ cup/ 4 oz/ 100 g lean salt pork
1 medium onion

Wash the dandelion leaves very well and tear into large pieces. Put into a pan with ½ pint/250 ml boiling salted water. Add diced pork and chopped onion and cook over high heat, stirring occasionally until the leaves are just tender. Drain and dress with butter, salt and pepper. Vinegar may be offered with these dandelion leaves too. Serve with crisp bacon and boiled potatoes.

Cucumbers are very susceptible to weather variations. They need light and plenty of water and manure to grow properly. There are two varieties: ridge cucumbers have rather knobbly skins and are more easily grown out of doors; greenhouse or frame (above) cucumbers are longer and smoother skinned but prefer to grow inside cloches, greenhouses or frames. Cucumbers prefer steamy heat to dry heat and thus cannot share the same greenhouse as other salad vegetables such as tomatoes.

French Dandelions with Bacon

½ lb/ 8 oz/ 225 g dandelion leaves
3 medium potatoes
1⅓ cups/ ½ lb/ 225 g bacon
2–3 tablespoons/ 30 ml wine vinegar
Pepper

Wash the dandelion leaves and drain well. Cook the potatoes and cut them in thin slices. Chop the bacon and cook in its own fat until just browned. Put the potatoes and dandelion leaves in a serving dish. Sprinkle with the bacon, vinegar and pepper and serve at once.

Dandelion Salad

1 large bunch young dandelion leaves
1 hard-boiled egg
2 slices of white bread
2 slices of bacon
2–3 tablespoons/ 30 ml oil
3–4 tablespoons/ 45 ml olive oil
1 tablespoon/ 15 ml wine vinegar
Salt and pepper
Pinch of sugar
½ teaspoon/ 2.5 ml French mustard

Wash the dandelion leaves, dry well, and put into a bowl. Chop the egg. Remove the crusts from the bread and cut the bread into small cubes. Chop the bacon and fry in its own fat until crisp, then drain well. Add the oil to the bacon fat in the pan, fry the bread cubes until golden, and drain well. Sprinkle the chopped egg, bacon and bread cubes on to the dandelion leaves. Mix the olive oil, vinegar, salt, pepper, sugar and mustard. Pour over the salad just before serving and toss lightly.

Dwarf Beans

see Beans, French

Edible-Pod Peas

see Peas, Edible-Pod

Eggplant/ Aubergine

The eggplant is known by many names, such as egg apple, mad apple, brinjal and aubergine. There is the Arabic batinjan, Spanish berenjena, Portuguese berinjela, Chinese ai-kwa, Japanese nanbu-naga nasu and Indonesian terong, and indeed the vegetable (or more correctly fruit) figures in a huge variety of exotic dishes.

The best eggplants to use are medium-size, firm, shiny and unwrinkled. When they are being used sliced in dishes, it is best to cut them and put the pieces into a colander with a liberal sprinkling of salt. The pieces should be left for 30 minutes for the juices to run out. Tomatoes, onions, wine, olive oil, garlic and basil are all natural accompaniments to eggplants, which are just as good served hot or cold.

Eggplant Dip

1 large eggplant
Salt and pepper
1 teaspoon/ 5 ml lemon juice
1 tablespoon/ 15 ml French dressing

Wipe the eggplant and broil or grill whole until the skin is burnt and the eggplant has collapsed and looks cooked through. Peel off the skin and allow the juices to escape. Mash the remaining pulp with salt, pepper, lemon juice and French dressing. Chill before serving as a dip, or spread on toast. This is sometimes known as 'mock caviar.'

Imam Baildi

3 medium eggplants
Salt and pepper
½ cup/ 4 fl oz/ 100 ml olive oil
4 large onions
¾ cup/ 6 fl oz/ 150 ml water
2–3 tablespoons/ 30 ml concentrated tomato purée
⅔ cup/ 2 oz/ 50 g breadcrumbs
½ teaspoon/ 2.5 ml curry powder
1 tablespoon/ 15 ml pine nuts
2 teaspoons/ 10 g chopped parsley
6 black olives

Wipe the eggplants and plunge them into boiling water. Cook for 15 minutes and put into cold water. Leave for 3 minutes, drain and cut in half lengthwise. Scoop out the center leaving a thin shell of skin and pulp. Put the skins into an ovenware dish, season with salt and pepper and pour over most of the olive oil, reserving 2 tablespoons/ 30 ml. Bake at 170°C/325°F/Gas Mark 3 for 30 minutes. Chop the onions and cook in the water until soft. Add the tomato purée, breadcrumbs, salt and pepper to taste, and the curry powder. Add the mashed pulp of the eggplant, the remaining olive oil and the pine nuts. Simmer together, stirring well, for 20 minutes. Put the mixture into the eggplant skins and sprinkle with chopped parsley and chopped olives. This dish may be eaten hot, but is better left to cool (not chill) for 3–4 hours. Almonds or peanuts may be substituted for the pine nuts. This dish has a romantic name and history, since Imam Baildi means 'the priest swooned.' The legend is that the gentleman was overcome by the exquisite dish presented by his proud host.

Italian Eggplant Salad*

2 large eggplants
Salt
12 medium tomatoes
2–3 tablespoons/ 30 ml olive oil
⅔ cup/ ¼ pint/ 125 ml dry white wine
2 garlic cloves
2 teaspoons/ 10 g chopped basil

Peel the eggplants thinly and cut them across in thick slices. Put into a colander, sprinkle with salt, and leave for 30 minutes for the juices to run out. Peel the tomatoes and slice them thinly into a serving dish. Heat the olive oil and fry the eggplant slices, turning them often so that they just color. Drain off any oil. Pour the wine, crushed garlic and basil into the pan and simmer until the liquid has reduced to a coating sauce. Stir well and pour over the tomatoes. Chill before serving, sprinkled with a little extra basil.

Below : Basil

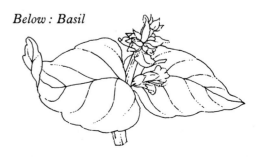

Italian Eggplant Salad

see page 65

**eggplants
salt
tomatoes
olive oil
dry white wine
garlic
basil**

Inset right: The eggplant or aubergine is basically a tropical vegetable which has been imported from southern Asia. Thus the successful gardener will need to be sure that his plants have lots of heat and sunshine.

Baked Eggplants in Tomato Sauce

2 large eggplants
Salt
12 large tomatoes
1 large sprig of basil
3 garlic cloves
4–5 tablespoons/ 60 ml olive oil
⅔ cup/ 2 oz/ 50 g breadcrumbs
Grated rind of 1 lemon
¼ cup/ 2 oz/ 50 g grated Parmesan
    cheese

Peel the eggplants thinly and cut them lengthwise in thick slices. Put into a colander, sprinkle with salt, and leave for 30 minutes for the juices to run out. Peel the tomatoes, remove the seeds, and cut them in large pieces. Mix them with chopped basil and crushed garlic. Put a little of the oil into a shallow ovenware dish and put in a layer of eggplant slices. Add a layer of tomato mixture and sprinkle with oil. Put on a second layer of eggplant, then tomato mixture and oil. Mix together the breadcrumbs, lemon rind and cheese and sprinkle on top of the tomato mixture. Bake at 200°C/ 400°F/Gas Mark 6 for 30 minutes and serve very hot.

Eggplant with Basil Sauce

2 large eggplants
4 tablespoons/ 1 oz/ 25 g flour
Salt and pepper
2 garlic cloves
2 large sprigs of basil
8 walnut halves
2–3 tablespoons/ 30 ml olive oil

Peel the eggplants thinly and cut them lengthwise in thick slices. Put into a colander, sprinkle with salt, and leave for 30 minutes for the juices to run out. Season the flour with salt and pepper and dip the eggplant slices in the mixture. Brush the grill tray with a little oil and put in the eggplant slices. Brush with oil and cook under a hot broiler/grill on both sides. Meanwhile make the sauce by pounding the garlic cloves, basil leaves and chopped walnuts together and gradually working in the oil (this can be done most easily in a blender). Serve the eggplants very hot with the sauce.

Indonesian Eggplants

4 small eggplants
2–3 tablespoons/ 30 ml peanut oil
1 large onion
1 garlic clove
⅔ cup/ 4 oz/ 100 g cooked prawns
    (or shrimps)
4–5 tablespoons/ 60 ml water
Salt and pepper
3 drops Tabasco sauce

Wipe the eggplants and cut into ½-in (1.25 cm) cubes without peeling. Put into a colander with a sprinkling of salt and leave for 30 minutes to drain off juices. Heat the oil in a heavy pan and cook the thinly sliced onion and chopped garlic for 2 minutes, stirring frequently. Add the eggplant cubes, prawns, warm water and seasoning, stir well, cover and simmer for 10 minutes. Serve warm with rice and a salad, or as part of an Indonesian *Rijstafel* (rice table).

Eggplant Fritters

2 large eggplants
6 tablespoons/ 1½ oz/ 40 g flour
1 egg
Salt and pepper
1 tablespoon/ 15 ml olive oil
3–4 tablespoons/ 45 ml water

Peel the eggplants thinly and cut them into thick slices. Put into a colander, sprinkle with salt, and leave for 30 minutes for the juices to run out. Make a batter with the flour, egg, salt, pepper, oil and water. Drain the pieces of eggplant and dip them in the creamy batter. Fry in deep hot oil until crisp and golden. Serve very hot with a hot tomato sauce.

Stuffed Eggplants

2 medium eggplants
¼ cup/ 2 oz/ 50 g butter
1 small onion
⅔ cup/ 4 oz/ 100 g mushrooms
4 large tomatoes
⅔ cup/ 2 oz/ 50 g fresh white bread-
    crumbs
1 lemon
1 teaspoon/ 5 g chopped marjoram
Salt and pepper
1 egg
3–4 tablespoons/ 45 ml olive oil

Wipe the eggplants and cut them in half lengthwise. Scoop out the flesh, leaving the skins whole. Chop the flesh finely. Melt the butter and cook the finely chopped onion until soft and golden. Add the finely chopped mushrooms. Peel the tomatoes, remove the seeds, and chop the flesh finely. Add the tomato pieces to the onion and mushroom mixture and cook gently until the juices run. Take off the heat and add to the eggplant flesh, breadcrumbs, lemon rind and juice, marjoram, salt and pepper. Bind with the egg and put the mixture into the eggplant skins. Put them into a greased ovenware dish and sprinkle with the olive oil. Cover and bake at 180°C/350°F/Gas Mark 4 for 45 minutes. Serve hot as a first course, or to accompany meat or fish.

Baked Eggplants with Cream Cheese

2 large eggplants
Salt
¼ cup/ 2 oz/ 50 g butter
2–3 tablespoons/ 30 ml oil
1 large onion
¾ lb/ 12 oz/ 350 g tomatoes
1 teaspoon/ 5 g chopped basil
1 tablespoon/ 15 g chopped parsley
Pepper
¾ cup/ 6 oz/ 150 g cream cheese
2–3 tablespoons/ 30 ml milk
2 tablespoons/ 1 oz/ 25 g grated
    Parmesan cheese
2 tablespoons/ 1 oz/ 25 g dry bread-
    crumbs
2 tablespoons/ 1 oz/ 25 g butter

Wipe the eggplants but do not peel. Cut in thick slices, sprinkle with salt and leave to drain in a colander for 30 minutes. Rinse in cold water and dry well. Heat the butter and oil and fry the eggplant slices until golden on both sides. Lift out the eggplants and drain well. Peel and slice the onion thinly and cook in the fat until soft and golden. Peel the tomatoes, remove the seeds and chop the flesh. Stir into the onion with the basil, parsley, salt and pepper and cook gently for 10 minutes. Divide the eggplants into three portions and put one layer in a greased ovenware dish. Top with half the tomato mixture. Cream the cream cheese with the milk and spread half on the tomato mixture. Put on more eggplants, then the remaining tomato mixture and cream cheese. Finish with a layer of eggplant. Top with a mixture of Parmesan cheese and breadcrumbs, and dot with flakes of butter. Bake at 180°C/350°F/Gas Mark 4 for about 40 minutes until the top is golden brown and the casserole is bubbling. This may be used to accompany lamb dishes, but is very good served by itself.

Lamb and Eggplant Bake

1½ cups/ 12 oz/ 350 g cooked ground lamb
2 medium eggplants
2 tablespoons/ 1 oz/ 25 g butter
2–3 tablespoons/ 30 ml olive oil
1 large onion
⅔ cup/ 4 oz/ 100 g mushrooms
1 tablespoon breadcrumbs
⅔ cup/ ¼ pint/ 125 ml concentrated tomato purée
1 large egg
Salt and pepper

Cut the eggplants in slices without peeling and sprinkle with salt. Leave to stand for 30 minutes. Drain thoroughly and fry in butter and oil until lightly browned on both sides. Remove from the pan and keep warm. Chop onions and mushrooms. Fry onion in the same pan until soft, then add mushrooms, breadcrumbs, stock, tomato purée, beaten egg and seasoning. Cover the bottom of a casserole with half the eggplant slices. Put the meat mixture on top and cover with the remaining eggplant slices. Bake uncovered at 180°C/350°F/Gas Mark 4 for 1 hour.

Endive, American

see Chicory, English

Endive, English

The endive (*cichorium endivia*) is called chicory in France and the USA. In England, endive is the name given to a salad plant with pale green curly leaves growing in a flattened crown, and with a slightly bitter taste. The leaves make an excellent salad but may also be cooked, using the same recipes as for lettuce.

Braised Endive

1 bunch endive
2 cups/ ¾ pint/ 375 ml beef stock
Salt and pepper
2 tablespoons/ 1 oz/ 25 g Parmesan cheese

Wash the endive and drain it well. Tear the leaves into large pieces and cook in boiling salted water for 8 minutes. Drain very thoroughly and put into a shallow ovenware dish. Pour on the beef stock and season well with salt and pepper. Bake at 180°C/350°F/ Gas Mark 4 for 20 minutes. Sprinkle with grated cheese before serving. This vegetable dish is particularly good with beef.

Escarole

This broad-leaved member of the endive and chicory family grows in rather flattened bunches of broad, curly-edged green leaves with a yellow center, a firm texture and slightly bitter flavor. Escarole is best washed in cold water, drained and eaten as salad with an oil and vinegar dressing. It may also be braised and served with butter and seasoning, or with a cream cheese or cheese sauce.

Italian Escarole Soup

1 large bunch escarole
½ cup/ 4 oz/ 100 g salt pork
1 large onion
4 tablespoons/ 1 oz/ 25 g flour
1 teaspoon/ 5 g salt
Pepper
11 cups/ 4 pints/ 2.25 liters chicken stock
½ cup/ 3 oz/ 75 g long grain rice
1 cup/ 4 oz/ 100 g fried bread cubes

Wash the escarole very thoroughly and shred it coarsely. Dice the salt pork and cook in its own fat until lightly browned. Add chopped onions and stir in the fat until soft and golden. Stir in the flour and gradually add the chicken stock. Bring to the boil and add the rice. Cover and simmer for about 15 minutes until the rice is tender. Add the escarole and cook for 5 minutes. Serve hot with a liberal garnish of fried bread cubes.

Below: Eggplants and curly English endive (called chicory in the United States).

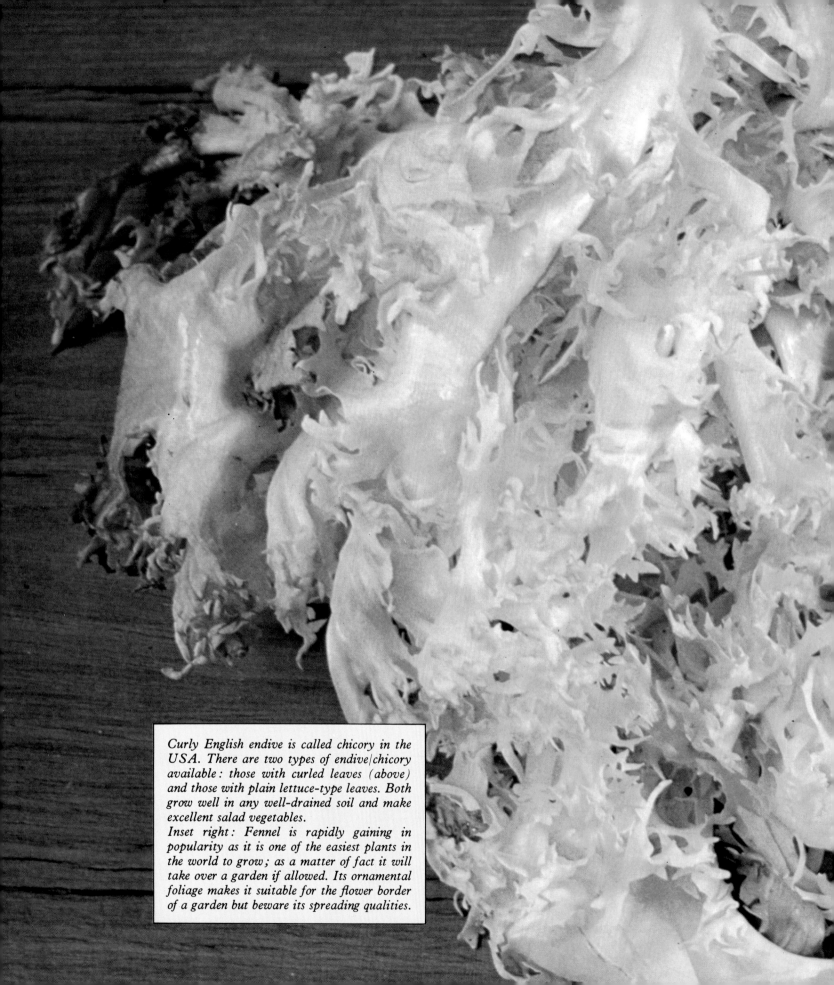

Curly English endive is called chicory in the USA. There are two types of endive/chicory available: those with curled leaves (above) and those with plain lettuce-type leaves. Both grow well in any well-drained soil and make excellent salad vegetables.

Inset right: Fennel is rapidly gaining in popularity as it is one of the easiest plants in the world to grow; as a matter of fact it will take over a garden if allowed. Its ornamental foliage makes it suitable for the flower border of a garden but beware its spreading qualities.

Fennel, Florence

There are two types of fennel, one being commonly used for the flavoring quality of its feathery leaves. The second type is a favorite vegetable, known variously as Florence fennel or finocchio, of which the swollen bulbous base is eaten. It is a particular favorite in Italian cooking. During growth, the plants are blanched like celery, and the root has a texture similar to celery, with a distinctive flavor of anise.

The bulbous base of fennel must be thoroughly washed and the stems trimmed off. Small 'bulbs' may be left whole, but larger ones should be cut across in half or quarters. To cook simply, boil in water until tender, drain very thoroughly and dress with butter or olive oil, salt and pepper and a pinch of mustard powder. Cooked fennel may also be drained and chilled and served in an oil and vinegar dressing. Fennel may also be braised like celery and indeed can be used in any favorite celery recipe.

Baked Fennel in Tomato Sauce

3 fennel bulbs
⅔ cup/ ¼ pint/ 125 ml olive oil
1 medium onion
3 garlic cloves
12 medium tomatoes
Salt and pepper
⅔ cup/ 2 oz/ 50 g fresh breadcrumbs
¼ cup/ 2 oz/ 50 g grated Parmesan cheese
Grated rind of ½ lemon

Trim the fennel and cut each bulb in half downwards, then cut across to give thin slices. Heat the oil and cook the sliced onion until soft and golden. Chop two garlic cloves and add to the oil, and then add the fennel slices. Stir over low heat until the fennel begins to color. Peel the tomatoes, remove the seeds and chop the flesh roughly. Add to the fennel with the salt and pepper and continue cooking over low heat for 5 minutes. Turn into a shallow ovenware dish. Mix the breadcrumbs, cheese, grated lemon rind and finely chopped garlic clove and sprinkle on top of the fennel. Bake at 200°C/400°F/Gas Mark 6 for 20 minutes until the top is crisp and golden.

Fennel Niçoise

3 fennel bulbs
2 medium onions
2 garlic cloves
4–5 tablespoons/60 ml oil
1 lb/ 500 g tomatoes
⅔ cup/ ¼ pint/ 125 ml dry white wine
Pinch of thyme
Salt and pepper

Trim the fennel and cut each bulb in quarters. Boil in salted water for 10 minutes. Drain well. Peel and chop the onions and garlic coarsely. Heat the oil and cook them until soft and golden. Add the fennel, and stir well. Peel the tomatoes and remove the seeds. Cut the flesh in large pieces and add to the onions and fennel. Pour in the wine and add the thyme, salt and pepper. Cover and simmer for 1 hour. This is delicious served as a first course, and may be sprinkled with grated Parmesan cheese.

Fennel Fritters

3 fennel bulbs
½ cup/ 2 oz/ 50 g flour
2–3 tablespoons/ 30 ml olive oil
Salt and pepper
⅔ cup/ ¼ pint/ 125 ml water
2 egg whites
Lemon wedges
Oil for frying

Trim the fennel and cut each bulb in half downwards, then cut across to give thin slices. Make a batter with the flour, oil, seasoning and water, adding a little more water if necessary to give a creamy consistency. Whip the egg whites to soft peaks and fold into the batter. Dip the fennel slices in the batter and fry in deep hot oil until crisp and golden. Serve hot with lemon wedges.

Fenugreek

The sprouts of this plant are used like bean sprouts and have a spicy curry flavor. The seeds and sprouts are rich in iron and vitamin A, and contain 29 percent protein. The seeds should be sprouted in a clean jar covered with a muslin (cheesecloth) lid, rinsing them three times in tepid water and then putting the container on its side in a temperature of 20–30°C (68–86°F), rinsing in water once or twice a day. They will take 4–5 days to grow to 3-in (7.5 cm) length, when they can be harvested. The raw sprouts may be eaten as part of a salad, or lightly cooked in a variety of dishes.

Fenugreek Soup

1 large potato
2 cups/ ¾ pint/ 375 ml water
1 lb/ 500 g fenugreek sprouts
⅔ cup/ ¼ pint/ 125 ml milk
Salt

Peel the potato and boil in the water until tender. Drain and reserve the liquid. Put the potato in a blender with most of the fenugreek sprouts and milk. Blend until smooth and put into a pan with the cooking liquid. Season and heat to boiling point, and garnish with the remaining sprouts.

Below: A bowl of fenugreek sprouts, an onion and a pair of gherkins.

Fenugreek Potatoes

1 lb/ 500 g potatoes
2–3 tablespoons/ 30 ml oil
½ teaspoon/ 2.5 ml turmeric
1 lb/ 500 g fenugreek sprouts
Salt and pepper

Cook the potatoes, cool and chop them roughly. Heat the oil in a thick pan and stir in the potatoes and turmeric powder. Cook for 5 minutes, stirring often. Add the fenugreek sprouts, salt and pepper, cover with a lid and cook for 5 minutes. Serve very hot.

Curried Fenugreek

1 small onion
2 tablespoons/ 30 ml oil
1 lb/ 500 g fenugreek sprouts
2 teaspoons/ 10 ml curry powder
1 teaspoon/ 5 g cornstarch
¼ cup/ 2 fl oz/ 50 ml water

Chop the onion finely and fry in the oil until soft and golden. Add the chopped fenugreek sprouts and curry powder. Continue cooking and stirring for 2 minutes. Mix the cornstarch and water and add to the sprouts. Simmer for 4 minutes until the mixture is thick. This is very good with chicken.

Finocchio

see Fennel, Florence

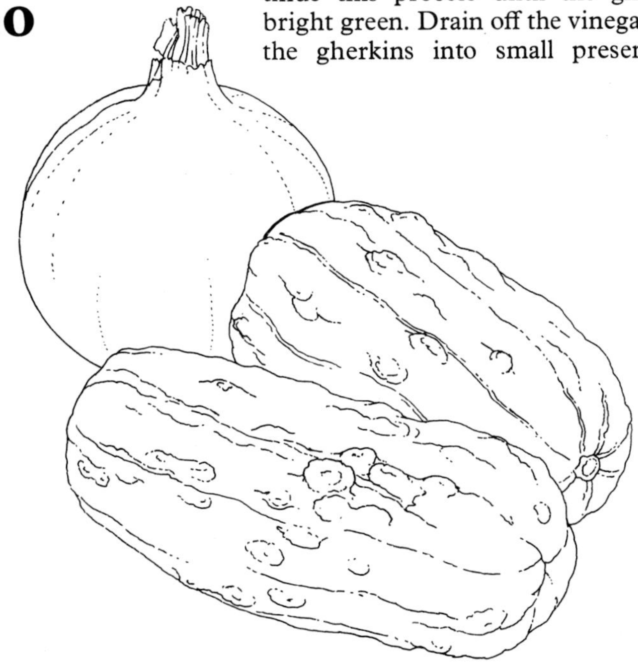

French Beans

see Beans, French

Gherkin

These very small cucumbers are known in France as cornichons and in Italy as cetriolini. The gherkin may be less than 1-in (2.5 cm) long without seeds. Traditionally the gherkin is pickled in vinegar, and pickled gherkins are used as a garnish and an appetizer, and may also be chopped to add piquancy to hot and cold sauces.

Pickled Gherkins

Gherkins
Salt
Water
Vinegar

The gherkins should be gathered on a dry day, wiped with a cloth and put into a large jar. Boil 5 cups/ 2 pints/ 1 liter water with ½ cup/ 4 oz/ 100 g salt and allow to get cold. Pour over the gherkins and leave them for 3 days. Drain off the brine and cover the gherkins with boiling vinegar. Leave for 24 hours, pour off vinegar, reboil it and pour over the gherkins. Leave for 24 hours. Continue this process until the gherkins are bright green. Drain off the vinegar and pack the gherkins into small preserving jars.

Cover with fresh cold spiced vinegar and cover with vinegar-proof lids.

Fried Gherkins

Fresh gherkins
Beaten egg
Breadcrumbs

Wipe the gherkins, dip in egg and breadcrumbs and fry in deep hot oil until golden brown. As an alternative, dip the gherkins in batter and fry like small fritters.

Good King Henry

This plant appears wild but used to be widely cultivated, particularly in eastern England. It is also known as good Henry, goosefoot, all-good, strawberry spinach, wild spinach, pigsweed and wild mercury. The leaves may be cooked like spinach (and were believed to be a preventative for scurvy), and the young shoots may be blanched during growth and then treated like asparagus, when they are sometimes known as 'blite' or 'blett.' These shoots should be tied in small bunches for boiling with a sprig of mint, and may then be served with cream sauce and garnished with cubes of fried bread.

Goosefoot

see Good King Henry

Green Peppers

see Peppers

Green Sprouting Broccoli

see Calabrese and Broccoli

Corn Chowder

see page 59

**slices of bacon
onion
potatoes
milk
cooked corn kernels
salt and pepper
rosemary
sugar**

Hamburg Parsley

This variety of parsley produces smallish white carrot-shaped roots and is sometimes known as root parsley, turnip-rooted parsley, or parsnip-rooted parsley. The foliage may be used as other parsley, and the fleshy root may be used raw or boiled and served with butter or cream sauce. The root itself is rather dry with a distinctive flavor rather like celeriac, and it was considered a delicacy in Victorian times.

Horse Beans

see Beans, Broad

Horseradish

The thickened long root of this plant is used as a very hot condiment, particularly with beef and fish. A piece of horseradish can be put into the water for poaching fish, and the fish may be garnished with grated horseradish and parsley. A little may also be used in fish pies, and it is a traditional accompaniment to blue carp. Apart from the traditional horseradish sauces, a little horseradish may be added to apple sauce for pork, and it is good in beet dishes. When grating fresh horseradish, be prepared to shed as many tears as when chopping onions.

Below: The thickened root (left) of the horseradish plant is used to make hot sauces. Kohlrabi is a hybrid cabbage that looks not unlike a turnip with more stems.

Cold Horseradish Sauce (1)

Fresh horseradish
Whipped cream
Pinch of salt

Grate the horseradish and mix with the cream and a pinch of salt. Chill before serving with roast beef, fish or smoked trout. The horseradish may be mixed with mayonnaise if preferred.

Cold Horseradish Sauce (2)

Fresh horseradish
Cooking apples
White vinegar
Pinch of sugar

Grate the horseradish and an equal quantity of apples. Mix well and cover with white vinegar. Add a pinch of sugar. Serve with salt meats.

Hot Horseradish Sauce

$\frac{2}{3}$ cup/ $\frac{1}{4}$ pint/ 125 ml white sauce (see page 10)
$\frac{1}{4}$ teaspoon/ 1.25 g mustard
Pinch of salt
2–3 tablespoons/ 30 ml red wine vinegar
2–3 tablespoons/ 30 ml grated horseradish

Mix all the ingredients together and serve hot with boiled or roast beef.

Horseradish Toasts

1 tablespoon/ 15 ml grated horseradish
2 tablespoons/ 1 oz/ 25 g grated cheese
1 tablespoon/ 15 ml cream
1 teaspoon/ 5 ml tarragon vinegar
Rounds of bread
Chopped parsley

Mix the cheese, horseradish, cream and vinegar and heat in a small basin over hot water or in a double boiler. Toast or fry the bread rounds on both sides. Spread on the horseradish mixture and sprinkle with chopped parsley. Serve as a savory at the end of a meal.

Russian Potatoes with Horseradish

1 lb/ 500 g potatoes
2–3 tablespoons/ 30 ml grated horseradish
Salt
Dill leaves
Soured cream or yogurt

Boil the potatoes until just tender, cool and chop coarsely. Mix with the horseradish, salt and some chopped dill. Put into a serving dish and coat with soured cream or yogurt.

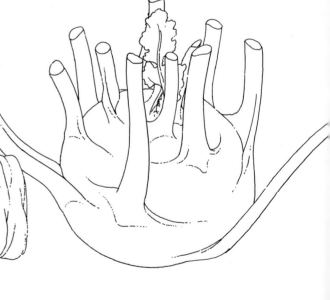

Hubbard Squash

see Squash

Indian Corn

see Corn

Indian Potato

see Yam

Kale

Kale, sometimes known as kail, borecole kale, cole or colewort is a type of cabbage with sprouting, curled, finely toothed leaves which do not form a solid head, and it is believed to be the original form of the great cabbage family. Kale stands through hard weather and is a true peasant cabbage and is usually served in rather simple dishes. The crisp leaves should be removed from their thickened stalks which are usually too fibrous to be pleasant eating. The leaves should be washed quickly, not soaked, and then cooked quickly in boiling salted water before dressing with butter, bacon fat or cheese. The slight bitterness of kale goes particularly well with rather crisp bacon and with sausages.

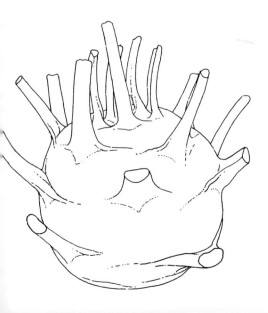

Creamed Kale

2 lb/ 1 kg kale
1 large onion
2–3 tablespoons/ 30 ml bacon fat
1 tablespoon/ 15 ml lemon juice
1⅓ cups/ ½ pint/ 250 ml white sauce
** (see page 10)**
⅜ cup/ 3 oz/ 75 g grated cheese

Wash the kale thoroughly, then cook in boiling water for 8 minutes. Drain and chop roughly. Chop the onion very finely and cook in the bacon fat until soft and golden. Add the lemon juice. Heat the white sauce, remove from the heat and stir in two-thirds of the cheese until melted. Add the onion mixture. Stir the sauce into the kale and put into a greased baking dish. Top with the remaining cheese and bake at 180°C/350°F/ Gas Mark 4 for 25 minutes until hot and golden brown. Serve with sausages or boiled ham.

Colcannon

1 lb/ 500 g cooked kale
1 lb/ 500 g cooked potatoes
6 scallions
2 tablespoons/ 1 oz/ 25 g butter
¾ cup/ 6 fl oz/ 150 ml milk
1 tablespoon/ 15 g chopped parsley
Salt and pepper

Chop the kale finely. Mash the potatoes with the finely chopped scallions, butter and hot milk until fluffy. Add the kale, parsley, salt and pepper. Serve very hot. This Irish dish was traditionally served on Hallowe'en, with a miniature thimble, horseshoe, button, sixpence and wedding ring wrapped in paper and dropped into the mixture. The finders would be rewarded with appropriate fortunes – the ring denoting happy marriage, the sixpence wealth, the horseshoe good fortune, the thimble a spinster and the button a bachelor.

Italian Kale

1 lb/ 500 g kale
4–5 tablespoons/ 60 ml olive oil
1 garlic clove
1 cup/ 3 oz/ 75 g coarse breadcrumbs
2 tablespoons/ 1 oz/ 25 g grated
** Parmesan cheese**

Cook the kale in boiling salted water until just tender. Drain, but do not press dry. Add the oil, crushed garlic, breadcrumbs and cheese, and stir lightly over medium heat for 5 minutes. Serve hot.

Kohlrabi

This is a hybrid of the cabbage family which is often described as being like a turnip growing on a cabbage root, although the flavor is more subtle than either of these vegetables. Kohlrabi is best if it has been grown quickly so that the base is tender and nutty, rather than growing woody when it is old.

The sprouting green leaves may be cooked in any way suitable for kale or spinach and may be dressed with butter and seasoning, or perhaps a little cream. The vegetable is, however, mainly grown for the swollen base which may be cooked in the same way as the turnip or celeriac. Most of the flavor is near the skin and it is better to steam the Kohlrabi before peeling and then to serve it sliced in butter or in a butter and lemon sauce. Cold cooked kohlrabi makes a good salad if cut in thin slices and dressed with oil and vinegar, or mayonnaise.

Ladies' Finger

see Okra

Lamb's Lettuce

see Corn Salad

Land Cress

see Cress, American

Leaf-Beet

see Chard

Leaf-Chard

see Chard

Leek

The leek was one of the divine plants worshipped by the ancient Egyptians, and it was later considered sacred to Latona, the mother of Apollo. There used to be competitions to see who could present the most magnificent leeks to Latona, who was said to prefer them raw. The Israelites in exile regretted their loss of the leeks of Egypt, along with their favorite onions and cucumbers. Perhaps it is this leek worship which is still commemorated by the great leek-growing competitions still held in Northern England, and by the adoption of the leek as one of the national emblems of Wales. The generally accepted story is that St David ordered the Welshmen to wear it in their caps after a great victory, still a traditional custom on St David's day.

The leek has a distinctive flavor but is not as strong as other members of the onion family and is particularly enjoyed in soups, or as a vegetable with white or cheese sauce. They must first be cleaned well as light earth gets between the layers and is difficult to remove. The roots should be trimmed off and then the green tops cut to within 1-in (2.5 cm) of the white bulb. Leeks may be split lengthwise before cooking, or cut in rings. They should be lightly cooked in salted water and very well drained, or else tossed in butter without coloring before adding to dishes.

Leek and Potato Soup

see page 80

leeks
potatoes
butter
chicken stock
salt and pepper
chives

Leek and Potato Soup

3 medium leeks
1 lb/ 500 g potatoes
2 tablespoons/ 1 oz/ 25 g butter
4 cups/ 1½ pints/ 750 ml chicken stock
Salt and pepper
1 tablespoon/ 15 g chopped chives

Cut off the roots and green tops from the leeks, and wash the leeks very thoroughly. Cut them into ½-in (1.25 cm) rings. Peel the potatoes and cut them in 1-in (2.5 cm) dice. Melt the butter in a thick saucepan and cook the leeks gently until soft but not colored. Add the potatoes and the stock and simmer until the potatoes are cooked but not broken. Season well and serve with a sprinkling of chives. The soup may be liquidized in a blender if preferred. If the soup is blended, with a little milk or thin cream added, and then chilled, it becomes *Crème Vichyssoise*.

Creamed Leeks

6 large leeks
Salt and pepper
1⅓ cups/ ½ pint/ 250 ml cream
1 tablespoon/ 15 g chopped parsley

Trim the leeks to remove the dark green tops and roots. Wash them very well. Put into boiling salted water and cook for 10 minutes. Drain thoroughly and cut each leek in four lengthwise. Put into a greased shallow ovenware dish. Season with salt and pepper and pour on the cream. Bake at 180°C/ 350°F/Gas Mark 4 for 30 minutes. Serve sprinkled with parsley. This is particularly good with ham or rare roast beef.

Leek Pie (1)

2 cups/ 8 oz/ 225 g basic pastry (see page 10)
6 large leeks
2 tablespoons/ 1 oz/ 25 g butter
1⅓ cups/ ½ pint/ 250 ml creamy milk
2 eggs
Salt and pepper
2 tablespoons/ 1 oz/ 25 g grated hard cheese

Line a pie plate with the pastry. Remove the roots and green tops from the leeks, and wash the leeks thoroughly. Cut them in thin slices and soften in the butter without coloring. Cool slightly and put into the pastry case. Beat together the milk and eggs until just blended. Season well and pour over the leeks. Sprinkle with the grated cheese. Bake at 200°C/400°F/Gas Mark 6 for 40 minutes until golden. Serve hot or cold.

Leek Pie (2)

2 cups/ 8 oz/ 225 g basic pastry (see page 10)
6 large leeks
1⅓ cups/ ½ pint/ 250 ml milk
Salt and pepper
⅜ cup/ 3 fl oz/ 75 ml cream

Roll out the pastry to fit the top of a pie dish. Cut off the roots and green tops from the leeks, and wash the leeks very thoroughly. Cut them into 1-in (2.5 cm) pieces. Cook the leeks with the milk, salt and pepper over low heat until they are tender. Put into a pie dish and stir in the cream. Cover with the pastry. Bake at 200°C/400°F/Gas Mark 6 for 30 minutes. Serve hot with hot or cold meat.

Leek Salad (1)

8 medium leeks
6–8 tablespoons/ 3 fl oz/ 90 ml olive oil
3–4 tablespoons/ 45 ml tarragon vinegar
1 garlic clove
Salt and pepper
½ teaspoon/ 2.5 g mustard

Trim off the roots and tops from the leeks, cutting about 1 in (2.5 cm) above the white part. Wash very carefully and cut into ½-in (1 cm) thick slices. Cook in boiling salted water for 7 minutes until just tender. Drain very thoroughly, rinse in cold water, and drain well again. Put the oil, vinegar, crushed garlic, salt, pepper and mustard in a bowl and mix well together. Pour over the leek rings and chill before serving.

Leek Salad (2)

1 lb/ 500 g leeks
⅔ cup/ ¼ pint/ 125 ml soured cream
1 garlic clove
1 teaspoon/ 5 ml horseradish sauce
1 teaspoon/ 5 g brown sugar
2–3 tablespoons/ 30 ml wine vinegar
Salt and pepper
Pinch of paprika

Trim the leeks to remove the dark green tops and roots. Cook in boiling salted water for 15 minutes until tender. Drain and put into a serving dish. Mix together the soured cream, crushed garlic, horseradish sauce, sugar, vinegar, salt and pepper and pour over the leeks. Leave to chill for 1 hour, then sprinkle on the paprika.

Grecian Leek Salad

6 large leeks
⅔ cup/ ¼ pint/ 125 ml olive oil
1⅓ cups/ ½ pint/ 250 ml dry white wine
⅔ cup/ ¼ pint/ 125 ml water
Salt and pepper
3 bay leaves
⅓ cup/ 2 oz/ 50 g coriander seeds

Trim the leeks to remove the dark green tops and roots. Wash them very well, and cut each leek into four lengthwise. Put into a large frying pan with all the other ingredients and bring to the boil. Reduce the heat and simmer, stirring frequently until the leeks are tender and the liquid reduced to half. Serve very hot, or chilled.

Below: The leek.

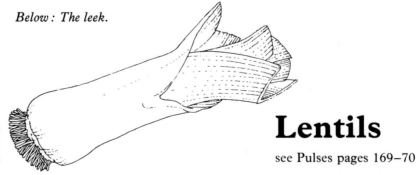

Lentils

see Pulses pages 169–70

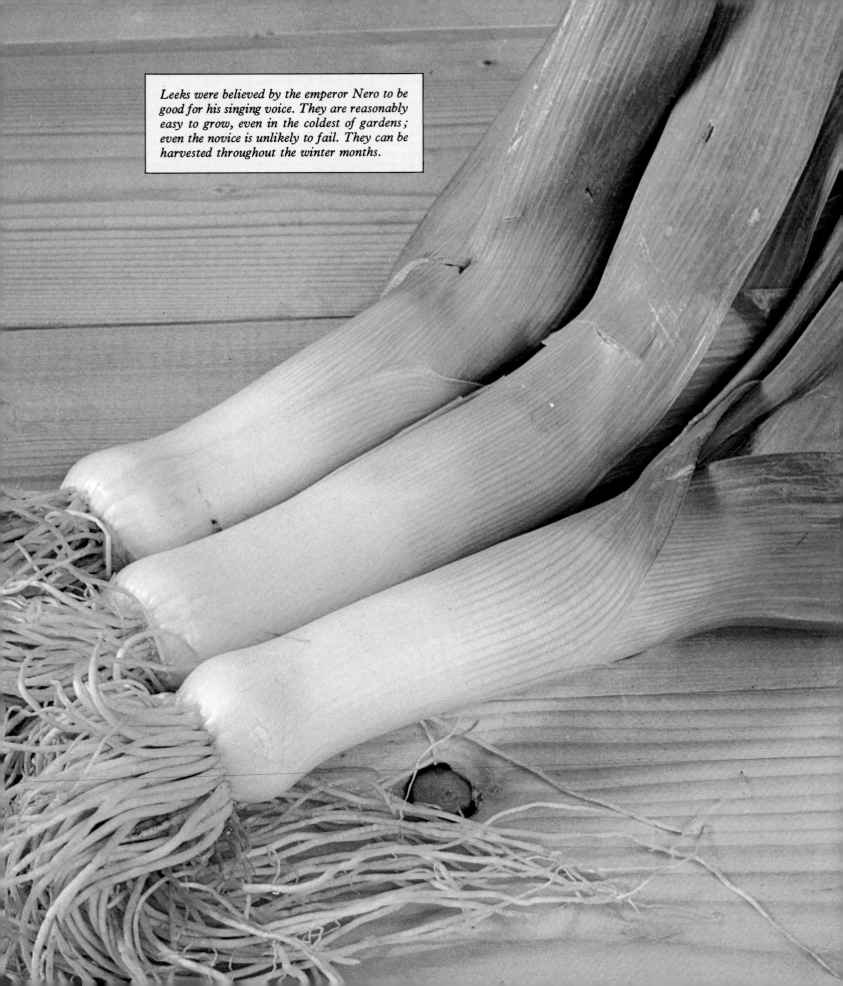

Leeks were believed by the emperor Nero to be good for his singing voice. They are reasonably easy to grow, even in the coldest of gardens; even the novice is unlikely to fail. They can be harvested throughout the winter months.

Lettuce

The lettuce in its many varieties has been a favorite vegetable for thousands of years. It was reputed to be the favorite plant of Adonis, and an ancient philosopher moistened the lettuce in his garden with good wine instead of water. While lettuce is too often only eaten as a salad, it has been cooked from earliest times. Apicius, the writer of an early cookbook, recommended that lettuce leaves should be cooked with onions in plenty of water, then drained and mixed with herbs, gravy, oil and wine.

Compact, round-headed cabbage lettuce are universally popular, and best of all are those of the iceberg variety with crisp crunchy leaves. The long-leaved cos lettuce is good for salads and cooked dishes.

Lettuce must be washed very carefully in plenty of cold water, and should then be thoroughly dried. It is easiest to do this in some form of mesh basket, and the lettuce can then be finished in a piece of thin cheesecloth, muslin or clean tea towel, but should not be pressed or patted or it will become limp and lifeless, and lose the crispness which is so essential for salads. Salad lettuce should never be cut but may be torn into bite-sized pieces. A really crisp lettuce is perfect with no more dressing than some sea salt, but an oil and vinegar dressing is most commonly used (three parts oil to one part wine vinegar or lemon juice gives a good dressing). Whatever dressing is chosen, it should not be used to cover the lettuce leaves until the moment of service. A pleasant garnish which is full of flavor is a mixture of chopped fresh herbs such as tarragon, chervil and chives.

Lettuce Soup

1 lb/ 500 g lettuce(s)
**4 cups/ 1½ pints/ 750 ml thin white
 sauce (see page 10)**
**6–8 tablespoons/ 3 fl oz/ 90 ml chicken
 stock**
Salt and pepper
Pinch of sugar
2 tablespoons/ 1 oz/ 25 g butter
2–3 tablespoons/ 30 ml cream
1 teaspoon/ 5 ml chopped chervil

Wash the lettuces well and cook in boiling water for 5 minutes. Plunge them into cold water, drain very thoroughly, and chop the lettuces roughly. Heat the sauce and add the lettuce. Simmer for 30 minutes and then put through a sieve or liquidize in a blender. Return to the saucepan with the stock, salt, pepper, sugar and butter. Reheat and just before serving stir in the cream. Serve sprinkled with chervil and with fried bread cubes if liked.

Iced Lettuce Soup

1 large cabbage lettuce
4 cups/ 1½ pints/ 750 ml chicken stock
1 tablespoon/ 15 g chopped chives
Salt and pepper
1 cup/ 8 fl oz/ 200 ml cream
1 tablespoon/ 15 g chopped parsley

Cut the lettuce into quarters and cut away any stalk or heavy veins from the leaves. Shred the lettuce very finely. Heat the stock and add the lettuce. Cover and simmer for 5 minutes. Take off the heat and add the chives and seasoning. Stir in the cream and chill for 3 hours before serving garnished with parsley.

Creamed Lettuce

4 small lettuces
¼ cup/ 2 oz/ 50 g butter
Salt and pepper
Pinch of sugar
2 egg yolks
4–5 tablespoons cream

Wash the lettuces well and cook them in boiling water for 5 minutes. Plunge them into cold water, drain and dry them, and cut them into eighths. Melt the butter and add the pieces of lettuce with salt, pepper and sugar. Simmer very gently, stirring often, for 2 hours until tender. Take off the heat and stir in the egg yolks beaten with cream. Reheat very gently without boiling. Serve hot with a garnish of fried bread cubes.

Baked Lettuce

4 small lettuces
2 slices of bacon
4 medium onions
2 cups/ ¾ pint/ 375 ml beef stock
Salt and pepper

Above: Lettuces come in many sizes and shapes. On the left is a celtuce, in the middle is a cos lettuce and on the right is a soft round cabbage-type lettuce.

Wash the lettuces very thoroughly, but keep them whole. Cook in boiling salted water for 5 minutes, then plunge into cold water. Take out straight away and drain very thoroughly. Put into an ovenware casserole with chopped bacon and sliced onions and cover with stock, seasoning well. Cover and cook at 150°C/300°F/Gas Mark 2 for 1½ hours. Take out the lettuces and press out moisture from them gently, returning them to the dish. Put the lettuces on a serving dish and keep warm. Simmer the cooking liquid until reduced by half, adjust seasoning and pour over the lettuces.

Braised Lettuce

4 small lettuces
1 tablespoon/ 15 ml olive oil
1 tablespoon/ ½ oz/ 15 g butter
1 small onion
1 slice of bacon
4 medium tomatoes
1 tablespoon/ 15 g chopped parsley
1 teaspoon/5 g sugar
Salt and pepper
Pinch of ground nutmeg

Wash the lettuces very thoroughly, but keep them whole. Bring a large pan of salted water to the boil and put in the lettuces. Bring to the boil again, then lift out the lettuces and drain them well. Heat the oil and butter together in a heavy pan. Add the chopped onion and bacon, and stir until soft and golden. Dip the tomatoes in boiling water to loosen the skins. Peel them and remove the pips. Cut the flesh into pieces, add to the onions and stir for 5 minutes. Put in the whole lettuces, parsley, sugar, salt, pepper and nutmeg. Cover tightly and simmer for 30 minutes.

Brazilian Baked Lettuce

2 medium lettuces
1⅓ cups/ ½ pint/ 250 ml natural yogurt
Salt and pepper
Pinch of nutmeg
2 hard-boiled eggs
1 medium cucumber
2 tablespoons/ 1 oz/ 25 g fine breadcrumbs
2 tablespoons/ 1 oz/ 25 g butter

The best lettuces to use for this dish are the very crisp iceberg type. Wash them very thoroughly and cook in boiling salted water for 5 minutes. Plunge into cold water, then drain very thoroughly and press out as much moisture as possible. Shred the lettuces very finely and put into a greased shallow oven-ware dish. Mix the yogurt with salt, pepper, nutmeg and chopped eggs and pour over the lettuce. Peel the cucumber and cut in very thin slices. Arrange on top of the lettuce and sprinkle with breadcrumbs. Put on thin flakes of butter. Bake at 200°C/400°F/Gas Mark 6 for 15 minutes until the top is crisp and golden. Serve immediately, cutting the dish in wedges.

Pennsylvania Wilted Lettuce Salad

1 large cabbage lettuce
4 slices of lean bacon
2–3 tablespoons/ 30 ml cider vinegar
½ cup/ 4 fl oz/ 100 ml whipping cream
Pinch of mustard powder

Wash the lettuce very well and drain off all moisture. Tear the lettuce into bite-sized pieces, but do not cut the leaves. Chop the bacon and cook in its own fat until crisp. Drain off all but 1 tablespoon/15 ml of the fat. Add the vinegar and cook for 30 seconds, stirring well. Stir in the cream and mustard powder, heating through but not boiling. Pour over the lettuce and serve at once.

Lima Beans

see Beans, Broad

Mad Apple

see Eggplant

Maize

see Corn

Mammoth Squash

see Squash

Mangetout

see Peas, Edible-Pod

Three different types of salad greens. Lettuces can be grown almost the whole year around and if you like your salads to be crisp and fresh, then growing your own ingredients can be a very rewarding experience.
Left to right : Chinese cabbage, cos lettuce and iceberg lettuce.

Marrow (also see Squash)

The vegetable marrow is a member of the family which includes squash and pumpkin, and recipes for them are interchangeable. Small marrows may be used as zucchini. An unusual variety is the spaghetti marrow whose flesh resembles cooked spaghetti in texture.

The marrow is a watery vegetable and is best steamed or cooked in water until only just tender before being very thoroughly drained and dressed with melted butter and seasoning. It may also be served with a white sauce or cheese sauce, or made into a purée with plenty of butter and parsley. A large marrow makes an excellent case for a stuffing of meat, onions and breadcrumbs, or of tomatoes and cheese. Because of its rather bland flavor, the marrow makes a useful bulk ingredient for chutney and for sweet preserves.

Stuffed Marrow*

1 large marrow
2–3 cups/ 1 lb/ 500 g cooked beef or lamb
¼ cup/ 2 oz/ 50 g bacon or ham
1 medium onion
4 tablespoons/ 1 oz/ 25 g flour
Salt and pepper
⅔ cup/ 2 oz/ 50 g fresh breadcrumbs
1 teaspoon/ 5 g chopped parsley
2 medium tomatoes
2 tablespoons/ 1 oz/ 25 g cooking fat

Peel the marrow and cut it in half lengthwise. Scoop out the seeds and pulp. Mince the meat with the bacon and onion, and mix with the salt and pepper, breadcrumbs and parsley. Dip the tomatoes in boiling water to loosen the skins. Peel them and remove the pips. Cut the flesh into pieces and mix with the meat. Fill the marrow and put the marrow into a greased ovenware dish. Put the cooking fat on top, and bake at 180°C/ 350°F/Gas Mark 4 for 1 hour, basting frequently with the pan juices. Serve with brown gravy or hot tomato sauce.

Sweet Marrow Pie

2 cups/ 8 oz/ 225 g basic pastry (see page 12)
¼ cup/ 2 oz/ 50 g jam
1 lb/ 500 g marrow
1 egg
Pinch of ground nutmeg
2 tablespoons/ 1 oz/ 25 g sugar

Line a dish with the pastry. Remember to keep the trimmings to decorate the top. Spread the pastry with a thin layer of jam. Boil the marrow until soft and put in a colander to drain off all liquid. When cold, add a well-beaten egg and the nutmeg, together with the sugar. Put into the pastry case and sprinkle a little more nutmeg on top. Decorate with a lattice made from strips of pastry. Bake at 200°C/400°F/Gas Mark 6 for 15 minutes, then reduce heat to 180°C/ 350°F/Gas Mark 4 for 15 minutes. Serve hot or cold. Currants or raisins may be added to the filling. This was a favorite old English recipe dating from the days when marrow was treated as a fruit rather than a vegetable.

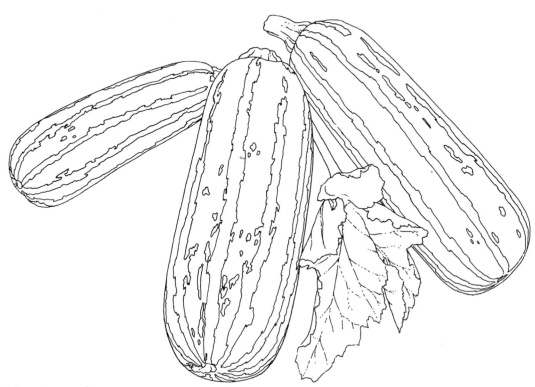

Above: Marrows (above), squashes, pumpkins and gourds are all cucurbits and the names are somewhat interchangeable. Marrows tend to be British and squashes and pumpkin, American.

Another version was made with marrow slices cooked with sugar, raisins and water in a pie dish until tender, then covered with a pastry crust. Sometimes the marrow was combined with pork in a savory pie. The dish was often known as 'million pie,' a 'million' being a kind of marrow.

Marrow and Apple Chutney

4 lb/ 2 kg prepared marrow
⅜ cup/ 3 oz/ 75 g block cooking salt
2 lb/ 1 kg apples
1 lb/ 500 g shallots or small onions
2 tablespoons/ 1 oz/ 25 g dried chilies
2 tablespoons/ 1 oz/ 25 g black
   peppercorns
2 tablespoons/ 1 oz/ 25 g root ginger
8 cups/ 3 pints/ 1.5 liters vinegar
1 lb/ 500 g sugar

Peel the marrow and remove the pith and seeds, then weigh the flesh. Cut the marrow into small pieces and sprinkle with salt between layers in a bowl. Leave to stand for 12 hours and drain very thoroughly. Peel the apples and shallots or small onions, and cut them in small pieces. Add to the drained marrow. Tie the chilies, peppercorns and ginger into a piece of cheesecloth and suspend in the saucepan. Simmer over low heat until the marrow is soft. Stir in the vinegar and sugar and simmer until the mixture is of the consistency of jam. Remove the spices. Pour into clean jars and cover tightly with vinegar-proof lids.

Marrow Jam

6 lb/ 3 kg prepared marrow
4 lemons
⅜ cup/ 3 oz/ 75 g root ginger
6 lb/ 3 kg sugar

Cut the peeled marrow into cubes and steam until just tender. Put into a bowl with the grated rind and juice of the lemons, the bruised root ginger tied in a muslin bag, and the sugar. Leave for 24 hours. Put into a pan and heat carefully until the sugar is dissolved. Cook until the marrow is transparent and the syrup is thick. Pour into hot jars. This is very good eaten as a dessert with cream.

Stuffed Marrow Rings

1 medium marrow
2–3 cups/ 1 lb/ 500 g cooked beef or
   lamb
2 cups/ 6 oz/ 150 g fresh white
   breadcrumbs
1 medium onion
1¼ cups/ ½ pint/ 250 ml stock
Salt and pepper

Cut the marrow into 2-in (5 cm) slices, removing seeds and pith, and cook in boiling water for 3 minutes. Drain well and arrange in a greased ovenware dish. Mince the meat and mix with the breadcrumbs, chopped onion, stock and seasoning. A little tomato purée or some chopped fresh herbs may be added for flavoring, and the stock may be thickened with a little cornstarch if a firmer texture is liked. Cook the mixture for 10 minutes, stirring well, and fill the marrow rings. Bake at 180°C/350°F/Gas Mark 4 for 30 minutes.

Sweet Marrow Pickle

8 lb/ 4 kg prepared marrow
5 cups/ 2 pints/ 1 liter white vinegar
3 lb/ 1.5 kg sugar
2 in/ 5 cm cinnamon stick
1 tablespoon/ ½ oz/ 15 g whole cloves

Peel the marrow and scoop out pith and seeds, then weigh the flesh for the recipe. Cut the marrow into pieces about 1½-in × ½-in (3.75 cm × 1.25 cm). Put the vinegar, sugar and spices into a saucepan and bring to the boil. Add the marrow and cook gently, stirring occasionally, until the marrow is translucent and tender, but not broken. Drain the marrow and cool it. Boil the vinegar syrup again, including any fluid which runs from the marrow while it is cooling. Put the marrow into clean jars. Reduce the vinegar syrup to 4 cups/ 1½ pints/ 750 ml, remove the spices and pour the boiling liquid on to the marrow. Cover tightly with vinegar-proof lids.

Morel

see Mushroom

Mung Beans

see Bean Sprouts

Mushrooms

Mushrooms have played a deadly role in history, although the actual fungus was not necessarily the cause. Agrippina disposed of Claudius by inserting a deadly poison into a fine morel, a species of which he was very fond, so that her son Nero could succeed as Emperor. She pretended to be inconsolable and raised the dead man to the rank of a god, which led Nero to call all mushrooms 'the food of the gods.' Sadly mushrooms were a favorite vehicle for introducing poison to unwanted husbands, and it is even said to Popes.

Most Englishmen have tended to eat only the common field mushroom although morels and blewits have been other favorites. The more experimental French are happy with many different varieties, but wise precautions are taken, and every mushroom or fungus sold in Paris shops has to be examined and passed by government experts. No hawker is allowed to sell mushrooms in the street, no mushroom may be sold on a second day, and a seller of inferior mushrooms can be banned from the markets. Those who wish to experiment with mushrooms are advised to buy a book which has very clear identification pictures and written details, and also a specialized cookery book. The rest will be happy with today's carefully cultivated mushrooms.

Freshness can be determined by a firm cap and fleshy stem. The button is a closed mushroom in the first stage of growth; the cup is slightly open showing delicate pinkish-brown gills; the fully ripe mushroom with an open cap is known as an open and has the most mature flavor. Mushrooms should be eaten very fresh, and certainly stored no longer than 3 days in a cool larder or refrigerator.

Mushrooms should not be washed as they quickly absorb water like a sponge. They need only be wiped clean with a damp cloth and should not be peeled either. The stem need only be slightly trimmed, or may be removed completely if the recipe requires it, but the stems are full of flavor and may be used in other recipes. Mushrooms should be cooked quickly, for only 2 or 3 minutes, so that they remain full of flavor.

A long green trailing marrow. Pumpkins, squashes, zucchinis, etc., belong to the same family as the marrow and recipes can be used interchangeably. Rich soil and lots of sun are essential for growing marrows but if these conditions are met they are easily cultivated and very prolific.

Mushroom Soup

1½ cups/ 8 oz/ 225 g mushrooms
1 small onion
¼ cup/ 2 oz/ 50 g butter
6 tablespoons/ 1½ oz/ 40 g flour
5 cups/ 2 pints/ 1 liter water
⅔ cup/ ¼ pint/ 125 ml milk
Salt and pepper
Pinch of ground nutmeg
⅔ cup/ ¼ pint/ 125 ml cream
1 tablespoon/ 15 ml chopped parsley

Wipe the mushrooms and chop them roughly. Chop the onion finely and soften in the butter for 5 minutes until golden. Add the mushrooms and continue cooking for 3 minutes. Remove from the heat and work in the flour, then gradually add the water and milk. Bring to the boil and then simmer for 10 minutes. Season with salt, pepper and nutmeg, and just before serving, stir in the cream and parsley. If liked, the mushroom mixture may be liquidized in a blender and reheated before adding the cream and parsley. Chicken or beef stock may be used instead of the water.

Mushrooms in Cream

3 cups/ 1 lb/ 500 g mushrooms
⅜ cup/ 3 oz/ 75 g butter
4 tablespoons/ 1 oz/ 25 g flour
1 cup/ 8 fl oz/ 200 ml cream
Thyme
Chopped parsley

Wipe mushrooms and toss in butter until just soft. Sprinkle with flour and add a pinch of thyme, salt and pepper. Add cream and cook gently for 5 minutes. Sprinkle with chopped parsley.

Mushrooms in Soured Cream

2 medium onions
3 cups/ 1 lb/ 500 g mushrooms
¼ cup/ 2 oz/ 50 g butter
Squeeze of lemon juice
⅔ cup/ ¼ pint/ 125 ml soured cream
Salt and pepper

Peel the onions and chop them finely. Wipe the mushrooms and cut them in thin slices. Melt the butter in a heavy saucepan, and cook the onions until soft and golden. Add the mushrooms and lemon juice and cook over gentle heat until the mushrooms are soft and the liquid has evaporated. Stir in the soured cream and reheat without boiling. Season well and serve hot.

Holstein Mushrooms

1 medium onion
2 hard-boiled eggs
2 cups/ 12 oz/ 350 g mushrooms
¼ cup/ 2 oz/ 50 g butter
4 tablespoons/ 1 oz/ 25 g flour
2⅔ cups/ 1 pint/ 500 ml milk
Pinch of salt
Pinch of paprika
2 tomatoes
1 tablespoon/ 15 ml dry sherry

Chop the onion and simmer in a little water until soft, then drain well. Slice the eggs. Wipe the mushrooms and leave them whole if they are small, otherwise chop roughly. Cook in the butter for 3 minutes, stirring well, then stir in the flour, milk, salt and paprika. Cook gently, stirring well, until the sauce is smooth. Peel the tomatoes and remove the seeds. Chop the flesh coarsely. Add the tomatoes, eggs and onions and heat through. Just before serving, add the sherry. Accompany with noodles or rice, or put into a pastry case. Two celery sticks may be substituted for the onions.

Mushroom Puffs with Tartare Sauce

1½ cups/ 8 oz/ 225 g button or cup
    mushrooms
Salt and pepper
¾ cup/ 3 oz/ 75 g flour
1 egg
⅔ cup/ ¼ pint/ 125 ml milk
1 garlic clove
Oil for frying

Tartare Sauce

5–6 tablespoons/ 75 ml mayonnaise
2–3 tablespoons/ 30 ml capers
1 tablespoon/ 15 ml chopped gherkins
Salt and pepper

Wipe the mushrooms. Season a little of the flour with salt and pepper and dust the mushrooms lightly with this mixture. Mix the rest of the flour and a little seasoning with the egg, milk and crushed garlic to make a smooth batter. Dip the mushrooms in batter and fry in hot deep oil until crisp and golden. Serve hot with sauce. Make this by mixing together the mayonnaise, capers, chopped gherkins and seasoning.

Mushrooms à la Grecque

1 medium onion
1 garlic clove
⅔ pint/ ¼ pint/ 125 ml oil
3–4 tablespoons/ 45 ml white wine
    vinegar
1 teaspoon/ 5 g chopped tarragon
2–3 tablespoons/ 30 g chopped parsley
1 bay leaf
1 cup/ 6 oz/ 150 g button mushrooms

Chop the onion finely and crush the garlic. Cook in 3 tablespoons/45 ml oil for 4 minutes. Add the remaining oil, vinegar and herbs and simmer gently for 20 minutes. Wipe the mushrooms and add them whole to the liquid. Simmer gently until they are just tender. Cool and chill for 2 hours. Serve with crusty bread.

Mushroom Pie*

1½ cups/ 12 oz/ 350 g basic pastry (see
    page 12)
1½ cups/ 8 oz/ 225 g button mushrooms
2 tablespoons/ 1 oz/ 25 g butter
2 eggs and 1 egg yolk
⅔ cup/ ¼ pint/ 125 ml natural yogurt
6–8 tablespoons/ 3 fl oz/ 90 ml cream
Salt and pepper
2 tablespoons/ 30 g chopped chives

Roll out the pastry to line a 9-in (22.5 cm) pie plate. Cover with foil and baking beads and bake at 190°C/375°F/Gas Mark 5 for 15 minutes. Remove beads and foil. Wipe the mushrooms and cut them in half. Melt the butter and toss the mushrooms in it for 2 minutes. Drain off the fat and put the mushrooms in the pastry shell. Beat together the eggs, egg yolk, yogurt, cream and seasoning and pour over the mushrooms. Sprinkle on the chives and bake at 190°C/

375°F/Gas Mark 5 for 30 minutes until golden. Serve hot or cold.

Pheasant Stuffed with Mushrooms

1 pheasant
1½ cups/ 8 oz/ 225 g mushrooms
3 tablespoons/ 3 oz/ 75 g butter
6 tablespoons/ 1½ oz/ 40 g flour
2 cups/ ¾ pint/ 375 ml stock
3–4 tablespoons/ 45 ml dry sherry
Salt and pepper

Wipe the pheasant and season inside and out with salt and pepper. Wipe the mushrooms and slice them. Melt half the butter and cook the mushrooms for 5 minutes. Cool and then put half the mushrooms inside the pheasant. Brown the bird in the rest of the butter and put into a casserole. Stir the flour into the pan juices and work in the stock and sherry. Season well and pour over the pheasant. Cover tightly and cook at 170°C/ 325°F/ Gas Mark 3 for 1½ hours, allowing 30 minutes longer for an older bird. Just before serving, stir in the remaining mushrooms. Mushrooms have a natural partnership with pheasant, and can be cooked in butter and used to stuff a pheasant for roasting. During the cooking the juices will run and form a delicious gravy.

Duxelles

3 cups/ 1 lb/ 500 g mushrooms
⅓ cup/ 2 oz/ 50 g shallots
¼ cup/ 2 oz/ 50 g butter

Mushroom stems may be used for this, or a mixture of whole mushrooms and stems. Shallots are essential for a subtle flavor. Wipe the mushrooms and peel the shallots. Chop very finely and cook in the butter until the mixture is very dry. Pack into small containers. The mixture will keep for 1 week in the refrigerator or 3 months in the freezer and is useful for adding to sauces, soups, stuffings and casseroles to give a rich flavor.

Mushroom Salad (1)

1 cup/ 6 oz/ 150 g button mushrooms
10 scallions
4–5 tablespoons/ 60 ml mayonnaise

1 teaspoon/ 5 ml dill seeds
Juice of 1 lemon
Salt and pepper
Crisp bacon

Wipe the mushrooms and cut into slices. Chop the onions and mix with the sliced mushrooms. Mix the mayonnaise with dill seeds, lemon juice, salt and pepper. Stir in the mushrooms and onions and sprinkle the salad with small pieces of crisp bacon.

Mushroom Salad (2)

3 cups/ 1 lb/ 500 g mushrooms
⅔ cup/ ¼ pint/ 125 ml olive oil
Salt and pepper
3 anchovy fillets
Juice of 1 lemon
1 tablespoon/ 15 g chopped parsley

Wipe the mushrooms and cut them in slices. Mix the oil, salt, pepper, chopped anchovies, lemon juice and parsley. Put the mushrooms into a serving dish and cover with the dressing. Stir well and chill for 30 minutes before serving.

Mushrooms à la Française

½ lettuce
¼ cup/ 2 oz/ 50 g butter
Salt and pepper
⅔ cup/ 4 oz/ 100 g button or cup mushrooms

Below : A button mushroom

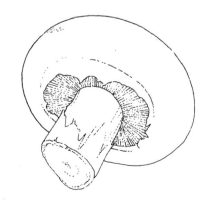

Wash the lettuce and shred coarsely. Put a layer of lettuce in a greased ovenware dish. Add half the butter cut in small pieces. Top with sliced mushrooms, salt and pepper, then the remaining lettuce and butter. Cover and cool at 180°C/350°F/Gas Mark 4 for 40 minutes.

Mushroom Sauce (for Chicken or Fish)

1 small onion
⅜ cup/ 1½ oz/ 40 g butter
⅔ cup/ 4 oz/ 125 g mushrooms
4 tablespoons/ 1 oz/ 25 g flour
1⅓ cups/ ½ pint/ 250 ml chicken or vegetable stock
2 teaspoons/ 10 ml lemon juice
Salt and pepper
3–4 tablespoons/ 45 ml cream

Chop the onion finely and cook in the butter until soft and golden. Chop the mushrooms finely and add to the onions. Cook and stir until the moisture has evaporated. Take off the heat and stir in the flour, stock, lemon juice, salt and pepper. Bring to the boil and then simmer for 5 minutes, stirring occasionally. Stir in the cream and serve hot.

Mushroom and Scallop Salad

3 cups/ 1 lb/ 500 g button mushrooms
8 scallops
⅔ cup/ 4 oz/ 100 g prawns or shrimps
⅔ cup/ ¼ pint/ 125 ml olive oil
Juice of ½ lemon
1 garlic clove
Salt and pepper
1 tablespoon/ 15 ml chopped parsley

Wipe the mushrooms and slice them thinly. Put into a serving dish and cover them with half the oil and lemon juice, the crushed garlic, salt and pepper. Simmer the scallops in a little water with a pinch of salt and piece of lemon rind, for 5 minutes, adding the red 'coral' of the fish only during the last minute. Drain well and cut each scallop across in two rounds. Mix with the cooked shelled prawns, and while still warm cover them with the remaining oil and lemon juice. Just before serving, stir the fish and mushrooms together in their dressing and sprinkle with parsley.

Mushroom Pie

see page 90

pastry
button mushrooms
butter
eggs
yogurt
cream
salt and pepper
chives

Potted Mushrooms

1 cup/ 6 oz/ 150 g button or cup
   mushrooms
1 garlic clove
$\frac{3}{4}$ cup/ 6 oz/ 150 g butter
Grated rind of $\frac{1}{2}$ lemon
Salt and pepper

Wipe the mushrooms and chop them roughly. Crush the garlic and fry in half the butter for 1 minute. Add the mushrooms and continue frying for 3 minutes. Drain the mushrooms, saving the cooking liquid. Put the mushrooms into a small serving dish. Add the remaining butter to the cooking liquid with the lemon rind, salt and pepper and heat until melted. Pour over the mushrooms and cool, then chill until set. Serve with hot toast.

Below : A bulb of garlic (left), two halves of a green pepper (top and right) and four okra (bottom).

Mustard, White

This European annual plant with small tender green leaves is usually cut 6–8 days after the seeds have been sown, to use with or without salad cress in sandwiches, salads and for garnishes.

Nanbu-naga Nasa

see Eggplant

Notchweed

see Purslane

Okra

Okra is sometimes known as ladies' finger because of the shape of these angular seed pods of the mallow family. Okra has a somewhat mucilaginous texture and is an essential ingredient of a range of soups in the southern States of America called gumbos (*gombo* or *gombaut* is the French name for okra) in which the vegetable acts as a thickening agent.

    Okra pods should be young, firm and unblemished. The stems should be broken off

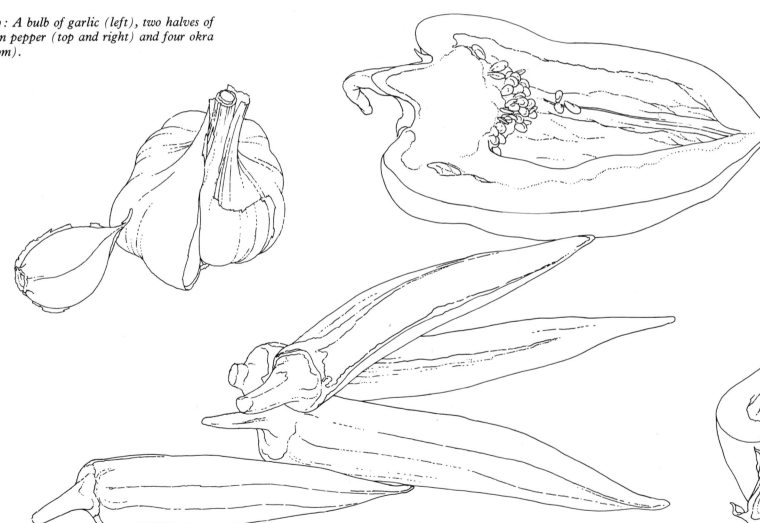

rather than cut, and the pods washed and dried thoroughly and refrigerated until used. If they are quickly blanched in boiling salted water before using in recipes, the texture will be firmer. Okra can be simply parboiled, then drained and fried in butter to be eaten very hot with salt and pepper. Served with a tomato or cream sauce, okra is a good accompaniment to fish or poultry, and to rice.

Okra Fritters

1 lb/ 500 g small okra
½ cup/ 2 oz/ 50 g flour
Salt and pepper
Basic Batter (see page 12)
¾ cup/ 6 oz/ 150 g butter
1 garlic clove
Few drops Tabasco sauce

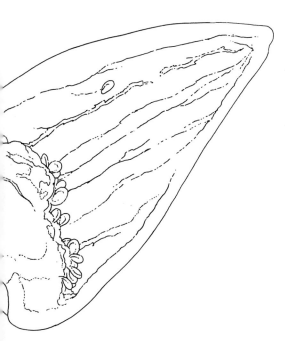

Halve the okra pods lengthwise and dust them with the flour seasoned with salt and pepper. Dip into basic batter and fry in deep hot oil until crisp and golden. While the fritters are cooking, melt the butter and add the crushed garlic and Tabasco sauce. Serve the fritters very hot with this butter sauce.

Brazilian Okra Salad

1 lb/ 500 g small okra
6–8 tablespoons/ 3 fl oz/ 90 ml oil
3–4 tablespoons/ 45 ml wine vinegar
Pinch of salt
Pinch of tarragon
2 teaspoons/ 10 g chopped chives
2 teaspoons/ 10 g chopped parsley
Few drops Tabasco sauce

Cut the okra pods in half lengthwise and cook in boiling salted water until just tender. Drain and cool and refrigerate for 1 hour. Mix the oil, vinegar, salt, tarragon, chives, parsley and Tabasco sauce and pour over the okra just before serving.

New Orleans Okra

1 lb/ 500 g small okra
2 tablespoons/ 1 oz/ 25 g butter
1 medium onion
1 medium green pepper
4 large tomatoes
Pinch of sugar
Pinch of marjoram
Salt and pepper

Cut the okra pods across in small slices. Melt the butter and cook the finely chopped onion and pepper until soft and golden. Add the okra and cook for 5 minutes, stirring well. Peel the tomatoes and cut them in pieces. Stir into the okra with the sugar and marjoram. Cover and simmer for 20 minutes, adding a little water if necessary, but the mixture should be rather dry. Season well with salt and pepper and serve hot with pork or ham.

Chicken Gumbo

1 medium onion
¼ cup/ 2 oz/ 50 g butter
1 medium green pepper
5 cups/ 2 pints/ 1 liter chicken stock
½ lb/ 8 oz/ 225 g small okra
½ lb/ 8 oz/ 225 g canned tomatoes
½ lb/ 8 oz/ 225 g cooked chicken
Salt and pepper

Chop the onion finely and cook in the butter until soft and golden. Add the finely chopped pepper and cook for 2 minutes. Stir in the stock, and the okra cut lengthwise. Add the tomatoes and their juice, chopped chicken, salt and pepper. Bring to boiling point and simmer for 45 minutes.

Onions

The onion has been a great favorite in the kitchens of the world for centuries to give a 'lift' to hundreds of savory dishes, but it has also been appreciated for its medicinal qualities. Onions are a stimulant to the digestion and are reputed to be an aid to sound sleep. The onion has high protein and mineral content, but is also high in calories because of its oil and sugar content.

The onion is perfect in many dishes or used as an accompaniment. They go well with grilled meat and sausages, and with potatoes, combine with cheese and are essential to many meat casseroles, pies and sauces. Salt and freshly ground pepper bring out the onion flavor, and a pinch of mustard powder or ground nutmeg will enhance it.

Raw onions may be used for salads – a combination of orange slices and onion rings is excellent with duck and game, while a little raw chopped onion improves tomato, beet and potato salads. To prepare onions for salads, they should be peeled and sliced thinly, then pushed apart to form rings which should be chilled in iced water before use.

Onions should not be used when sprouting or if spongy, or with thick soft necks. The best onions to use are firm and hard, with thin tight necks and crisp skin. Old onions are stronger in flavour than new ones, but boiling reduces the strength of flavour. It is important not to add too much fat to onion dishes as they contain plenty of their own oil. Spanish and Bermuda onions have the sweetest flavor of all.

Onion peeling can be a troublesome business, causing tears and smelly hands. Peeling the onion under cold running water is supposed to help matters, while some cooks hold a knife or crust of bread in their

teeth. The French prefer to peel the onion and leave it to stand for a few minutes before chopping without tears. To clear the hands of onion smells, wash them in cold water and salt, or in cold water followed by a rub with fresh parsley, celery tops or lemon before washing with soap and cold water. A sprig of parsley, a clove, a coffee bean or a little sugar carefully chewed will help to freshen the breath after eating onions; a drink of strong black coffee or milk will also help.

Old English Onion Soup

4 large onions
1⅓ cups/ ½ pint/ 250 ml water
11 cups/ 4 pints/ 2.25 liters milk
2 blades mace
½ cup/ 4 oz/ 100 g unsalted butter
2 egg yolks
1 tablespoon/ 15 g chopped parsley

Slice the onions thinly and simmer gently in the water with a lid on until just soft. Add the milk, mace and butter and simmer for 30 minutes. Beat the egg yolks in a bowl and add a little of the cooking liquid. Blend together and then stir into the soup off the heat. Stir in the parsley and serve at once with squares of toast.

Onions à la Grecque

1 lb/ 500 g small pickling onions
⅔ cup/ ¼ pint/ 125 ml water
⅔ cup/ ¼ pint/ 125 ml red wine
Juice of ½ lemon
4–5 tablespoons/ 60 ml olive oil
2–3 tablespoons/ 30 ml concentrated
  tomato purée
2 tablespoons/ 1 oz/ 25 g sugar
1 sprig rosemary
Salt and pepper
1 tablespoon/ 15 g chopped parsley

Drop the onions in boiling water, simmer for 1 minute, and then peel. Put the water, wine, lemon juice, olive oil, tomato purée, sugar, rosemary, salt and pepper into a wide shallow saucepan and bring slowly to the boil, stirring well to blend the ingredients. Add the onions, cover and simmer for 25 minutes until the onions are tender. Lift out

Left : Onions. Inset : Okra

the onions and put into a bowl. Boil the sauce for 5 minutes until thick. Take out the rosemary and pour over the onions. Sprinkle with the parsley and serve cold.

French Onion Soup

1½ lb/ 750 g onions
¼ cup/ 2 oz/ 50 g butter
8 cups/ 3 pints/ 1.5 liters beef stock
Salt and pepper
4 slices French bread
½ cup/ 4 oz/ 100 g grated hard cheese

Peel the onions and cut them in thin slices. Melt the butter and cook the onions until soft and golden. Add the stock, salt and pepper and bring to the boil. Simmer for 25 minutes. Just before serving, cut thick slices from a French loaf and cover each slice with grated cheese. Toast under a hot broiler or grill until the cheese melts. Put a slice in each individual bowl, or put them all into a soup tureen. Pour the soup over the toast and serve very hot.

Onion Sambal

2 medium onions
1 garlic clove
1 tablespoon/ 15 g chopped mint
⅔ cup/ ¼ pint/ 125 ml natural yogurt
1 teaspoon/ 5 ml chili paste
Few drops of Tabasco sauce
Salt and pepper
1 teaspoon/ 5 g sugar

Peel the onions and slice them thinly. Crush the garlic and mix with the remaining ingredients. Spoon over the onion slices and mix well. Serve with curry or other spiced dishes.

Crisp Onion Rings

1 large onion
Milk and water
Salt and pepper
Flour
1 egg yolk

Peel the onion and cut into ¼-in (0.5 cm) slices. Push out the slices to make rings, and soak the rings in equal quantities of milk and water for 30 minutes. Drain the rings thoroughly, season with salt and pepper and

coat lightly with flour. Beat the egg yolk with 2 tablespoons/ 30 ml milk. Coat the onion rings with this mixture. Dip into more flour and leave on a wire cooling-rack until they have dried slightly. Deep-fry in hot oil until crisp and golden. Drain and serve very hot with cheese or meat.

Oriental Onions

¾ lb/ 350 g button onions
2–3 tablespoons/ 30 ml oil
2 tablespoons/ 1 oz/ 25 g butter
2 slices pineapple
1 red pepper
1 tablespoon/ 15 ml vinegar
Juice of ½ lemon
2 tablespoons/ 1 oz/ 25 g soft brown
  sugar
Pinch of ground ginger
Salt and pepper

If fresh pineapple is unobtainable, a small can of crushed pineapple may be used. Peel the onions. Heat the butter and oil in a thick saucepan and add the onions. Cook gently until golden brown. Put the finely chopped pineapple, chopped red pepper, vinegar, lemon, sugar, ginger, salt and pepper into another pan and simmer for 10 minutes. Pour over the onions and continue simmering until the onions are just tender. Serve hot or cold. This is particularly good with ham, pork, chicken or duck.

Braised Onions

6 medium onions
½ cup/ 4 oz/ 100 g cooking fat
1⅓ cups/ ½ pint/ 250 ml beef stock
2 tablespoons/ ½ oz/ 15 g flour
Salt and pepper
Juice of ½ lemon

Peel the onions. Melt the cooking fat in a heavy pan and put in the onions. Cover and cook gently until the onions are golden. Drain off the fat. Pour the stock onto the onions, cover and simmer until they are soft but not broken. Take 1 tablespoon/ 15 ml of the dripping and heat in a small thick pan. Work in the flour and then the stock drained from the onions. Heat gently, stirring well, until the mixture is creamy. Season to taste with salt and pepper and stir in the lemon juice. Pour over the onions and serve with beef or lamb.

Stuffed Onions

4 large onions
$\frac{1}{2}$ lb/ 8 oz/ 225 g cooked beef or lamb
1 cup/ 3 oz/ 50 g fresh white
   breadcrumbs
$\frac{2}{3}$ cup/ $\frac{1}{4}$ pint/ 125 ml brown gravy
1 teaspoon/ 5 ml concentrated tomato
   purée
Salt and pepper
2 tablespoons/ 1 oz/ 25 g cooking fat

Peel the onions and put them into a saucepan. Just cover with water and boil until
just tender. Drain well and scoop out the
center of the onions with a sharp pointed
knife. Chop this flesh finely. Mince the beef
or lamb and mix with the chopped onion.
Keep a few crumbs for topping, and mix the
rest of the breadcrumbs with the meat,
gravy, tomato purée and seasoning. Put the
onions into an ovenware dish and fill the
centers with the meat mixture. Top with
flakes of fat and sprinkle on the remaining
breadcrumbs. Bake at 200°C/400°F/Gas
Mark 6 for 45 minutes. Serve with some
extra gravy. If desired, a little grated cheese
may be added to the breadcrumbs for the
topping.

Onions Braised in Cider

6 large onions
2–3 tablespoons/ 30 ml oil
1⅓ cups/ ½ pint/ 250 ml cider
1 bay leaf
1 sprig of rosemary
Salt and pepper

Peel the onions. Heat the oil in a large sauce-pan and turn the onions in the oil. Pour on the cider and add the herbs and seasoning. Cover and simmer for 45 minutes until the onions are tender. Lift out the onions and put into a serving dish. Boil the cooking liquid until syrupy. Take out the herbs and pour over the onions. These onions are particularly good with roast beef.

Jacket Onions

6 large onions
Butter
Salt and pepper

Remove any loose skin from the onions, but leave on as much skin as possible. Put them in a baking tin and put at the bottom of the oven set at 190°C/375°F/Gas Mark 5 for 1 hour until tender. The softness of the onions can be tested by inserting a skewer. Serve hot with plenty of butter and season-ing. It is a good idea to cook these in the same oven as roast meat or a casserole, as they go particularly well with beef.

Mexican Onion Soup

3 large onions
2 tablespoons/ 1 oz/ 25 g butter
1 tablespoon/ 15 ml oil
2 egg yolks
½ teaspoon/ 2.5 g mustard powder
3⅓ cups/ 1¼ pints/ 625 ml milk
3⅓ cups/ 1¼ pints/ 625 ml chicken stock
¼ cup/ 2 oz/ 50 g grated hard cheese
Pinch of ground coriander
Salt and pepper

Peel the onions and slice them thinly. Cook in the butter and oil, stirring often, until they are soft and golden. Beat the egg yolks, mustard powder and milk. Remove the onions from the heat and stir in the egg mixture gradually. Bring the chicken stock

to the boil. Add to the soup and reheat gently, stirring often, but do not boil. Stir in the cheese, coriander, salt and pepper and serve hot.

Onion Sauce

3 large onions
2⅔ cups/ 1 pint/ 500 ml white sauce
(page 10)
Salt and pepper
4–5 tablespoons/ 60 ml cream

Peel the onions and chop them coarsely. Simmer in just enough water to cover until they are tender. Drain well and add to the white sauce with salt and pepper. Press through a sieve, or liquidize until smooth in an electric blender. Reheat and stir in the cream. This sauce is particularly good with lamb.

Glazed Onions

1 lb/ 500 g small pickling onions
¼ cup/ 2 oz/ 50 g butter
3 tablespoons/ 1½ oz/ 40 g sugar
Salt and pepper
⅓ cup/ 3 fl oz/ 75 ml sherry
1⅓ cups/ ½ pint/ 250 ml water
2 teaspoons/ 10 g chopped parsley

Peel the onions and keep them whole. Melt the butter and add the onions. Toss over low heat for 10 minutes until the onions are golden. Stir in the sugar, salt, pepper, sherry and water. Continue cooking over low heat, stirring frequently until the onions are cooked and the liquid forms a glaze. These are excellent served with roast beef.

Pissaladière

2½ cups/ 10 oz/ 275 g bread flour
Pinch of salt
1½ teaspoons/ 8 g dried yeast
½ cup/ 3 oz/ 75 g anchovy fillets
1 lb/ 500 g onions
⅔ cup/ ¼ pint/ 125 ml olive oil
Pepper
3 tomatoes
⅔ cup/ 4 oz/ 100 g black olives

Sift the flour and salt into a warm bowl. Dissolve the yeast in 6–8 tablespoons/90 ml warm water and leave for 10 minutes until frothy. Stir the yeast liquid into the flour

Below : Onions are fairly easy to grow, preferring a medium soil that is firm.

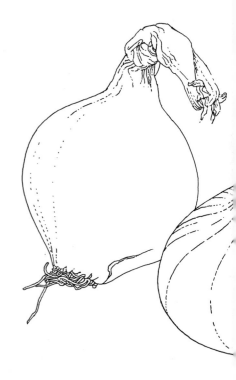

and work together until smooth, adding a little more warm water if necessary to make a firm dough. Knead until smooth and put into an oiled bowl. Cover with a damp cloth and leave in a warm place. Soak the an-chovies in a little cold water, changing the water several times. Peel the onions and slice into thin rings. Heat half the oil and cook the onions very gently for 40 minutes, stirring well so that the onions soften almost to a purée without coloring. Season with salt and pepper. Peel the tomatoes and cut them in thin slices. Roll the dough into a large circle and put on a greased baking sheet, rolling up the edges to form a rim. Prick well with a fork. Spread the onions on the dough, top with tomato slices, drained anchovy fillets and olives arranged in a lattice pattern. Sprinkle on the remaining oil and bake at 200°C/400°F/Gas Mark 6 for 30 minutes. The tomatoes may be omitted if preferred.

Pickled Onions

4 lb/ 2 kg small button onions
1 tablespoon/ 15 g whole allspice
1 tablespoon/ 15 g black peppercorns
7½ cups/ 3 pints/ 1.5 liters vinegar

Shallots may be used instead of small onions. Peel them and pack into clean dry jars. Put the allspice and peppercorns into a saucepan with vinegar and bring to the boil. Take off the heat and leave until cold. Pour over the onions and cover tightly with vinegar-proof lids. Store for 3 months before use.

Onions, Green

see Scallion

Onions, Spring

see Scallion

Onions, Welsh

The Welsh onion or ciboule has a leek-like bulb with tubular leaves and grows in small clusters. When a little onion flavoring is needed, it is convenient to break off one or two small bulbs from a cluster, leaving the main plant still in the ground; it is therefore a useful permanent source for small onions, as the plant is perennial. The flavor is delicate, and the onion may be used raw or cooked in place of scallions.

Oyster Plant

see Salsify

Pak-Choi

This Chinese vegetable is also known as Bok-Choi. The leaves are dark green and shiny with broad white midribs like chard. The blanched hearts of Pak-Choi are a great Chinese delicacy, but normally the leaves and ribs are cooked quickly by stir-frying. The leaves are crisp and should not be overcooked.

Sage and Onion Tart*

2 cups/ 8 oz/ 225 g basic pastry (see page 12)
3 medium onions
2 tablespoons/ 1 oz/ 25 g butter
⅔ cup/ ¼ pint/ 125 ml creamy milk
1 egg
1 tablespoon/ 15 g fresh sage
1 teaspoon/ 5 g fresh parsley
½ cup/ 4 oz/ 100 g bacon
Salt and pepper

Line a 9-in (22.5 cm) pie plate with the pastry. Peel the onions. Chop them finely and toss in hot butter until soft and golden. Beat the milk and egg together and add the finely chopped herbs, chopped bacon, salt and pepper. Add the softened onions and butter and put into the pastry shell. Bake at 200°C/400°F/Gas Mark 6 for 35–40 minutes until the pastry is crisp and the filling golden.

Onion Quiche

2 cups/ 8 oz/ 225 g basic pastry (see page 12)
3 medium onions
1 garlic clove
3–4 tablespoons/ 45 ml oil
2 tablespoons/ 1 oz/ 25 g butter
⅔ cup/ ¼ pint/ 125 ml cream
2 eggs
Salt and pepper
2 tablespoons/ 1 oz/ 25 g grated Parmesan cheese

Roll out the pastry to line an 8-in (20 cm) pie plate and prick the base. Peel the onions and slice them, and crush the garlic. Heat the oil and butter and fry the onion and garlic gently for 5 minutes. Put into the pastry shell. Beat the cream, eggs, salt and pepper and pour over the onions. Sprinkle with the cheese. Bake at 190°C/375°F/Gas Mark 5 for 40 minutes.

Sage and Onion Tart

see page 101

pastry
onions
butter
milk
egg
sage
parsley
bacon
salt and pepper

Inset left : Variegated sage

Inset right : Onions should be harvested in the autumn and dried in the sun (weather permitting) with their roots facing south or in a dry well-ventilated greenhouse before they are stored.

Stir-Fried Pak-Choi

1 medium head Pak-Choi
2 teaspoons/ 10 ml peanut oil
½ teaspoon/ 2.5 g salt
1 tablespoon/ 15 ml cider vinegar
2 tablespoons/ 1 oz/ 25 g sugar
2 teaspoons/ 10 ml soy sauce
4 teaspoons/ 10 g cornstarch
⅓ cup/ 3 fl oz/ 75 ml hot water

Rinse the Pak-Choi and strip the leaves from their stems. Cut the stems diagonally into 2-in (5 cm) lengths and tear the leaves into chunks. Heat the oil in a thick shallow pan and stir-fry the stem pieces for 2 minutes. Mix the salt, vinegar, sugar, soy sauce, cornstarch and water in a bowl. Add the green leaves to the pan and stir in the hot sauce at once. Cook for about 15 seconds, stirring all the time while the sauce thickens. Serve immediately. If desired small strips of cooked pork, beef, chicken or shrimps may be stirred in with the green leaves.

Parsley, Hamburg

see Hamburg Parsley

Parsnip

Parsnips were prized long before the advent of Christianity, and much enjoyed by both the ancient Greeks and Romans. The infamous emperor Tiberius was particularly fond of parsnips and had them specially imported from France and Germany to Capri. It became the traditional vegetable to eat in England with salt fish on Ash Wednesday and other penitential days, and perhaps this is the reason so many people seem to dislike its distinctive flavor. The flavor is greatly improved if parsnips stand through two or three frosts. Plainly boiled parsnips are certainly not to everyone's taste, but they are delicious if turned into a purée with butter, plenty of seasoning and a little cream. Parboiled parsnips can also be finished by frying in butter until just crisp, or by roasting round a joint of beef, pork or lamb for the last 30 minutes of cooking time.

Parsnip Balls

1 lb/ 500 g parsnips
½ cup/ 4 oz/ 100 g butter
1 tablespoon/ 15 ml milk
Salt and pepper
1 egg
1⅓ cup/ 4 oz/ 100 g breadcrumbs

Cook the parsnips, mash them and mix with the butter, milk and seasoning. Heat and stir until the mixture is thick. Cool and beat in a little of the egg to give a smooth mixture. Shape into balls and roll in the remaining egg, then dip into breadcrumbs. Fry in hot fat until golden, and serve hot.

Chicken and Parsnip Pie

7 cups/ 1½ lb/ 750 g cooked chicken
1 large onion
1 lb/ 500 g parsnips
2⅔ cups/ 1 pint/ 500 ml white sauce (see page 10)
3–4 tablespoons/ 45 ml sherry
Pinch of nutmeg
2½ cups/ 12 oz/ 300 g rough puff pastry

Dice the chicken. Cook the onion and parsnips in a little water until tender, and cut into dice. Arrange chicken and vegetables in a pie dish. Flavor the white sauce with sherry and nutmeg and season well, and mix with the chicken and vegetables. Cover with the pastry and bake at 200°C/425°F/Gas Mark 6 for 20 minutes, then at 190°C/375°F/Gas Mark 5 for 25 minutes.

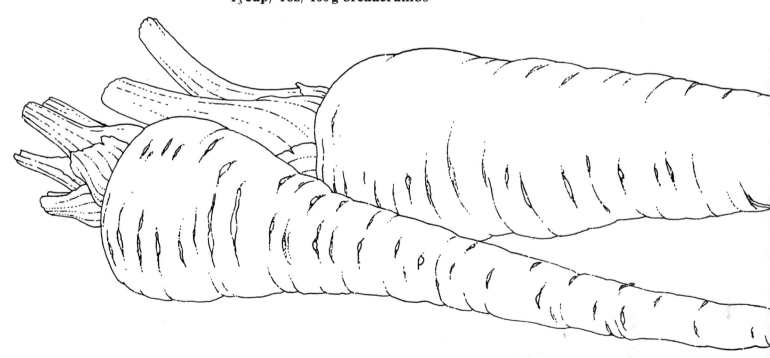

Parsnip Chips

2 lb/ 1 kg parsnips
Oil for frying
Sea salt

Peel the parsnips and cut them into very thin lengthwise strips, discarding any hard core. Put the strips into a bowl of iced water with some extra ice cubes and leave to stand for 1 hour. Drain very thoroughly and dry with kitchen paper. Fry a few at a time in hot lard or oil (do not use olive oil). Drain with a slotted spoon and finish draining on kitchen paper. While still hot, sprinkle with sea salt and eat at once.

Parsnip Salad

2 lb/ 1 kg parsnips
Mayonnaise or French dressing
Lettuce leaves
1 tablespoon/ 15 g chopped parsley

Peel the parsnips, cut in pieces and cook in boiling salted water until tender. Cool and cut into matchstick-sized pieces. Cover and chill. Just before serving, shred the lettuce leaves and arrange in a bowl. Put the parsnips on top and cover with mayonnaise or French dressing. Sprinkle with parsley. This is

sometimes known as 'Poor Man's Lobster Salad' because of the texture and slight sweetness.

Sweet Parsnip Pie

1½ cups/ 12 oz/ 350 g basic pastry (see page 12)
2 lb/ 1 kg parsnips
1 teaspoon/ 5 g salt
3–4 tablespoons/ 45 ml clear honey
¼ teaspoon/ 1.25 g ground ginger
½ teaspoon/ 2.5 g ground cinnamon
Pinch of ground mace
½ teaspoon/ 1.25 g grated orange rind
1 tablespoon/ 15 ml lemon juice
3 egg yolks

Line a pie plate with the pastry, reserving enough to make a top lattice of pastry strips. Prick the pastry, cover with foil and baking beads and bake at 200°C/400°F/Gas Mark 6 for 10 minutes. Remove the foil and beads. Peel the parsnips and cut into pieces. Boil in lightly salted water until tender. Drain well and mince or mash them thoroughly. Mix in the honey, spices, orange rind, lemon juice and egg yolks and pour into the pastry case. Cover with a lattice of pastry strips. Bake at 230°C/450°F/Gas Mark 8 for 20 minutes. Serve warm with cream. This is an Elizabethan dish which was a traditional harbinger of spring; fresh primrose flowers were set in the lattice crosses.

Parsnip-rooted Parsley

see Parsley, Hamburg

Pattypan

see Squash

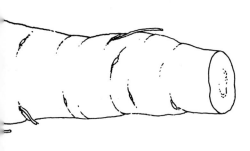
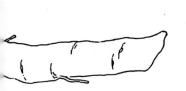

Left: Parsnips are able to grow up to three feet (90 cm) into the soil (although this is not to be desired). Deep, well-cultivated soil is essential. Like other roots, parsnips will fork if the soil is stony. One way to prevent this forking is to push a crowbar about 18 inches (45 cm) into the soil. Rotate it to make a hole and fill the hole with sifted soil and peat. This allows the parsnip to grow with the minimum of difficulty.

Peas, Asparagus

Sometimes known as the winged pea, the asparagus pea has thin green rectangular pods which should be gathered when about 2 in (5 cm) long. The pods are simmered in a little water for 10 minutes and served with butter and seasoning, as a dish by themselves or with meat or poultry.

Peas, Dried

see Pulses, page 162–73

Peas, Edible-Pod or Snow

Peas which are grown for their edible pods are known variously as edible-pod peas, sugar peas, Chinese peas, snow peas, or mangetout. The pods have no parchment lining like shelling-peas, and when the tiny peas inside are very small and the pods are still almost flat, the pods should be topped and tailed, boiled quickly, drained and eaten whole with butter and seasoning. The pods should remain slightly crisp during cooking or they become limp and tasteless. The edible-pod pea is popular in Eastern cooking as they can be stir-fried very successfully.

Chinese Peas and Mushrooms

1 lb/ 500 g edible-pod peas
3 cups/ 1 lb/ 500 g button mushrooms
2–3 tablespoons/ 30 ml peanut oil
1 tablespoon/ 15 ml soy sauce

Wash the pea pods and remove their tops and tails. Wipe the mushrooms and slice finely. Heat the oil in a large shallow pan and stir-fry the mushrooms for 2 minutes over high heat. Add the pea pods and continue stir-frying for 2 minutes. Stir in the soy sauce and serve at once.

Ham and Pea Salad

see page 108

shelled peas
cooked ham
button mushrooms
potatoes
oil
wine vinegar
salt and pepper
lettuce
chives

Peas, Green

Peas were one of the earliest vegetables to be appreciated by mankind, but these were of the dried and split variety which provided nourishing year-round food (see Pulses, p. 173). The green pea as we know it was first cultivated by a French gardener called Michaux in the fifteenth century, and for some time the vegetables were called Michaux after him. There are many varieties of garden peas, but the tiny French *petit pois* are most favored by gourmets.

To cook peas in the most simple way, put them into boiling salted water with a sprig of mint and a pinch of sugar. Bring to the boil and then simmer until the peas are just tender. Drain well and serve hot with a seasoning of salt and pepper and a knob of butter.

Green Pea Soup

2 lb/ 1 kg shelled peas
2 tablespoons/ 1 oz/ 25 g butter
1 small onion
1 small lettuce
Fresh mixed herbs
Salt and pepper
Crisp bacon

Put peas, butter, grated onion, shredded lettuce, and a small bunch of herbs in a pan with a tight-fitting lid. Cook slowly for 10 minutes. Add stock, salt and pepper, and simmer for 1½ hours. Put through a sieve or liquidize. Reheat and serve garnished with small pieces of crisp bacon.

Venetian Rice and Peas

⅜ cup/ 3 oz/ 75 g butter
1 small onion
½ cup/ 4 oz/ 100 g cooked ham
1¾ cups/ 12 oz/ 350 g shelled peas
1½ cups/ 12 oz/ 350 g long grain rice
5 cups/ 2 pints/ 1 liter chicken stock
¼ cup/ 2 oz/ 50 g grated Parmesan cheese

Melt ¼ cup/ 2 oz/ 50 g butter and cook the chopped onion until soft and golden. Add the diced ham, peas and rice and stir well until the butter has been absorbed. Pour in half the stock and cook for 5 minutes, stirring occasionally. Add more stock without stirring and continue adding stock until it has all been used. Stir occasionally, but very gently so that the peas do not break, and cook until the mixture is creamy. Stir in remaining butter and cheese and serve hot.

Gourmet Peas

2½ cups/ 1 lb/ 500 g shelled peas
2 celery stalks
3 scallions
½ teaspoon/ 2.5 g salt
1 cup/ 8 fl oz/ 200 ml chicken stock
4–5 tablespoons/ 60 ml dry white wine
¼ cup/ 2 oz/ 50 g butter
Pepper
4 teaspoons/ 10 g cornstarch

Put the peas into a heavy saucepan with the thinly sliced celery, chopped scallions, salt and chicken stock. Cover and cook over low heat until the peas are almost tender while the celery remains slightly crisp. Stir in the wine, butter and pepper. Mix the cornstarch with a little water and blend into the peas. Cook over gentle heat, stirring occasionally for about 2 minutes until the sauce thickens.

Below : Green peas in their pods.

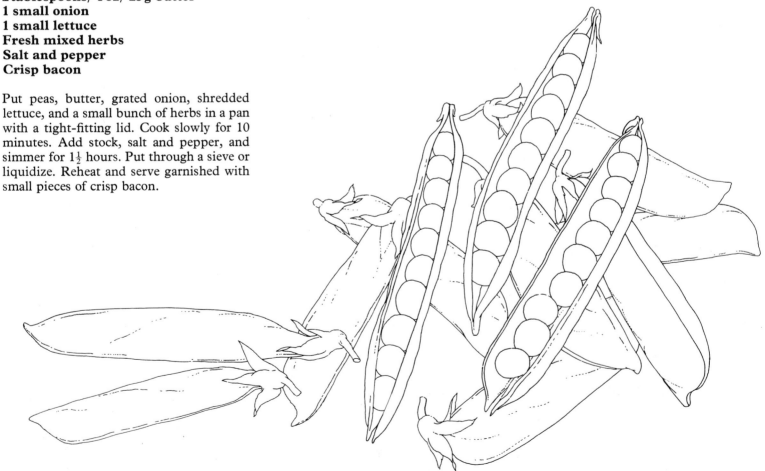

Creamed Peas

2½ cups/ 1 lb/ 500 g shelled peas
⅔ cup/ ¼ pint/ 125 ml water
¼ cup/ 2 oz/ 50 g butter
Salt and pepper
1 teaspoon/ 5 g sugar
Sprig of mint
⅔ cup/ ¼ pint/ 125 ml whipping cream

Put the water, butter, salt, pepper, sugar and mint into a saucepan and heat until the butter melts. Add the peas and cook quickly until the peas are tender. Remove the mint and stir in the cream. Heat very gently and serve hot. This is very good with chicken.

Green Peas with Lettuce

2 tablespoons/ 1 oz/ 25 g butter
12 scallions
1 small lettuce
2½ cups/ 1 lb/ 500 g shelled peas
Salt and pepper
Pinch of ground nutmeg
1 teaspoon/ 5 ml honey
1 sprig of tarragon
1 sprig of thyme
1 sprig of chervil

Melt the butter in a thick saucepan. Chop the onions finely. Wash the lettuce well and chop it finely. Put the onions and lettuce into the pan, and top with the peas. Season well with salt and pepper, and add the nutmeg and honey. Chop the herbs and add them to the peas. Add 3–4 tablespoons 45 ml water, cover tightly, and simmer gently for 12 minutes. Serve very hot with meat or fish.

Peas with Onions

2½ cups/ 1 lb/ 500 g shelled peas
½ cup/ 4 oz/ 100 g lean salt pork
12 small white onions
1 teaspoon/ 5 g flour
1¼ cups/ ½ pint/ 250 ml chicken stock
2 tablespoons/ 30 g chopped parsley
Salt and pepper

Dice the salt pork finely and boil in a little water for 2 minutes. Drain thoroughly and fry in its own fat in a heavy pan with a lid.

When the pork begins to brown, add the peeled onions and cook until the onions are tender and the pork is crisp. Drain off surplus fat. Work the flour into the mixture and cook for 1 minute. Add the stock and bring to the boil. Cover and simmer until the onions are tender. Add the peas, parsley, salt and pepper, cover and simmer until the peas are just tender.

Braised Peas

2½ cups/ 1 lb/ 500 g shelled peas
1 large lettuce
1 teaspoon/ 5 g sugar
⅔ cup/ ¼ pint/ 125 ml boiling water
Salt and pepper

Line a heavy saucepan (with a tight-fitting lid) with washed lettuce leaves. Add the peas and sprinkle with sugar. Add the boiling water. Cover with washed lettuce leaves, put on the lid, and cook over medium heat for 15 minutes until the peas are just tender. Remove the lettuce leaves. Season the peas with salt and pepper and toss in a little butter.

Italian Peas

2½ cups/ 1 lb/ 500 g shelled peas
1 medium onion
¾ cup/ 6 oz/ 150 g cooked ham
¼ cup/ 2 oz/ 50 g butter
Bunch of mixed herbs
Salt and pepper
2 cups/ ¾ pint/ 375 ml chicken stock

Chop the onion and ham finely and cook in the melted butter until the onion is just golden. Add all the remaining liquid and bring to the boil. Boil until the liquid is absorbed and serve hot.

Pea Pod Soup

2 lb/ 1 kg pea pods
1 medium onion
3 medium potatoes
5 cups/ 2 pints/ 1 liter milk
Salt and pepper
1 egg yolk
1 teaspoon/ 5 g chopped mint

Use the pods from shelling ordinary garden peas, not edible-pod peas. Remove strings and stems from the pea pods, together with as much of the inner parchment as possible. Wash the pods well and put into a pan with the sliced onion and potatoes. Add the milk and seasoning and simmer until the potatoes are soft. Put through a sieve or liquidize in an electric blender. Reheat the soup. Beat the egg yolk with a little of the liquid and stir in just before serving. Garnish with mint. A little crumbled crisp bacon or some fried bread cubes go well with this soup.

Japanese Peas and Prawns

2½ cups/ 1 lb/ 500 g shelled peas
1½ cups/ 8 oz/ 225 g cooked shelled
   prawns (or shrimps)
1 tablespoon/ 15 ml peanut oil
1½ cups/ 8 oz/ 225 g button mushrooms
12 scallions
2 cups/ ¾ pint/ 375 ml chicken stock
½ teaspoon/ 2.5 g sugar
Pinch of monosodium glutamate
2–3 tablespoons/ 30 ml soy sauce

Cut each prawn into 2 pieces. Heat the oil in a large shallow pan and stir-fry the prawns over high heat for 1 minute. Add the peas, thinly sliced mushrooms and chopped scallions and continue stir-frying for 1 minute. Add the chicken stock, sugar, monosodium glutamate and soy sauce, and simmer, stirring well for 3 minutes. Serve hot.

Ham and Pea Salad*

2½ cups/ 1 lb/ 500 g shelled peas
1½ cups/ 12 oz/ 350 g cooked ham
⅔ cup/ 4 oz/ 100 g button mushrooms
3 medium potatoes
4–5 tablespoons/ 60 ml oil
2–3 tablespoons/ 30 ml wine vinegar
Salt and pepper
Lettuce leaves
1 tablespoon/ 15 g chopped chives

Cook the peas and also the potatoes and cool completely. Mix the peas, diced ham and thinly sliced mushrooms. Cut the potatoes in thin slices. Just before serving, arrange lettuce leaves on individual plates. Put a layer of potato slices on top, and then a mound of the mixture of peas, ham and mushrooms. Mix the oil, vinegar and seasoning and pour over the salad. Sprinkle with chives.

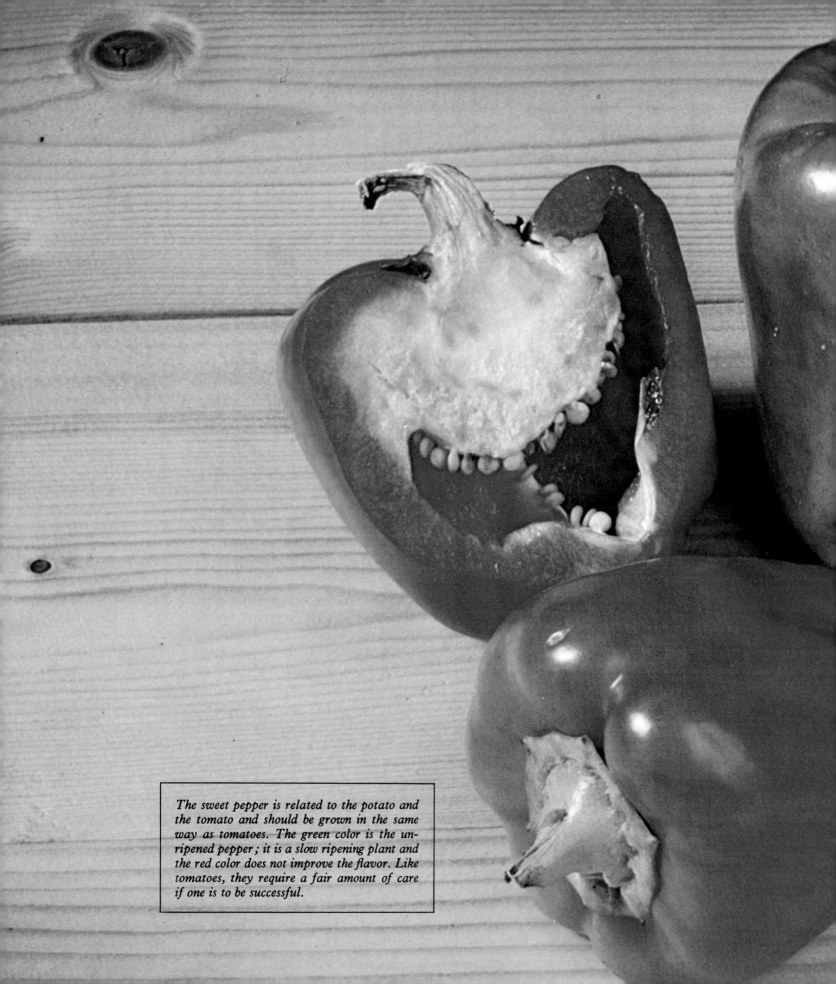

The sweet pepper is related to the potato and the tomato and should be grown in the same way as tomatoes. The green color is the unripened pepper; it is a slow ripening plant and the red color does not improve the flavor. Like tomatoes, they require a fair amount of care if one is to be successful.

Peppers

The sweet pepper or capsicum, often known as Spanish pepper, and most commonly as green or red peppers were natives of tropical America, but spread to Asia and Africa in early days, and the plant is now a great favorite in the Mediterranean countries. It is the ingredient from which paprika is made which gives color and flavoring to many Hungarian and Austrian dishes. A little chopped pepper gives flavor and texture to salads, while stuffed peppers make a distinctive vegetable dish.

Peppers should be fresh, firm and glossy, with no wrinkling or soft spots. The seeds must be discarded as they are very fiery, and the thin inner membrane is also commonly discarded.

Spanish Pepper and Onion Soup

2 large green peppers
2 large onions
$\frac{1}{2}$ cup/ 2 oz/ 50 g butter
2–3 tablespoons/ 30 ml olive oil
6 tablespoons/ 1$\frac{1}{2}$ oz/ 40 g flour
2$\frac{2}{3}$ cups/ 1 pint/ 500 ml chicken stock
Salt and pepper
2 cups/ $\frac{3}{4}$ pint/ 375 ml milk
4–5 tablespoons/ 60 ml cream

Remove the seeds and membranes from the peppers and chop the flesh finely. Peel the onions and chop finely. Heat the butter and oil, and cook the peppers and onions over low heat for 5 minutes, stirring well, until soft and golden. Remove from the heat and stir in the flour. Add the stock and stir well. Bring to the boil, season and simmer for 25 minutes. Cool and liquidize in an electric blender, or put through a sieve. Reheat with the milk and adjust the seasoning. Stir in the cream and serve hot. If preferred, the soup may be served chilled.

Peppers in Tomato Sauce

6 green peppers
4 tablespoons/ 1 oz/ 50 g flour
1 egg yolk
1 tablespoon/ 15 ml olive oil
3 tablespoons/ 45 ml water
Salt and pepper
1 small onion
1 garlic clove
8 large tomatoes
1 teaspoon/ 5 g chopped basil

Halve the peppers and take out the seeds and membranes. Cut each piece in half again lengthwise. Make a batter with flour, egg yolk, oil, water, salt and pepper, and mix well until the batter is like thick cream. Dip the peppers into the batter and deep-fry in hot oil until crisp and golden. Make the sauce by softening the chopped onion and crushed garlic in a little oil, then adding skinned chopped tomatoes, basil and seasoning to taste. Simmer until the sauce is thick. Drain the pepper pieces and serve hot with the sauce.

Shrimp Soufflés in Green Peppers

4 large peppers
1 small onion
2 tablespoons/ 1 oz/ 25 g butter
2 tablespoons/ $\frac{1}{2}$ oz/ 15 g flour
1 cup/ 8 fl oz/ 200 ml milk
3 eggs and 1 egg white
$\frac{1}{2}$ teaspoon/ 2.5 g chopped parsley
$\frac{1}{2}$ teaspoon/ 2.5 g chopped chives
Salt and pepper
Pinch of ground nutmeg
$\frac{1}{2}$ teaspoon/ 2.5 ml Worcestershire sauce
1 cup/ 6 oz/ 150 g cooked shrimps
1 tablespoon/ 15 ml brandy

Pre-heat oven to 220°C/425°F/Gas Mark 7. Cut a slice from the bottom of the peppers so that they stand firmly. Scoop out the seeds and membranes and put the peppers into a buttered ovenware dish. Chop the onion very finely and cook in the butter for 2 minutes, stirring well. Work in the flour and then the milk, and cook over low heat, stirring well until creamy. Take off the heat and cool slightly and then add the egg yolks one at a time, stirring well. Return to low heat and add the herbs and seasonings and cook until thick, stirring well. Add coarsely chopped shrimps and cook gently for 2 or 3 minutes. Cool and stir in the brandy, then fold in the stiffly beaten egg whites. Put the mixture into the peppers. Bake for 20 minutes until the soufflés have risen and are golden-brown on top.

Portuguese Sardine Salad*

2 red peppers
8 oz/ 225 g sardines in oil
2–3 tablespoons/ 30 g chopped parsley
3–4 tablespoons/ 45 ml olive oil
1 tablespoon/ 15 ml wine vinegar
1 teaspoon/ 5 ml lemon juice
1 teaspoon/ 5 g grated onion
Pinch of pepper

Roast the peppers under the broiler or grill, or over a flame until the skin blisters and burns. Rub off the skin and cut the peppers into very thin rings, discarding the seeds and membranes (canned or bottled peppers may be used and will need no preparation before slicing). Arrange the slices in a shallow dish and top with the drained sardines. Sprinkle with the parsley. Mix the oil, vinegar, lemon juice, onion and pepper and pour over the sardines just before serving.

Stuffed Green Peppers

4 large or 6 small green peppers
$\frac{1}{4}$ cup/ 2 oz/ 50 g butter
$\frac{1}{2}$ lb/ 8 oz/ 225 g fresh ground beef
1 small onion
1 garlic clove
1 teaspoon/ 5 g marjoram
1 tablespoon/ 15 g chopped parsley
2 teaspoons/ 10 ml tomato purée
2–3 tablespoons/ 30 ml stock
$\frac{3}{8}$ cup/ 3 oz/ 75 g cooked long-grain rice
Salt and pepper
2 tablespoons/ 1 oz/ 25 g fresh bread-crumbs

Slice the top off each pepper and keep on one side, and remove the seeds. Put the peppers in a pan and cover with boiling water. Boil for 5 minutes and drain. Melt the butter, add the meat and brown it all over, together with chopped onion and garlic. Take off the heat and stir in rice, chopped tops of peppers, oregano, parsley, tomato purée and stock. Season and mix well. Fill the peppers with this stuffing. Rub the remaining butter with the breadcrumbs and use this mixture to top each pepper. Put into a buttered ovenware dish and bake at 180°C/350°F/Gas Mark 4 for 45 minutes.

Red potatoes (left) and white potatoes. Potatoes come in more than one hundred varieties and new types are being developed every day to resist insects and diseases and to provide more food value. Potatoes store quite well provided that it is not too cold (frost will ruin potatoes) or too warm (potatoes will sprout if it is too humid and warm). Inspection throughout the winter to remove any sprouts and to discard those which seem to be rotting will preserve your supply of potatoes until the next crop is ready to be harvested.

Mexican Salsa Fria

2 chili peppers
1 large green pepper
2 tomatoes
1 medium onion
2 garlic cloves
1 tablespoon/ 15 g parsley
1 teaspoon/ 5 g salt
½ teaspoon/ 2.5 g ground coriander
Few drops of Tabasco sauce

Chop the chili peppers finely and mix with finely chopped green pepper. Peel the tomatoes and cut the flesh into pieces. Add to the peppers with the finely chopped onion, mashed garlic, minced parsley, salt, coriander and Tabasco sauce. Stir well and leave to stand for 4 hours before serving. This relish is very hot and spicy and is very good with such Mexican dishes as Chili con Carne.

Tunisian Pepper Relish

6 medium tomatoes
2 medium green peppers
1 garlic clove
Juice of 2 lemons
2 teaspoons/ 10 g salt
5–6 tablespoons/ 75 ml olive oil

Wipe the tomatoes. Cut the peppers in halves and remove the seeds and membranes. Put in a pan of boiling water and cook for 10 minutes. Add the whole tomatoes and simmer for 5 minutes. Drain thoroughly. Remove skins and cores from the tomatoes and squeeze the tomatoes to push out the seeds. Cut the peppers and tomatoes into small pieces and put into a colander to drain. Put them on a chopping board and use a sharp knife to chop them very finely, gradually adding the crushed garlic, lemon juice, salt and oil. Continue chopping until the mixture is quite smooth. Serve with plenty of crusty bread and butter, or with fried potatoes.

Turkish Pepper Salad

2 medium green peppers
2 tablespoons/ 1 oz/ 25 g raisins
2 scallions
2 tablespoons/ 1 oz/ 25 g pine nuts

5–6 tablespoons/ 75 ml olive oil
2–3 tablespoons/ 30 ml lemon juice
Pinch of paprika
Salt and pepper

Remove the seeds and membranes from the peppers and cut the flesh into thin strips. Soak the raisins in a little warm water for 15 minutes and then drain them very well. Mix together the green peppers, raisins, finely chopped scallions and pine nuts and put into a bowl. Mix the oil, lemon juice, paprika, salt and pepper and pour over the contents of the bowl. Stir well and serve immediately with a casserole dish or shish kebab.

Peperonata

4 large red peppers
6 large tomatoes
¼ cup/ 2 oz/ 50 g butter
2–3 tablespoons/ 30 ml olive oil
1 medium onion
Salt
1 garlic clove
Chopped basil

Cut the peppers in half and take out the seeds. Cut the flesh in strips. Dip the tomatoes in boiling water to loosen the skins and peel them. Remove the pips and chop the flesh. Heat the butter and oil together and add the thinly sliced onion. Stir until soft and golden. Add the peppers and cover. Simmer for 15 minutes, then add the tomatoes, salt and crushed garlic. Simmer until the peppers and tomatoes are soft and the oil is almost absorbed, leaving a fairly dry mixture. Sprinkle with basil and serve hot or cold.

Chinese Steak and Peppers

2 large green peppers
2 lb/ 1 kg good cut of steak
4 tablespoons/ 60 ml peanut oil
Salt and pepper
1 medium onion
1 garlic clove
1 celery stalk
1 cup/ 8 fl oz/ 200 ml beef stock
2 tablespoons/ ½ oz/ 15 g cornstarch
2–3 tablespoons/ 30 ml water
2–3 tablespoons/ 30 ml soy sauce

Remove the seeds and membranes from the peppers and cut the flesh in chunks. Cut the steak into very thin diagonal slices. Heat the oil and cook a few slices of steak at a time with the lid on over high heat. When just brown, remove from the oil with a slotted spoon and season well with salt and pepper. When all the steak has been cooked, keep it warm. Add the pepper pieces to the oil with the chopped onions, diagonally-cut celery and crushed garlic. Stir over high heat until the onions begin to soften. Add the stock and steak slices, cover tightly and cook on high heat for 3 minutes. Mix the cornstarch and water with the soy sauce and blend into the other ingredients. Simmer uncovered, stirring constantly until the sauce thickens. Serve at once with rice.

Roast Peppers

4 large peppers
4 garlic cloves
½ cup/ 4 fl oz/ 100 ml olive oil
1 teaspoon/ 5 ml salt

Wash the peppers and roast them at 180°C/ 350°F/Gas Mark 4 for 20 minutes until the skin blisters and blackens and may be pierced easily with a sharp knife. Crush the garlic and heat in the olive oil, adding the salt. Skin the peppers, remove membranes and seeds, and cut the flesh in 1-in (2.5 cm) strips. Put into a glass preserving jar, pour on the oil and seal. When cool, store in the refrigerator. Use in rice dishes, or to garnish dishes, or in salads.

Pepper and Onion Relish

12 green peppers
12 red peppers
15 large onions
11 cups/ 4 pints/ 3.25 liters white vinegar
2 cups/ 1 lb/ 500 g sugar

Remove the seeds and membranes from the peppers and chop the flesh very finely. Peel and chop the onions finely. Put into a bowl and pour on boiling water to cover. Drain well. Cover with cold water, bring to the boil and drain. Put the vinegar, sugar and salt in a saucepan and bring to the boil. Add the peppers and onions and bring quickly to the boil, stirring well. Boil for 1 minute.

Pour into preserving jars and screw on lids tightly. Use all green or all red peppers if preferred. This may be eaten as a pickle, or the vegetables can be drained and added to casseroles.

Pe-tsai

see Cabbage, Chinese

Picridie

see Scorzonera

Pigsweed

see Good King Henry

Potato

The potato is one of the most basic vegetables, delicious cooked in dozens of ways as an accompaniment to protein foods, and also a useful extender when prepared as part of a dish. Spain is credited with the first use of the potato around 1553, and John Hawkins introduced the potato to England in 1563 (although some authorities think this was the sweet potato). Potatoes as we now know them were brought from North Carolina in 1585/6 by colonists sent out by Sir Walter Raleigh, and they were first cultivated on his Irish estate near Cork. Ireland became the home of the potato, and many of the best recipes originate there, but potato blight caused the disastrous famine of 1845–49 and as a result at least 800,000

Irish emigrants sailed for the United States and Canada.

In the kitchen, potatoes add flavor, moisture and quantity to dishes, without affecting the flavor of accompanying foods. Whatever the color of their skins, potatoes are either floury or waxy in texture. Floury potatoes which cook to a fluff are best for mashing and for baking in their skins; waxy potatoes are the ones to use for frying and for salads.

Boiled Potatoes

Potatoes may be boiled in their skins and peeled while hot or they may be peeled first. Just cover in the pan with cold salted water, bring to the boil and cook until tender. Drain well and put over low heat for a second or two to drive off steam. Put *new potatoes* in boiling salted water with a sprig of mint and cook until just tender. For the best mashed or creamed potatoes, mash them while hot and add a knob of butter and hot milk, beating well and seasoning with pepper and a pinch of grated nutmeg.

Roast Potatoes

Use even-sized potatoes and peel them. Put into cold salted water, bring just to the boil and drain well. Put into hot fat and cook at 200°C/400°F/Gas Mark 6 until tender, basting occasionally. For a deliciously crisp skin, draw a fork down the potatoes all round the surface before putting into the hot fat.

Fried Potatoes

Choose waxy potatoes, peel and cut as desired. Rinse in plenty of cold water to remove loose starch and dry very thoroughly in a cloth. Fry in clean hot fat until golden and drain very well before serving. For the best chips, cook them in hot deep fat until white and just tender. Lift out of the fat and reheat the fat, then plunge the potatoes in again and cook until golden and crisp. *French-fried* or *chip* potatoes should be $\frac{1}{4}$-in thick; *allumettes* should be the thickness of a match; *straw* potatoes should be finer than a match and *hair* potatoes are finest of all.

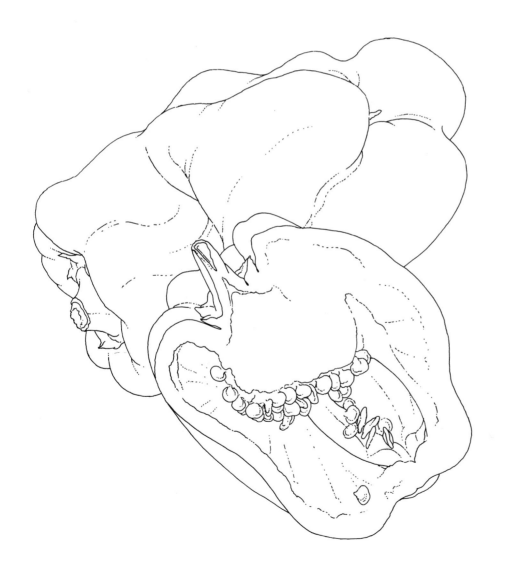

Left: Sweet peppers or capsicums.

Portuguese Sardine Salad

see page 112

red peppers
sardines in oil
parsley
olive oil
wine vinegar
lemon juice
onion
pepper

Potato Salads

Use waxy potatoes and cook them in their skins whether old or new. Drive off all steam when cooked and peel the potatoes quickly. Toss in French dressing or Mayonnaise while still warm and add more dressing just before serving. Add a little grated onion or chopped chives for maximum flavor.

Potato Soup

1 lb/ 500 g potatoes
2 onions
2 tablespoons/ 1 oz/ 25 g cooking fat
2⅔ cups/ 1 pint/ 500 ml water
2⅔ cups/ 1 pint/ 500 ml milk
Salt and pepper
2 tablespoons/ 1 oz/ 25 g seed pearl
tapioca

Melt the dripping in a saucepan. Peel and slice the potatoes and onions. Cook gently in fat for 10 minutes covering the saucepan. Pour in the water. Cook until vegetables are tender. Rub through a sieve. Reheat and add milk and seasoning. Shake in tapioca. Boil for 10 minutes or until tapioca is cooked.

Yvette's Sauté Potatoes

Potatoes
Flour
Oil for frying
Sprig of rosemary

Peel potatoes and cut them into neat small cubes. Dry the cubes well in a clean tea-towel or on a paper towel. Roll the potatoes in flour to cover them completely. Heat a little oil in a frying pan and put in the cubes, which should not be covered by the oil. Turn often and leave until golden on the outside and cooked inside. When the cubes start to brown, turn down the heat and put a lid on, and then turn the cubes only occasionally. Sprinkle with rosemary and serve very hot.

Dauphine Potatoes

¾ lb/ 12 oz/ 350 g potatoes
Salt and pepper

2 tablespoons/ 1 oz/ 25 g grated
Parmesan cheese
¼ cup/ 2 oz/ 50 g butter
⅔ cup/ ¼ pint/ 125 ml water
¾ cup/ 3 oz/ 75 g flour
2 eggs
Oil for frying

Peel the potatoes and cut them in pieces. Cook in salted water until just tender and drain them. Mash the potatoes and add the salt and pepper with the cheese. Put the butter and water into a saucepan and heat until the fat has just melted. Add the flour and beat until the mixture leaves the sides of the pan. Cool slightly and gradually add the beaten eggs, beating until they are absorbed. Mix well with the mashed potatoes. Drop spoonfuls of the mixture into a pan of hot oil and fry until puffed and golden, turning the potatoes half way through cooking. Drain and serve at once.

Duchess Potatoes

1 lb/ 500 g boiled potatoes
2 tablespoons/ 1 oz/ 25 g butter
1 egg
Salt and pepper

Mash the potatoes very thoroughly and work in the butter and beaten egg. Season well and pipe into pyramids on a greased baking sheet. Brush with a little more beaten egg and bake at 180°C/350°F/Gas Mark 4 for 25 minutes. The potatoes are·particularly good if sprinkled with flaked or chopped almonds.

Bakehouse Potatoes

1 lb/ 500 g potatoes
2 medium onions
2 tablespoons/ 1 oz/ 25 g butter
1⅓ cups/ ½ pint/ 250 ml stock
Salt and pepper

Peel and slice the potatoes and put into an ovenware dish. Slice the onions and cook in the butter until golden. Mix with the potatoes, pour over the stock and add knobs of butter. Season well. Bake at 190°C/375°F Gas Mark 5 for 1 hour until the potatoes are tender. A small leg of lamb may be cooked on top of these potatoes and the cooking time should then be extended by 30 minutes. Add a sprig of rosemary and some slivers of garlic to the lamb for maximum flavour.

Potatoes come in an infinite number of shapes, sizes, textures and tastes. They will grow in almost any soil and can be harvested throughout late summer and fall. Below are five different varieties.

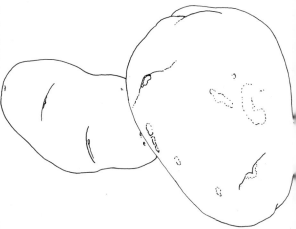

Parisian Potatoes

1 lb/ 500 g large potatoes
Butter for frying
Salt

Peel the potatoes and using a potato or melon scoop gouge small balls out of the potatoes. Cook them in boiling salted water until just tender but not broken. Drain very well and toss in butter until golden. Sprinkle with salt before serving.

Savoy Potatoes

1 lb/ 500 g potatoes
2 medium onions
4 slices of bacon or ham
2 tablespoons/ 1 oz/ 25 g butter
1⅓ cups/ ½ pint/ 250 ml stock
Salt and pepper
¼ cup/ 2 oz/ 50 g grated Cheddar cheese

Peel the potatoes and slice them thickly. Slice the onions thinly. Chop the bacon and

cook in the butter until lightly colored. Drain the bacon and keep on one side. Cook the onion in the fat in the pan until soft and golden. Toss the potatoes in the fat with the onion. Return the bacon to the pan with the stock and seasoning. Put into an ovenware dish and sprinkle with cheese. Bake at 190°C/375°F/Gas Mark 5 for 1 hour.

Anna Potatoes

1½ lb/ 750 g potatoes
½ cup/ 4 oz/ 100 g butter
Salt and pepper

Peel the potatoes and cut them into thin slices. Wash the slices and dry them thoroughly. Butter a shallow ovenware dish and arrange a layer of overlapping potato slices. Season well and pour over a little melted butter. Continue in layers. Cover the dish and bake at 200°C/400°F/Gas Mark 6 for 1 hour, removing the cover for the last 15 minutes. Cut in wedges to serve.

Baked Potatoes*

Potatoes for baking should have the skins brushed with melted butter or cooking fat, and pricked to allow the steam to escape. Bake 1–1¼ hours at 200°C/400°F/Gas Mark 6. To serve, mark a cross on top of the potato, squeeze gently, held in a cloth, sprinkle with salt and place a knob of butter in the cross. The potatoes may be cut in half, the cut side wiped dry, and placed cut side down on a greased pan. This will reduce the cooking time to 30–40 minutes. Variations for baked potato fillings:

When the potato has been baked, scoop out the flesh, mash, and add any of the variations listed below:
1. Chopped cooked meat, beef, ham, bacon and garnish with parsley.
2. Flaked fish and butter.
3. Chopped grilled kidney, garnished with fried onion rings.
4. Chopped boiled egg and mayonnaise, garnished with sieved egg yolk.
5. Chopped fried mushrooms.
6. Raisins and cubes of cheese.
7. Minced ham and savory sauce.
8. Grated cheese and egg yolk.
9. Flaked salmon and lemon juice.
10. Chopped chives and tomato purée.
11. Flaked cooked kipper fillets and lemon juice.
12. Cottage cheese and chopped chives.
13. Scrambled egg and chopped fried bacon.
14. Minced chicken and sautéed chopped mushrooms.

Scalloped New Potatoes

⅜ cup/ 3 oz/ 75 g butter
1½ lb/ 750 g new potatoes (all similar in size, scraped)
⅔ cup/ 2 oz/ 50 g fresh breadcrumbs
Salt and pepper

Melt ¼ cup/ 2 oz/ 50 g butter in a medium-to-large saucepan. Add the whole potatoes. Spread them out so they cover the base of the pan in one layer, and cover. Cook very slowly to prevent butter from burning. Turn the potatoes over several times during cooking so they become golden all over. Cook for ½–1 hour, (depending on size of potatoes). When tender, add remaining butter. Turn the heat up and add the breadcrumbs and seasoning. Cook 3–4 minutes, stirring continuously until the breadcrumbs have absorbed the butter, and have turned crisp and golden.

Foil Potatoes

4 large potatoes
¼ cup/ 2 oz/ 50 g butter
2 medium onions
Salt and pepper
Parsley

Peel potatoes and cut crosswise in 4 slices. Spread butter thickly between each slice and on top. Re-assemble potatoes with onion slices between. Season with salt and pepper and wrap each potato tightly in double foil. Bake at 170°C/325°F/Gas Mark 3 for 1½ hours. Open foil and sprinkle with parsley, or brown in the oven.

Scots Potato Fritters

6 large potatoes
2 eggs
1 tablespoon/ 15 g breadcrumbs
1 tablespoon/ 15 g lean ham

Parboil the potatoes and cut them in thick slices. Beat up the eggs with the finely grated breadcrumbs and grated ham. Dip each slice of potato in this mixture and fry in plenty of hot fat.

Swiss Potato Cake

2 lb/ 1 kg potatoes
¼ cup/ 2 oz/ 50 g Gruyere cheese
⅜ cup/ 3 oz/ 75 g butter
1 medium onion
Salt and pepper

Wash the potatoes and boil them in their skins for 10 minutes. Cool and peel and then grate with a coarse grater into a bowl. Stir in the cheese. Melt 1 tablespoon/ 15 g butter; cook the finely chopped onion till soft and golden. Add to the potato mixture and season well. Melt the remaining butter in a thick frying pan and press in the potato mixture. Cook until golden brown on one side, then turn the potato cake and cook on the other side until golden, which will take about 15 minutes. Serve very hot.

Baked Potatoes

see page 119

stuffed with
top center – creamed mushrooms topped
with chives
left – grated cheese and parsley
right – scrambled egg
Almost everything goes well with baked
potatoes!

Deviled New Potatoes (1)

1 lb/ 500 g new potatoes
¼ cup/ 2 oz/ 50 g butter
2 teaspoons/ 10 g mustard powder
1 tablespoons/ 15 g concentrated
    tomato purée
2 tablespoons/ 30 ml chutney
2 tablespoons/ 30 ml vinegar
1 tablespoon/ 15 ml Worcestershire
    sauce
Salt and pepper

Use very small potatoes and scrape them. Cook in salted water for 10 minutes until partly boiled. Drain well. Melt the butter and stir in the mustard, tomato purée, chutney, vinegar, sauce, salt and pepper. Simmer for 5 minutes. Add the potatoes, cover the pan and cook very gently for 12 minutes.

Deviled New Potatoes (2)

1 lb/ 500 g small new potatoes
2 tablespoons/ 1 oz/ 25 g butter
4–5 tablespoons/ 60 ml whipping
    cream
1 teaspoon/ 5 ml French mustard
Few drops of Worcestershire sauce
Chopped chives

Scrape the potatoes and put them into boiling, salted water. Cook until just tender, drain well and toss in the butter. Stir together the cream, mustard sauce and chives. Pour over the potatoes and shake the pan gently. Serve hot with grilled steak or chops.

Jamaican Sugar Potatoes

1 lb/ 500 g new potatoes
¼ cup/ 2 oz/ 50 g butter
4 –5 tablespoons/ 60 ml clear honey
2 tablespoons/ 1 oz/ 25 g soft brown
    sugar
Salt and pepper

Use very small potatoes and scrape them. Cook in salted water for 10 minutes until partly boiled. Drain well. Heat the butter until it melts and add the honey. Add the potatoes and cover, and cook very gently for 15 minutes, shaking the pan occasionally to coat the potatoes. Add the brown sugar and simmer for 5 minutes. These are particularly good with ham.

Italian Potato Salad

6 medium potatoes
1 bunch scallions
⅜ cup/ 3 fl oz/ 75 ml red wine
¾ cup/ 7 fl oz/ 165 ml olive oil
2 teaspoons/ 10 ml wine vinegar
Salt and pepper
12 anchovy fillets
2 teaspoons/ 10 g chopped chervil

Boil the potatoes in their skins, cool and peel them. Cut in slices and put into a serving dish. Chop the onions and mix with the wine, oil, vinegar, salt and pepper, chopped anchovies and chervil. Pour over the potatoes, mix well, and leave to stand for 30 minutes before serving.

Potato Scones

12 oz/ 350 g potatoes
1 teaspoon/ 5 g mustard powder
1½ cups/ 6 oz/ 150 g flour
¼ cup/ 2 oz/ 50 g butter
Salt and pepper
2–3 tablespoons/ 30 g chopped parsley

Peel the potatoes, cut them in pieces, and boil in salted water until just tender. Drain well and mash the potatoes. Mix with the mustard, flour, melted butter, salt, pepper and parsley. Chill for 1 hour. Roll out on a lightly floured surface and cut into 12 triangles. Cook on a lightly greased heavy frying pan or griddle until lightly golden. Turn the scones and cook on the other side. Serve hot with butter. The parsley may be omitted.

Welsh Potato Cakes*

1 lb/ 500 g boiled potatoes
1 cup/ 4 oz/ 100 g flour
1 teaspoon/ 5 g baking powder
1 egg
2 tablespoons/1 oz/ 25 g butter
2 tablespoons/ 1 oz/ 25 g sugar
Pinch of salt

Mix all the ingredients except the butter. Melt the butter and mix thoroughly with the rest. Roll out 1 in (2.5 cm) thick. Bake on a griddle, or at 220°C/425°F/Gas Mark 7 for 20 minutes. Serve hot with a lot of butter. Cold potato can be fried with bacon.

Welsh Onion Cake

1 lb/ 500 g potatoes
1½ cups/ 8 oz/ 225 g onions
½ cup/ 4 oz/ 100 g butter
Salt and pepper

Use a well-buttered cake tin. Peel the potatoes, slice them fairly thinly and arrange in a layer on the bottom of the tin. Sprinkle a layer of finely chopped onion on the potatoes, add flakes of butter, salt and pepper. Continue in layers until the tin is full, finishing with a layer of potatoes and a few flakes of butter. Cover with foil and bake at 180°C/350°F/Gas Mark 4 for 1 hour. Eat with hot or cold meat.

Hot Potato Salad

2 lb/ 1 kg new potatoes
2 tablespoons/ 1 oz/ 25 g butter or
** bacon fat**
1 teaspoon/ 5 g flour
3–4 tablespoons/ 45 ml vinegar
4 scallions
4 slices of bacon
2 tablespoons/ 1 oz/ 25 g sugar
1 teaspoon/ 5 g salt
1 tablespoon/ 15 g chopped parsley

Scrub the potatoes and cook them in boiling salted water until just tender. Drain them and reserve the cooking liquid. Melt the fat in a pan, stir in the flour and salt and cook for 1 minute. Add the potatoes and chopped bacon, cover and cook over very low heat shaking the pan occasionally. Serve hot, garnished with parsley.

Welsh Hot Pot

1 lb/ 500 g potatoes
½ lb/ 8 oz/ 225 g onions
½ lb/ 8 oz/ 225 g bacon
Salt and pepper

Slice potatoes fairly thickly, slice onions and cut bacon in neat pieces. Arrange in alternate layers in a casserole, season with salt and pepper. Cover with a lid and cook at 170°C/325°F/Gas Mark 3 for 2 hours. Remove lid and continue cooking for 20 minutes. Another version of this made in a saucepan and with the addition of water used to be called 'The Miser's Feast,' with the miser eating the mashed up potatoes one day, and saving the slices of bacon to eat a second day.

Champ

8 large potatoes
6 scallions
¾ cup/ 7 fl oz/ 200 ml milk
Salt and pepper
Butter

Let the peeled potatoes stand in cold water for 1 hour. Drain and cover with cold salted water and boil until tender. Drain well and dry off by putting a folded cloth on top and returning the pot to a gentle heat for a few minutes. Chop the scallions very finely using the green tops as well as the bulbs, put

them into a bowl and cover with boiling water. Drain the onions and add to the milk. Bring to the boil and pour on to the mashed potatoes, with pepper and salt to taste. When very light and fluffy, pile up on individual plates, making a well in the middle, and put a piece of butter in the well. The potato is scooped up into the melted butter as it is eaten. Sometimes this is known as *thump* or *stelk* in Ireland. Another version, called *colcannon* includes chopped boiled curly kale or cabbage. The Welsh mixture of vegetables is a *stwns* and is a mixture of potatoes and turnip, potatoes and peas, or potatoes and broad beans, sometimes with buttermilk poured over.

Boxty

2 large raw potatoes
3 cups/ 12 oz/ 350 g mashed potatoes
4 tablespoons/ 1 oz/ 25 g flour
1 teaspoon/ 5 g baking soda
1 teaspoon/ 5 g salt

Grate the raw potatoes and squeeze out the liquid. Add to the mashed potatoes and salt. Mix the soda with the flour and add to the potatoes. Roll out ½ in (1.25 cm) thick in a circle. Cut in 4 quarters and put on an ungreased griddle. Cook on gentle heat for 30–40 minutes, turning bread once. The quarters should be well-browned on both sides. A teaspoon of caraway seeds can be added to the dough.

Potato, Indian

see Yam

Potato, Sweet

see Sweet Potato

Pulses

see pages 162–73

Pumpkin

Giant orange pumpkins are one of the most delightful sights in markets and vegetable stores on the cooler fall days, and they are traditionally hollowed out to make Jack o'Lantern faces for Hallowe'en. One of the largest achieved fame as Cinderella's coach in the seventeenth century French fairy tale. The original French name was *citrouille* referring to the citrus yellow color, but today's name of *potiron* derives from the Arabic word for morel mushroom, when the French called them 'huge mushrooms.' The word 'pumpkin' comes from *pepon*, the Greek word for melon. Indeed all the names indicate warm sunny origins from which the favorite recipes come.

As with other members of the squash and gourd family, the pumpkin is ruined by over-exposure to water. It is best to peel and cut the flesh into small pieces, simmering in very little water, or steaming until tender. Drain off surplus liquid and then mash to a purée before using in recipes. The pumpkin purée may be served simply as a vegetable accompaniment to meat if well-seasoned and dressed with butter. In sweet dishes, the pumpkin is enhanced by ginger, nutmeg and cinnamon, and by brandy or rum.

Pumpkin Soup (1)

4 cups/ 2 lb/ 1 kg prepared pumpkin
Milk
Salt and pepper
Pinch of nutmeg

Peel the pumpkin, remove the seeds and membrane before measuring the flesh. Cook in just enough water to cover until tender, then put through a sieve. Add enough milk to give a creamy consistency, and reheat, seasoning well with salt, pepper and nutmeg. Serve with a garnish of fried bread cubes. The soup may be made with chicken stock, and a little cream may be added for richer flavor. Another good garnish is a handful of peeled shrimps or prawns dipped in lemon juice.

Welsh Potato Cakes

see page 122

boiled potatoes
flour
baking powder
egg
butter
sugar
salt

Pumpkin Soup (2)

4½ cups/ 2 lb/ 1 kg prepared pumpkin
½ lb/ 8 oz/ 225 g potatoes
½ lb/ 8 oz/ 225 g tomatoes
1 celery stick
1 large onion
1 leek
½ cup/ 4 oz/ 100 g butter
4 cups/ 1½ pints/ 750 ml chicken stock
2⅔ cups/ 1 pint/ 500 ml milk
Salt and pepper
Pinch of sugar
4–5 tablespoons/ 60 ml cream
Few drops Tabasco sauce

Chop the pumpkin, potatoes, tomatoes and celery and simmer in the stock for 20 minutes. Drain and sieve the vegetables. Chop the onion and leek and cook in half the butter until soft but not colored. Stir in the vegetable purée, then add the milk, salt, pepper and sugar. Reheat and stir in the cream and Tabasco sauce, together with the remaining butter.

New England Baked Pumpkin

This is an old recipe which was considered 'a proper supper dish for a growing child.' Take a small and very ripe pumpkin with a hard shell. Slice off the stem end to form a cover with a handle. Scoop out the seeds and stringy fibers. Fill the cavity with creamy milk, put back the cover and bake in a low oven 150°C/300°F/Gas Mark 3 for 4 hours. Fill with milk to the brim and eat from the shell with a spoon.

Sicilian Pumpkin

2¼ cups/ 1 lb/ 500 g prepared pumpkin
1 teaspoon/ 5 ml olive oil
1 small garlic clove
⅜ cup/ 3 fl oz/ 75 ml dry white wine
1 sprig of mint
Pinch of sugar
1 teaspoon/ 5 ml lemon juice
¼ pint/ 125 ml whipping cream
Salt and pepper

Cut the pumpkin into small cubes and sprinkle with salt. Leave for an hour and drain off any liquid. Heat the oil and add the pumpkin and finely chopped garlic. Brown lightly and add the wine, mint and sugar. Simmer gently until the pumpkin is tender but not broken. Take out the mint. Add the lemon juice, cream and seasoning, and stir gently over very low heat for 5 minutes.

Pumpkin Pie

2 cups/ 8 oz/ 225 g basic pastry (see page 12)
1½ cups/ 12 oz/ 350 g pumpkin purée
4 eggs
1 cup/ 8 oz/ 225 g sugar
½ teaspoon/ 2.5 g ground cinnamon
Pinch of ground allspice
Pinch of ground ginger
2 tablespoons/ ½ oz/ 15 g flour
3 tablespoons/ 1½ oz/ 40 g butter
⅔ cup/ ¼ pint/ 125 ml cream

Prepare the pumpkin by dicing the flesh and steaming it until tender before rubbing through a sieve. Line a pie plate with the pastry. Prick well all over, cover with foil and baking beads, and bake at 200°C/400°F/ Gas Mark 6 for 20 minutes. Remove the foil and beads. Mix the pumpkin purée with the egg yolks, sugar, spices, flour, melted butter and cream. Whip the egg whites with a pinch of salt to soft peaks, and fold lightly into the pumpkin mixture. Pour into the pastry shell and bake at 170°C/325°F/ Gas Mark 3 for 50 minutes. If liked, add some mixed dried fruit or some nuts to the pumpkin mixture before baking.

South African Pumpkin Fritters

2 cups/ 1 lb/ 500 g cooked pumpkin
¾ cup/ 3 oz/ 75 g flour
1 teaspoon/ 5 g baking powder
2 eggs
Pinch of salt
Lard for frying
Sugar
Ground cinnamon
Lemon wedges

Squeeze as much liquid from the pumpkin as possible and then mash the cooked flesh with the flour and baking powder. Work in the well-beaten eggs and the salt to make a soft mixture. Fry in large spoonfuls in hot lard in a frying pan. Cook on both sides and serve hot, sprinkled thickly with sugar, cinnamon and lemon wedges.

Caribbean Soup

4 cups/ 2 lb/ 1 kg pumpkin
1 large onion
2 large carrots
2 tomatoes
4 cups/ 1½ pints/ 750 ml chicken stock
2 teaspoons/ 10 g chopped chives
Sprig of parsley
Pinch of paprika
Pinch of salt
⅔ cup/ ¼ pint/ 125 ml cream

Do not peel the pumpkin but cut it in 4 or 5 pieces and cook for 15 minutes in boiling salted water. Drain well and scoop out the flesh from the skin. Cut it in small pieces and simmer in the chicken stock with the chopped onion, chopped carrots and tomatoes, half the chives and the sprig of parsley. Simmer with a lid on until the vegetables

Below : Pumpkins belong to the same family as squashes, marrows and gourds. Pumpkins however have made themselves popular, not just as items for the gourmet's table but as the carved lantern for Hallowe'en.

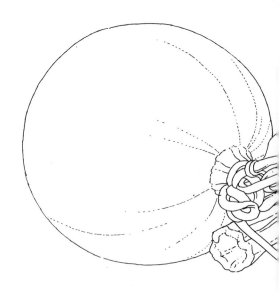

are tender. Put through a sieve and cool. Season with paprika and salt, and stir in half the cream. Chill completely and swirl in the remaining cream.

Pumpkin Custards

1 cup/ 8 oz/ 225 g cooked pumpkin
1⅓ cups/ ½ pint/ 250 ml milk
2–3 tablespoons/ 30 ml clear honey
Pinch of ground nutmeg
Pinch of ground cloves
2 eggs

Mash the pumpkin and beat with the milk, honey and spices until smooth, or blend the ingredients together in an electric blender. Beat in the beaten eggs and pour into six individual greased ovenware dishes. Put into a shallow pan of hot water and bake at 170°C/325°F/Gas Mark 4 for 20 minutes

until the custards are set and golden. Cool to room temperature before serving.

Pumpkin Pickle

12 cups/ 5 lb/ 2.5 kg prepared pumpkin
8 cups/ 3 pints/ 1.5 l white vinegar
3 lb/ 1.5 kg sugar
1 tablespoon/ ½ oz/ 15 g celery salt
2 pieces root ginger
2 cinnamon sticks
1 tablespoon/ ½ oz/ 15 g mustard seeds
10 whole cloves

Peel the pumpkin and scoop out pith and seeds before weighing the pumpkin. Cut the flesh into small pieces. Boil the vinegar and sugar together, pour over the pumpkin and leave overnight. Drain off the liquid and add the spices tied in a cheesecloth bag. Bring

to the boil and then add the pumpkin pieces. Simmer for 3 hours, stirring occasionally. Remove the spice bag. Pour the pickle into clean jars and cover tightly with vinegar-proof lids. Store for 1 month before use.

Pumpkin Preserve

12 cups/ 5 lb/ 2.5 kg prepared pumpkin
4 lb/ 2 kg sugar
1 cup/ 8 oz/ 225 g butter
6 lemons

Peel the pumpkin and remove the seeds before weighing. Cut into pieces and steam for 30 minutes. Drain in a cheesecloth bag for 24 hours. Weigh the remaining pulp (4 lb [2 kg] is needed for the remaining ingredients). Put into a pan with sugar, butter, the grated rind and the lemon juice. Bring to the boil slowly, and then boil gently for 20 minutes. Pour into hot jars and cover. Do not try to keep this preserve more than 2 months because of the fat content. Use as a tart or pie filling.

Pumpkin and Cranberry Jam

1½ cups/ 8 oz/ 225 g cranberries
9 cups/ 4 lb/ 2 kg prepared pumpkin
2⅔ cups/ 1 pint/ 500 ml water
1 teaspoon/ 5 g cream of tartar
4 lb/ 2 kg sugar

Put the cranberries with the diced pumpkin flesh, water and cream of tartar into a pan and simmer for about 1 hour until tender. Stir in the sugar until dissolved, then boil hard to setting point. This is very good used as a tart filling.

Purslane

This plant is often considered to be a weed but it used to be cultivated and widely used although the leaves are somewhat bitter. The large tender leaves can be used in salad, made into sandwiches, or cooked briefly and served with butter or cream sauce. Purslane may be used in spinach recipes. Sea purslane or notchweed may be cooked like spinach, or the stems can be pickled in vinegar.

Radishes comprise one of the best catch crops. They require a rich, moisture-retaining soil and should be grown quickly as they become too hot and spongy if grown slowly. They should take only three to four weeks from sowing to eating.

Radish

The radish is usually treated as a raw salad vegetable whether it is red or white, is spherical, olive-shaped or tapering. Radishes for this purpose are best washed well and then chilled in iced water until serving time. They may be sliced into a salad or left whole, but are delicious eaten on their own with fresh butter and sea salt. The rat-tailed radish comes from Southern Asia and is grown for its seed pods which are eaten freshly picked and raw, or pickled – the root is not edible. The Oriental radish or daikon is larger and has a more spongy texture than the other varieties but the flavor is similar.

Chinese Radish Salad

36 salad radishes
½ teaspoon/ 2.5 ml salt
2 tablespoons/ 1 oz/ 25 g soft brown
   sugar
2–3 tablespoons/ 30 ml wine vinegar
1 teaspoon/ 5 ml oil

Trim the radishes and wash them well. Drain thoroughly and crush the radishes lightly with a weight. Sprinkle with salt and leave to stand for 30 minutes. Drain off the liquid and put the radishes in a serving dish. Mix the sugar, vinegar and oil and pour over the radishes just before serving.

Steamed Radishes

36 salad radishes
8 scallions
¼ cup/ 2 oz/ 50 g butter
4–5 tablespoons/ 60 ml water

Scrub the radishes and trim them. Chop the scallions and cook in the butter until soft and golden. Add the radishes and water and cover. Cook on high heat for 2 minutes, then reduce heat and simmer for 5 minutes. Drain thoroughly and serve hot with butter and seasoning, or with white sauce or pan juices from roast meat.

Rampion

A European weed of the Canterbury Bell family which used to be cultivated in England for the sake of the long spindle-shaped fleshy roots in the winter. The plant has almost gone out of use, but may be sliced in salads, or cooked in the same way as salsify.

Red Cabbage

see Cabbage

Red Peppers

see Peppers

Root Parsley

see Parsley, Hamburg

Runner Beans

see Beans, Runner

Rutabaga

see Turnip, Yellow

Salsify

This plant is often known as the oyster plant or vegetable oyster since it has a distinct oyster flavor. The young grassy leaves

Below: Salsify is a biennial plant which means it takes two years to complete the cycle from seed to seeding. However the root can be harvested annually.

may be blanched and used in salads, but the long white root is more commonly eaten.

To prepare salsify, scrape the roots and cut them into 2-in (5 cm) lengths, then leave in cold water with a few drops of lemon juice to prevent discoloration. Cook either in salted water with a little lemon juice, or simmer in stock, or toss in butter. Cooked salsify may be eaten with butter and seasoning, and is particularly good with chicken. It may also be made into a purée, or served with a cream sauce, cheese sauce or Hollandaise sauce. Cooked salsify may also be cooled and served in oil and vinegar dressing.

Italian Salsify

1 medium onion
2 tablespoons/ 1 oz/ 25 g butter
1 lb/ 500 g salsify
2 tablespoons/ ½ oz/ 15 g flour
2 egg yolks
1 teaspoon/ 5 ml lemon juice
2–3 tablespoons/ 30 ml stock
1 tablespoon/ 15 g chopped parsley
Fried bread cubes

Chop the onion finely and cook in the butter until soft and golden. Scrape and clean the salsify and cut in 1-in (2.5 cm) pieces. Put into the frying pan and stir over low heat for 15 minutes. Stir in the flour and continue cooking gently for 10 minutes. Beat the egg yolks with the lemon juice and stock and stir into the pan off the fire. Reheat gently without boiling and serve hot with a garnish of parsley and fried bread cubes.

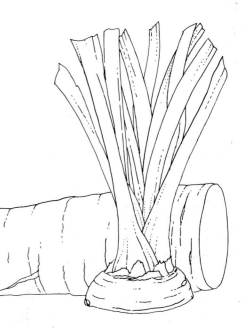

Salsify with Fresh Herbs

see page 132

salsify
butter
parsley
chives
thyme
lemon wedges

Salsify with Fresh Herbs*

1 lb/ 500 g salsify
¼ cup/ 2 oz/ 50 g butter
1 tablespoon/ 15 g chopped parsley
2 teaspoons/ 10 g chopped chives
1 teaspoon/ 5 g chopped thyme
Lemon wedges

Wash and scrape the salsify, and soak in cold water with a squeeze of lemon juice. Cut in 1-in (2.5 cm) slices and cook in just enough water to cover until tender. Drain very well and put into a pan with the butter and herbs. Toss over low heat for two or three minutes, and serve very hot with lemon wedges.

Salsify Fritters

1 lb/ 500 g salsify
Salt and pepper
Pinch of cayenne pepper
Beaten egg
Fine breadcrumbs
Oil for frying
Lemon wedges

Scrape the salsify and boil in salted water with a squeeze of lemon juice until tender. Drain, season with salt, pepper and cayenne pepper and mash well. Form into small flat cakes and dip in egg and breadcrumbs. Fry in hot oil and serve with lemon wedges. An alternative way of preparing fritters is to cook short lengths of salsify, dip them in batter and deep-fry until golden.

Salsify, Black

see Scorzonera

Samphire

This plant is found on the north coast of Norfolk (England) on the edge of tidal waters and marshes, and is eaten during late July and August. Traditionally, it was pickled, although it is claimed that rock samphire from Wales (known as cress, marine) is better for this purpose. In Norfolk the samphire was heated for pick-ling in the village baker's oven.

To eat fresh, pick from areas where the tide has washed the samphire well. Wash well in fresh water and pick out any weeds. Boil in fresh water for 10 minutes and serve with melted butter. Eat like asparagus, biting off the fleshy parts (it is often known as 'poor man's asparagus'). Samphire can also be served with roast meat, or as a vegetable garnished with cubes of fried bread.

Pickled Samphire (1)

Do not wash the samphire, but leave the sea salt on it. Put the samphire in a flat bowl, cover with salt and spring water and leave for 24 hours. Put into a clean pan and cover with good vinegar. Set the pan over a very slow fire and let it come slowly to the boil. Take off while the samphire is still green and crisp. Put into pickling jars, pour on the hot vinegar and leave until cold. Seal tightly. Use after a week or two.

Pickled Samphire (2)

Pick and wash the samphire in fresh water. Take off the roots and cook it in water with just an egg-cup full of vinegar so the taste of the vinegar cooks in it. Put into preserving jars with the pickling vinegar. It can be eaten straight away but it lasts right through the winter.

Savoy Cabbage

see Cabbage

Scallion

The spring onion or scallion is a small member of the onion family which grows quickly and is available in all but the coldest weather. Both the green tops and the small white bulbs may be used raw in salads as they have a delicate flavor and crisp texture. Although a large quantity is needed, scallions can be substituted for leeks when these are not available for recipes. The little white bulbs may be cooked with peas to give a subtle onion flavor, and are useful for savory pies. Bunches of scallions may be lightly cooked until just tender and then served just warm in a French dressing. Scallions are also widely used in Oriental cooking since they can be quickly stir-fried and have a very delicate flavor when cooked in this way. They are also used in Chinese and Korean soups.

Scallop Squash

see Squash

Below: Scorzonera or black salsify (right) and the ever-popular scallions.

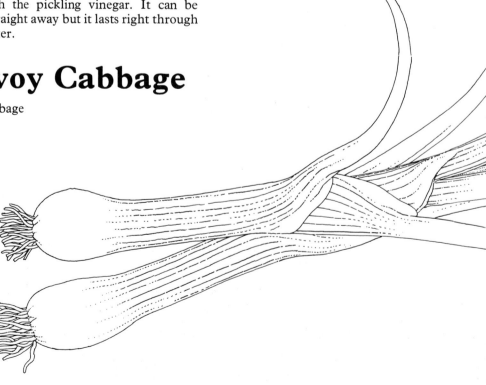

Scorzonera

This is sometimes known as black salsify as it is closely related to the salsify with white roots. Scorzonera however has black cylindrical roots instead of white tapering ones, but the flavor is similar. It can be used for all salsify recipes. If a few roots are left in the ground, young shoots will be produced in the spring which can be used like chards. French scorzonera or picridie is a related variety which is grown for the sake of its leaves rather than its roots which are coarse. The leaves are cut two or three times from the same root to use as salad.

The roots of scorzonera should not be peeled, cut or scraped before boiling as the plant juices run out and much of the flavor is lost. It is best boiled first, then peeled, and is excellent mashed to a purée with cream and butter. A sauce made from this purée may be used as a substitute for oyster sauce.

Seakale

Seakale is sometimes known as sea kail or sea cole, and is a native of sea coasts of Western Europe. It is cultivated for its leaf-stalks which are bleached and forced for cold weather, but seakale which is not forced and is cut in the warmer months is better in flavor. The crisp leaves may be cooked until tender and served with butter, seasoning and a little crisp bacon.

The green tops of unforced seakale may also be used as a salad if well washed and dried, torn in small pieces and served with French dressing and a good sprinkling of herbs. When seakale is cooked, it quickly becomes hard if overcooked. It is best steamed until tender and can then be dressed with melted butter or white sauce. Seakale may also be simmered gently in vegetable stock until tender, and it is very good if drained, covered with cheese sauce and baked in a hot oven until golden brown.

Seakale-Beet

see Chard

Shallot

This member of the onion family has small dark bulbs joined in a cluster while growing. The flavor is mild, and the shallot is essential to classic French cooking, particularly for flavoring sauces. Shallots are seldom used as a vegetable, but are often pickled in place of small onions. They are also excellent braised in stock and served in a brown or white sauce.

Sauce Béarnaise (for Beef or Lamb)

1 tablespoon/ 15 g chopped shallot
½ teaspoon/ 2.5 g tarragon
5–6 tablespoons/ 75 ml wine vinegar
3 egg yolks
1⅛ cups/ 9 oz/ 250 g butter
Salt and pepper
Pinch of chervil

The shallot should be chopped very finely. Put it into a saucepan with the tarragon and vinegar and simmer until all the liquid has evaporated. Take from the heat and stir in 3–4 tablespoons/ 45 ml cold water. Add the egg yolks and beat well. Put over a very low heat and stir until the yolks thicken. Melt the butter in a separate saucepan and add to the egg mixture drop by drop at first, then a little more at a time. Do not use the liquid at the bottom of the melted butter as this will spoil the consistency of the sauce. Stir while the butter is added and finally season with salt and pepper and a pinch of chervil. Serve warm and not hot.

Sauce Bordelaise (for Steak)

1 tablespoon/ 15 g chopped shallot
½ cup/ 4 fl oz/ 100 ml dry red wine
1 teaspoon/ 5 g crushed peppercorns
1 sprig of thyme
⅜ cup/ 3 fl oz/ 75 ml beef stock
1 tablespoon/ 15 ml melted butter
2 teaspoons/ 5 g flour
Salt

The shallot should be chopped very finely. Add the wine, peppercorns and thyme and cook until the liquid is reduced by two-thirds to one-third. Add the beef stock and the butter and flour mixed together and cook until thick. Season with salt and put the sauce through a fine sieve. A little more butter may be added just before serving if the sauce tastes acid. Sometimes, a little lemon juice and cubed cooked bone marrow is added.

Shantung Cabbage

see Cabbage, Chinese

Silver Beet

see Chard

Snow Peas

see Peas, Edible Pod

The onions pictured here have been called spring onions, green onions, salad onions and scallions depending upon their country (or province within a country) of origin. They are quite easy to grow in a home garden and if planted between rows of other vegetables such as carrots, help to deter dreaded pests from attacking other vegetables.

Sorrel

There are a number of varieties of sorrel, but all have the same acid flavor which some people enjoy but which others hate. French sorrel is the mildest and the best to use in the kitchen, but wood and mountain sorrels may be used although they have a sharp flavor. The Indian sorrel, also known as masha or sour-sour is used in the East to flavor soups, stews, salads and curry, and for making a refreshing drink.

French sorrel may be eaten raw when young and small, and can be included in salad. Sorrel is also used in spinach recipes.

Sorrel Purée

2 lb/ 1 kg sorrel
¼ cup/ 2 oz/ 50 g butter
4 tablespoons/ 1 oz/ 25 g flour
2⅔ cups/ 1 pint/ 500 ml beef stock
Salt and pepper
Pinch of sugar
2 egg yolks
3–4 tablespoons/ 45 ml cream

Remove the stalks from the sorrel and wash the leaves several times in several bowls of clean water. Put it into a pan with the water clinging to the leaves, cover and simmer on low heat until tender and much reduced in volume. In another pan, melt half the butter and work in the flour. Add the stock, plenty of seasoning and sugar and simmer, stirring well, for 5 minutes. Add the sorrel, cover and leave to simmer for 30 minutes. Put through a sieve or liquidize in an electric blender. Reheat, and just before serving stir in the egg yolks beaten with the cream. Do not boil once the egg mixture has been added. Stir in the remaining butter and serve hot with fish or poultry, or top with poached eggs.

Sorrel Soup

2 lb/ 1 kg sorrel
2 tablespoons/ 1 oz/ 25 g butter
4 cups/ 1½ pints/ 750 ml milk
Salt and pepper
2 egg yolks
2–3 tablespoons/ 30 ml cream
Fried bread cubes

Remove the stalks from the sorrel and wash the leaves several times in several bowls of clean water. Put into a pan with the water clinging to the leaves and add the butter. Cover and cook over low heat for 10 minutes. Stir in the milk gradually and season well. Bring to the boil. Mix the egg yolks and cream. Take the soup off the heat, stir in the egg mixture and serve at once with a garnish of fried bread cubes.

Spanish Pepper

see Peppers

Spinach

A native of Asia, spinach was introduced to Europe in the sixteenth century and is one of the vegetables which is either loved or deeply hated. Few children enjoy the strong flavor but were encouraged to eat it by the example of Popeye, whose strength derived from eating large quantities of the vegetable.

Spinach needs to be cleaned very thoroughly and should be rinsed in three or four bowls of fresh water. The spinach may be cooked with leaf ribs intact but the thick stalks should be discarded. If a purée is to be the ingredient of a recipe, it is easier to remove the leaves from the leaf ribs before cooking. An old way of cooking spinach was in vast quantities of water, but this produces dreadful results and ruins both flavor and texture. Spinach is best shaken after washing to get rid of surplus water, and should then be cooked only in the water which remains on the leaves with a knob of butter or bacon fat in a closed pan until just tender with the moisture almost evaporated. Always allow plenty of spinach for a dish, as it shrinks a great deal in cooking. Spinach goes particularly well with bacon and with cheese and these two ingredients will enhance spinach dishes.

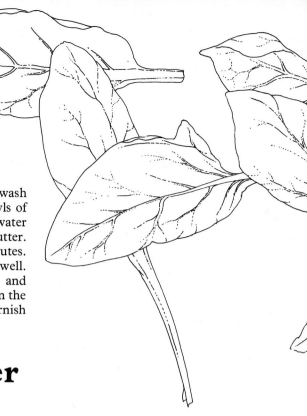

Spinach is somewhat difficult to grow but the taste of fresh spinach from the garden is worth some extra effort. Summer varieties do not like hot, dry weather and the winter types tend not to grow in cold, wet weather. Rich soil will help all types. When harvesting, remember not to strip the plant completely as this will certainly cause it to die.

Spinach Soup

2 lb/ 1 kg spinach
1 medium onion
1 small green pepper
¼ cup/ 2 oz/ 50 g butter
1 teaspoon/ 5 g sugar
Salt and pepper
1 teaspoon/ 5 g tarragon
½ cup/ 4 fl oz/ 100 ml cream
Milk
Crisp bacon

Strip the spinach stems from the leaves. Wash the leaves very well and drain. Chop the onion and pepper finely and soften in the butter for 5 minutes. Stir in the spinach, sugar, salt and pepper and tarragon. Cover tightly and cook until the spinach is tender. Put through a sieve, or purée in a blender. Add cream and enough milk to thin to the consistency of cream. Reheat gently and sprinkle with small pieces of crisp bacon.

Creamed Spinach

2 lb/ 1 kg spinach
2 tablespoons/ 1 oz/ 25 g butter
2 tablespoons/ ½ oz/ 15 g cornstarch
4 tablespoons/ 60 ml creamy milk
1 teaspoon/ 5 ml lemon juice

Cook the spinach with a little salt, then drain and chop finely. Make a thick sauce with the butter, milk, lemon juice and cornstarch. Stir in the spinach and simmer for 5 minutes.

Spinach Soufflé

½ cup/ 4 oz/ 100 g cooked spinach purée
¼ cup/ 2 oz/ 50 g butter
4 eggs and 1 egg white
⅔ cup/ ¼ pint/ 125 ml cream
½ cup/ 4 oz/ 100 g grated Cheddar cheese
Salt and pepper

Preheat the oven to 190°C/375°F/Gas Mark 5. Put the spinach into a pan with the butter and heat through. Mix well and put into a bowl. Separate the eggs and beat the yolks and cream together. Stir into the spinach with the cheese and season well. Beat the egg whites to stiff peaks and fold into the spinach mixture. Spoon into a greased 5 cups/ 2 pints/ 1 liter soufflé dish. Bake for 35 minutes and serve at once.

Italian Spinach Balls

2 lb/ 1 kg spinach
¼ cup/ 2 oz/ 50 g butter
1 small onion
¼ cup/ 2 oz/ 50 g grated Parmesan cheese
2 eggs
2 cups/ 6 oz/ 150 g dry breadcrumbs
Fat for frying

Wash the spinach very thoroughly and remove the stems. Chop the leaves and cook with half the butter until tender. Drain off the liquid and press the spinach until almost dry. Melt the remaining butter and add to the spinach with the finely chopped onion, cheese, eggs and half the breadcrumbs. Leave to stand for 15 minutes, then form into balls about the size of a walnut. Roll the spinach balls in the remaining breadcrumbs and deep-fry a few at a time until crisp and brown. Serve hot, sprinkled with a little more grated Parmesan cheese, or with a meaty pasta sauce.

Baked Spinach with Eggs*

1 lb/ 500 g spinach
2–3 tablespoons/ 30 ml olive oil
1 medium onion
8 eggs
Salt and pepper
Pinch of chopped basil
1 tablespoon/ 15 g chopped parsley
¼ cup/ 2 oz/ 50 g grated Parmesan cheese
2 large tomatoes
8 black olives

Use a shallow heavy pan which can be used on top of the stove and in the oven. Preheat the oven to 180°C/350°F/Gas Mark 4. Wash the spinach very well, remove the stalks and chop the leaves roughly. Heat the oil in the pan and fry the thinly sliced onions until soft and golden, stirring them often. In a large bowl, beat the eggs with a wire beater and add the salt, pepper, basil, parsley, cheese and spinach. Put into the pan with the onion slices and cook over low heat, lifting from the bottom with a wide spatula as the eggs run through the mixture and set, which will take about 3 minutes. Slice the tomatoes thinly and arrange on top with the

stoned and sliced olives. Put into the oven and cook for 8 minutes until lightly browned. Serve very hot. Any leftovers may be eaten chilled with plenty of crusty bread.

Spinach Quiche

3 cups/ 12 oz/ 300 g basic pastry (see page 12)
2 lb/ 1 kg spinach
¼ cup/ 2 oz/ 50 g butter
2 eggs
2–3 tablespoons/ 30 ml whipping cream
1 cup/ 8 oz/ 225 g cream cheese
¼ cup/ 2 oz/ 50 g grated Parmesan cheese
¼ teaspoon/ 1.25 g ground nutmeg
Salt and pepper

Roll out the pastry to line a 10-in (25 cm) pie plate. Prick with a fork, line with foil and dried beads and bake at 220°C/425°F/Gas Mark 7 for 10 minutes. Remove the beads and foil and leave to cool. Wash the spinach very thoroughly and drain well. Put into a saucepan with the butter, but no water, and cover. Cook for 10 minutes until the spinach is tender. Take off the lid and cook gently until all excess moisture has evaporated. Put into a bowl and chop roughly. Mix together the eggs, cream, cream cheese, Parmesan cheese, nutmeg, salt and pepper. Stir this into the spinach and put into the pastry shell. Bake at 220°C/425°F/Gas Mark 7 for 30 minutes until set and golden. Serve hot or cold.

Syrian Spinach Salad

1 lb/ 500 g spinach
1 teaspoon/ 5 g salt
6 scallions
1 tablespoon/ 15 ml lemon juice
1 tablespoon/ 15 ml olive oil
¼ cup/ 2 oz/ 50 g salted walnuts

Wash the spinach very thoroughly and remove the stems. Shake the leaves dry and pat them in paper towel to remove surplus moisture. Tear leaves into large pieces and put into a shallow dish with the salt. Stir in the salt very thoroughly and leave the spinach to stand for 15 minutes. Drain and squeeze dry. Put into a serving bowl with the finely sliced scallions, lemon juice and oil. Toss lightly and sprinkle with chopped nuts.

Baked
Spinach with Eggs

see page 137

spinach
olive oil
onion
eggs
salt and pepper
basil
parsley
Parmesan cheese
tomatoes
black olives

Spinach and Bacon Salad

2 lb/ 1 kg spinach
8 slices of bacon
1⅓ cups/ 4 oz/ 100 g small bread cubes
1 garlic clove
2–3 tablespoons/ 30 ml lemon juice
Salt and pepper
¼ teaspoon/ 1.25 g French mustard
5–6 tablespoons/ 75 ml peanut oil

Wash the spinach very thoroughly, take off the stalks, and pat the leaves dry in paper towels. Chop the bacon and cook in its own fat until crisp. Drain thoroughly. Cook the bread cubes and crushed garlic in the remaining bacon fat until the bread is crisp and golden. Drain thoroughly. Mix a dressing with the lemon juice, salt, pepper, mustard and oil. Just before serving, tear the spinach leaves into small pieces and toss in the dressing with the bacon and bread cubes, and serve at once.

Spinach Beet

A type of beet grown for its leaves and midribs and not for the roots. Spinach beet may be used in spinach or chard recipes.

Spring Cabbage

see Cabbage

Sprouts

see Brussels Sprouts

Sprouts, Bean

see Bean Sprouts

Squash (see also Marrow)

There are many varieties of squash which belong to the same family as the marrow, pumpkin and zucchini, so that recipes are interchangeable. While it is difficult to categorize squash exactly as there are so many variations and regional names, the smaller summer squashes include crooknecks, pattypan, butternut and scallop. The harder-skinned larger winter squashes include banana, acorn, Hubbard, turban, mammoth, Cushaw, Canada crookneck and winter crookneck. A favorite way of cooking squash is to bake the halves until tender and serve with butter and honey or brown sugar but the squash also lends itself to savory stuffings, or may be used as purée for soup or pie fillings.

Squash Soup

3 cups/ 1 lb/ 500 g Hubbard squash
¼ teaspoon/ 1.25 g ground ginger
2 tablespoons/ 1 oz/ 25 g brown sugar
4⅓ cups/ 1¼ pints/ 675 ml chicken stock
Salt and pepper
⅔ cup/ ¼ pint/ 125 ml cream
2–3 tablespoons/ 30 ml sherry

Cut the squash into cubes and steam it over boiling water. Mash the squash with the ginger, sugar, stock and seasoning. For a smoother soup, use a blender. Reheat and just before serving stir in the cream and sherry.

Strawberry Spinach

see Good King Henry

String Beans

see Beans, Runner

Succory

see Chicory, English

Sugar Peas

see Peas, Edible-Pod

Summer Cabbage

see Cabbage

Swede

see Turnip, Yellow

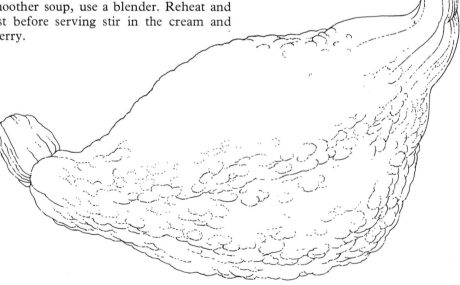

Above : Hubbard squash

Sweetcorn

see Corn

Sweet Pepper

see Peppers

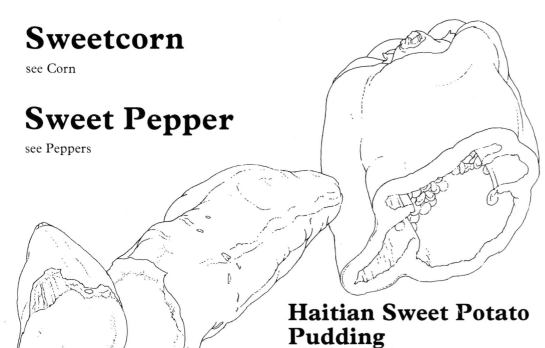

Above : The sweet potato (left) and the sweet pepper. The former has always been popular in the United States and is only beginning to gain fame in the United Kingdom. The latter is popular around the world.

Sweet Potato

The sweet potato or batata is often confused with the yam which it resembles, but which is of a different plant family. The sweet potato comes in two main types, one yellowish in color, with mealy flesh which becomes rather dry when cooked; the other orange or reddish-orange in color with moister, softer, sweeter flesh. The vegetable is best cooked without peeling for high nutritive value, and small sweet potatoes will have a less fibrous texture. They may be simply baked or boiled and are good with pork, ham and poultry. Their sweetness is very distinctive and in tropical countries they may be sliced or mashed and served with milk, sugar and spice or grated coconut. In Brazil the sweet potato is made into a spiced sweet pudding, and in Thailand and the East Indies it is sometimes preserved in syrup as a sweetmeat.

Haitian Sweet Potato Pudding

1½ cups/ 12 oz/ 350 g cooked sweet
  potatoes
2 small bananas
1 cup/ 8 fl oz/ 200 ml milk
2 tablespoons/ 1 oz/ 25 g sugar
Pinch of salt
Pinch of ground nutmeg
Pinch of ground cinnamon
2 egg yolks
⅓ cup/ 2 oz/ 50 g seedless raisins

Mash the potatoes and bananas and gradually work in the milk. Add the sugar, salt, spices and egg yolks and beat well until smooth. Chop the raisins and stir into the mixture. Put into a greased casserole and bake at 150°C/300°F/Gas Mark 2 for 1 hour until set, firm and golden. Serve hot or cold in thin slices.

Brazilian Sweet Potato Soup

1 lb/ 500 g sweet potatoes
⅜ cup/ 3 oz/ 75 g butter
1 medium onion
2–3 tablespoons/ 30 g chopped parsley
Salt and pepper
3 cups/ 1½ pints/ 750 ml water
½ teaspoon/ 2.5 g grated orange rind
Pinch of ground mace
2 tablespoons/ ½ oz/ 15 g cornstarch
2½ cups/ 1¼ pints/ 675 ml milk
⅓ cup/ 2 oz/ 50 g salted peanuts

Peel the sweet potatoes and cut them in cubes. Melt half the butter and stir in the sweet potatoes and thinly sliced onion. Stir until coated with the butter and then add the parsley, plenty of seasoning and the water. Cover and bring to the boil, and then simmer until the vegetables are soft. Mash the vegetables in the liquid but do not make a purée. Add the orange rind and mace. Blend the cornstarch with a little milk, and stir into the soup with the remaining milk. Heat through and add coarsely chopped peanuts and the remaining butter. Serve very hot.

Louisiana Sweet Potatoes

4 medium sweet potatoes
4 eating apples
1 tablespoon/ ½ oz/ 15 g sugar
3–4 tablespoons/ 45 ml water
3–4 tablespoons/ 45 ml milk
¼ cup/ 2 oz/ 50 g butter
⅓ cup/ 2 oz/ 50 g dark soft brown sugar
Pinch of salt
Pinch of ground cinnamon
¼ cup/ 1 oz/ 25 g seedless raisins
¼ cup/ 1 oz/ 25 g pecan nuts

Peel and cook the sweet potatoes. Do not peel the apples but take out the cores and cut the apples across in three slices. Reserve the top slices. Put the other slices in an ovenware dish, sprinkle with sugar and pour in the water. Bake at 190°C/375°F/Gas Mark 5 for 15 minutes. Mash the sweet potatoes with the milk, butter, brown sugar, salt and cinnamon. Peel and chop the reserved apple slices and stir the apple pieces into the sweet potato mixture with the raisins and chopped pecans. Put a large spoonful of the mixture on the apple slices and continue baking for 15 minutes. Serve hot with chicken.

Swiss Chard

see Chard

Terong

see Eggplant

Sweet potatoes (or batata) were the first potatoes to be brought to Europe from South America by Spanish explorers in the sixteenth century. Sweet potatoes should not be mistaken for yams.

Tomato

The tomato, one of our most useful vegetables (or fruit) is a comparative newcomer to the world's kitchen. As a member of the Deadly Nightshade family, it was considered dangerous when introduced to Italy from Peru in the sixteenth century. The tomato came via Morocco and was originally known as *Pomi de' Mori*, or apples of the Moors. This was translated by the French *Pommes d'Amour* and thus 'love apple' or 'golden apple' was a common name until the twentieth century.

The tomato is delicious eaten on its own, but lends its flavor to hundreds of different dishes since it blends so well with many other vegetables and herbs. Its texture makes it particularly suitable for sauce-making, while the rich color lends an appetizing look to any dish in which it is included. The best-flavored tomatoes are the large ugly ones favored in Europe, but today's commercial tomato has to be uniform in size, shape and color and is sadly dull in flavor. While we associate tomatoes with savory dishes, many early recipes were for sweetmeats, and many people still like to add a pinch of sugar to tomatoes to counter the slight acidity of the fruit.

Raw tomatoes make delicious salads and sandwiches, while plainly cooked ones make good edible garnishes to meat and fish. Tomatoes may be grilled or fried, or baked with or without a stuffing. When tomatoes are incorporated in recipes, it is usually best to peel them. This may be done by turning the tomato over a low flame until the skin wrinkles, splits and slips off *or* by dipping the tomato into boiling water to loosen the skin. The pips are not pleasing in dishes and may be removed before cooking.

Tomato Soup

1 lb/ 500 g tomatoes
$2\frac{2}{3}$ cups/ 1 pint/ 500 ml stock
1 small onion
1 bay leaf
Sprig of parsley
Sprig of thyme
3 tablespoons/ $1\frac{1}{2}$ oz/ 40 g butter
5 tablespoons/ $1\frac{1}{2}$ oz/ 40 g flour
$\frac{2}{3}$ cup/ $\frac{1}{4}$ pint/ 125 ml milk
1 teaspoon/ 5 g sugar
Salt and pepper

Chop the tomatoes without peeling them. Put them into a pan with the stock, chopped onion, bay leaf, parsley and thyme. Simmer for 1 hour and put through a fine strainer. Melt the butter and work in the flour. Add the tomato purée and stir over a gentle heat until the mixture comes to the boil. Stir in the milk, sugar, salt and pepper. Reheat gently. Serve hot with fried or toasted bread cubes. Tomato soup is also delicious served with a garnish of whipped cream and finely chopped parsley.

Iced Tomato Soup

8 tomatoes
4 small white onions
4 garlic cloves
Strip of lemon rind
4–5 tablespoons/ 60 ml water
6–7 tablespoons/ 90 ml concentrated tomato purée
$\frac{1}{2}$ cup/ 2 oz/ 50 g flour
$2\frac{2}{3}$ cup/ 1 pint/ 500 ml chicken stock
1 teaspoon/ 5 ml Tabasco sauce
1 teaspoon/ 5 g sugar
Salt and pepper
2–3 tablespoons/ 30 ml sherry
1 teaspoon/ 5 ml lemon juice
$\frac{2}{3}$ cup/ $\frac{1}{4}$ pint/ 125 ml cream
Thin cucumber slices

Combine thinly sliced tomatoes and onions, chopped garlic, lemon rind and water and simmer gently for 10–15 minutes. Add tomato paste and cook a further three minutes. Stir in flour made into a paste in some of the measured stock. Add remaining stock, Tabasco sauce, sugar, salt and pepper. Bring soup to the boil stirring constantly. Sieve the soup through a fine strainer and add sherry and lemon juice. Chill for 2 hours. Stir in cream and serve garnished with thin cucumber slices.

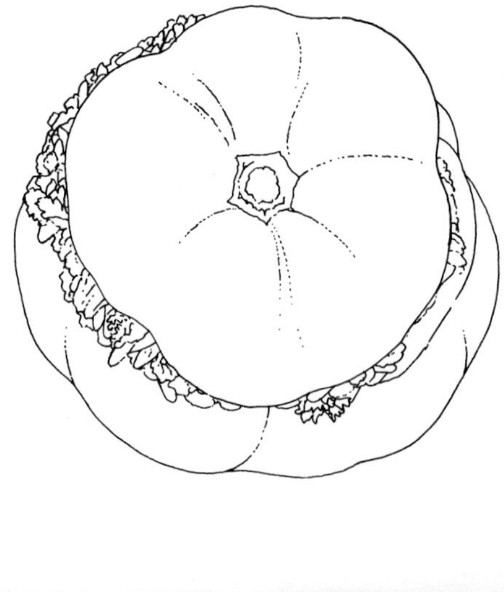

Basic Tomato Sauce

2 tablespoons/ 1 oz/ 25 g butter
1 tablespoon/ 25 g oil
$1\frac{1}{2}$ cups/ 8 oz/ 225 g onion
1 celery stick
1 medium carrot
2 slices of bacon
2 garlic cloves
3 lb/ 1.5 kg very ripe tomatoes
2 tablespoons/ 1 oz/ 25 g sugar
2 teaspoons/ 10 ml wine vinegar
$\frac{2}{3}$ cup/ $\frac{1}{4}$ pint/ 125 ml red wine
1 teaspoon/ 5 g salt
Pepper
$\frac{1}{2}$ teaspoon/ 2.5 g basil or marjoram
1 teaspoon/ 5 g parsley

Heat the butter and oil together. Chop the onion, celery, carrot, bacon and garlic and fry until golden, stirring well until the fat has been absorbed. Peel the tomatoes and remove the seeds. Chop roughly and add to the pan with all the other ingredients. Simmer for 30 minutes, stirring occasionally. This sauce may be kept in the refrigerator up to 48 hours, or can be frozen, and is a useful standby to use as a sauce, or as a base for a variety of dishes. The sauce may be used as it is, or put through a sieve, or liquidized in an electric blender.

Italian Stuffed Tomatoes*

6 large tomatoes
1 tablespoon/ 15 ml oil
1 small onion
$1\frac{1}{3}$ cups/ 4 oz/ 100 g fresh breadcrumbs
$1\frac{1}{4}$ cups/ 8 oz/ 225 g canned tuna fish
$\frac{1}{4}$ cup/ 2 oz/ 50 g anchovy fillets
2–3 tablespoons/ 30 g chopped parsley
4 stuffed olives
Salt and pepper

Cut the tomatoes in half and scoop out their centers, keeping the pulp. Heat the oil and cook the finely chopped onion over low heat until soft but not colored. Take off the heat and add the tomato pulp, breadcrumbs, flaked tuna fish and chopped anchovies. Add the parsley and finely chopped olives and season to taste. Pile into tomato halves and put on a greased baking (cookie) sheet. Bake at 190°C/375°F/Gas Mark 5 for 10 minutes. Serve hot or cold.

Left: Stuffed tomato.

Tomatoes are perhaps the most popular and useful of vegetables available in today's market. They can be eaten raw or cooked, singly or as an accompaniment. Tomatoes can be grown by anyone who has access to sunshine and will thrive either outdoors or indoors.

Tomato Soufflé

2 tablespoons/ 1 oz/ 25 g butter
⅜ cup/ 1½ oz/ 40 g flour
½ teaspoon/ 2.5 g mustard powder
¾ cup/ 7 fl oz/ 175 ml milk
1½ tablespoons/ 23 ml concentrated
    tomato purée
Salt and pepper
4 eggs
5 tablespoons/ 1½ oz/ 40 g grated
    Parmesan cheese
6 tomatoes

Preheat oven to 200°C/400°F/Gas Mark 6.
Grease a 4-cup/ 1½ pint/ 750 ml soufflé dish.
Melt the butter, stir in the flour and mustard
and cook for 1 minute. Gradually stir in the
milk and bring to the boil, stirring well to
give a smooth sauce. Simmer for 3 minutes.
Take off the heat and beat in the tomato
purée, salt, pepper, egg yolks and half the
cheese. Beat the egg whites to stiff peaks and
fold into the tomato mixture. Skin the
tomatoes, remove the seeds, and chop the
flesh neatly. Fold the tomato pieces into the
soufflé mixture. Sprinkle with remaining
cheese. Put the dish into a roasting pan with
enough water to come half way up the sides
of the dish. Cook in a hot oven for 30
minutes. Serve at once.

Tomato Water-Ice

1 lb/ 500 g ripe tomatoes
2⅔ cup/ 1 pint/ 500 ml water
Juice of 1 lemon
3 apples
¾ cup/ 6 oz/ 150 g sugar
2 tablespoons/ 30 ml apricot jam
1 teaspoon/ 5 g ground ginger
⅜ cup/ 3 fl oz/ 75 ml rum
⅜ cup/ 3 fl oz/ 75 ml Curaçao
¼ cup/ 2 oz/ 50 g preserved ginger

Slice the tomatoes and cook them with the
water, lemon juice, sliced apples, sugar, jam
and ground ginger. Simmer until the
tomatoes are soft. Put through a sieve and
cool. Stir in the rum, Curaçao and finely
chopped preserved ginger. Put into a
freezing tray and freeze in the ice-making
compartment of the refrigerator until solid.
Scoop out into tall glasses to serve. A little
red food coloring may be added if the
tomato purée is pale.

*Tomatoes are easy to
grow provided they
have rich soil, sun and
lots of water. They
prefer a south-facing
wall if possible and
should be well
protected from wind
and well supported as
the stems break easily
with the weight of the
ripening vegetable.
The redness comes not
from the sun's light
but from its warmth.
Thus tomatoes will
turn red even if locked
in a dark but warm
drawer.*

Provençal Tomatoes

6 large tomatoes
4–5 tablespoons/ 60 ml olive oil
Salt and pepper
1 garlic clove
3 tablespoons/ 45 g chopped parsley
⅔ cup/ 2 oz/ 50 g fresh breadcrumbs

Cut the tomatoes in half. Heat the oil and cook the tomatoes, cut side down, for 5 minutes. Put into a baking dish and sprinkle with salt and pepper, finely chopped garlic, parsley and breadcrumbs. Sprinkle with the oil left in the frying pan. Bake at 190°C/ 375°F/Gas Mark 5 for 25 minutes and serve hot. These are delicious with roast or broiled meat, omelettes or plain boiled rice.

Anchovy and Tomato Salad

Peel tomatoes and slice them into a bowl. Arrange strips of anchovy on top and some chopped black olives. Pour French dressing over the mixture, made from three parts oil to one part vinegar, with a little crushed garlic, sea salt and freshly ground black pepper. Chill before serving.

Ratatouille

4 large tomatoes
2 medium eggplants
1 large green pepper
2 medium onions
2 zucchini
2–3 tablespoons/ 30 ml olive oil
2 tablespoons/ 1 oz/ 25 g butter
1 garlic clove
Chopped parsley

Dip the tomatoes in hot water to loosen the skins, and peel them. Cut the flesh into slices. Wipe the eggplants and slice them without peeling. Take the seeds out of the green pepper and cut the flesh in slices. Peel and slice the onions. Wipe the zucchini and peel them without slicing. Put the oil and butter in a heavy pan and heat together. Add all the vegetables, salt, pepper and crushed garlic clove. Stir well, cover tightly and simmer for 1 hour until the vegetables are tender and the oil has been absorbed. Sprinkle thickly with chopped parsley and serve hot or cold.

French Tomato Salad

For the best results, use large fully-flavored tomatoes which are firm, fleshy and ripe. Skin the tomatoes and slice them across evenly. Arrange in a bowl and top with some finely chopped shallots or onions, and some chopped parsley or basil. Cover with French dressing, made from three parts oil to one part vinegar, with plenty of sea salt and freshly ground black pepper. Chill before serving.

Housewife's Tomato Salad

The French housewife knows that ripe tomatoes and hard-boiled eggs are a perfect combination. Sometimes she serves a big bowl filled with alternate layers of sliced tomatoes, hard-boiled eggs and chopped chives. Each layer should be sprinkled with salt, pepper, oil and vinegar, and a pinch of sugar on the tomatoes. A more elegant first-course is made by slicing large tomatoes downwards to form a 'fan' and filling each gap between slices with a slice of egg. Each individual tomato is topped with a swirl of creamy mayonnaise and chopped herbs.

Celery and Tomato Salad

Peel tomatoes and slice them into a bowl. Chop some celery finely and sprinkle on top. Pour over French dressing, made from three parts oil to one part vinegar, with sea salt and freshly ground black pepper. Chill before serving.

Baked Tomatoes and Eggs

Large tomatoes
Eggs
Salt and pepper

Cut lids off tomatoes and scoop out the seeds. Break an egg into each one, season and bake at 180°C/350°F/Gas Mark 4 for 15 minutes. Add a little cream or grated cheese before baking if desired.

Green Tomato Chutney

2 lb/ 1 kg green tomatoes
2 lb/ 1 kg apples
⅔ cup/ 4 oz/ 100 g shallots
2 tablespoons/ 1 oz/ 25 g garlic
2 cups/ 1 lb/ 500 g soft brown sugar
1 tablespoon/ ½ oz/ 15 g salt
1½ teaspoons/ 8 g cayenne pepper
1⅓ cups/ 8 oz/ 225 g seedless raisins
Juice of 2 lemons
2⅔ cups/ 1 pint/ 500 ml vinegar

If shallots are not obtainable, small onions may be used. Do not peel the tomatoes, but chop them finely. Peel the apples and shallots and chop them finely. Peel and chop the garlic. Mix all the ingredients together and simmer gently for 2½ hours, stirring frequently. The chutney will be rich brown in color and the consistency of jam. Put into clean jars and cover tightly with vinegar-proof lids.

Red Tomato Chutney

4 lb/ 2 kg/ red tomatoes
2 cups/ 1 lb/ 500 g prepared squash
1⅓ cups/ 8 oz/ 225 g onions
1 tablespoon/ ½ oz/ 15 g salt
Pinch of cayenne pepper
¼ teaspoon/ 1.25 g ground cinnamon
¼ teaspoon/ 1.25 g ground cloves
¼ teaspoon/1.25 g ground allspice
¼ teaspoon/ 1.25 g ground mace
¼ teaspoon/ 1.25 g paprika
1½ cups/ 12 oz/ 350 g sugar
1⅓ cups/ ½ pint/ 250 ml vinegar

Wipe the tomatoes and cut them in small pieces. Peel the marrow and remove the seeds and pith before measuring. Cut the squash in small pieces and mix with the tomatoes and chopped onions. Put through the grinder and mince coarsely. Put into a saucepan with the salt and spices, and simmer for 1½ hours, stirring occasionally. Add the sugar and vinegar and stir well. Continue simmering until brown and thick. Put into sterilized jars and cover with vinegar-proof lids.

Italian
Stuffed Tomatoes

see page 144

tomatoes
oil
onion
breadcrumbs
tuna fish
anchovy fillets
parsley
stuffed olives
salt and pepper

Pickled Green Tomatoes

2 lb/ 1 kg green tomatoes
1⅓ cups/ 8 oz/ 225 g onions
Block cooking salt
1 cup/ 8 oz/ 225 g sugar
2⅔ cups/ 1 pint/ 500 ml white vinegar

Wipe the tomatoes and peel the onions. Cut them in thin slices and put into a bowl. Sprinkle generously with salt. Leave for 24 hours, stir well and drain off the salt and liquid completely. Stir the sugar and vinegar together and bring to the boil. Add the tomatoes and onions and simmer for 1 hour until tender. Pour into clean jars and cover at once with vinegar-proof lids.

Right : White turnips are popular in Europe and Britain although they are not unknown in the Far East or the USA.

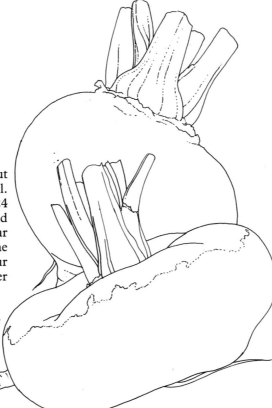

Green Tomato Jam (1)

3 lb/ 1.5 kg green tomatoes
4 cups/ 2 lb/ 1 kg sugar
1 lemon

Cut the tomatoes in very thin slices and put in layers in a bowl with the sugar. Leave for 24 hours. Put into a pan with the lemon cut in very small pieces. Simmer until the jam turns golden, pour into jars and cover. Use as a pie filling, topped with thick cream.

Green Tomato Jam (2)

2 lb/ 1 kg green tomatoes
Rind of 1 sweet orange
3 cups/ 1½ lb/ 750 g sugar

Shred the orange rind very finely and simmer in as little water as possible until tender. Cut up the tomatoes and simmer with the orange rind until tender. Stir in the sugar until dissolved, then boil hard to setting point. Pour into hot jars. Serve with toast or use as a pie filling.

Red Tomato Jam

6 lb/ 3 kg ripe tomatoes
¾ cup/ 6 fl oz/ 150 ml lemon juice
2 teaspoons/ 10 ml citric or tartaric
    acid
12 cups/ 6 lb/ 3 kg sugar

Skin the tomatoes. Cut them into pieces and put into a pan with the lemon juice and acid. Simmer to a pulp. Stir in the sugar until dissolved, then boil hard to setting point. Pour into hot jars.

Tomato Jelly

3 lb/ 1.5 kg ripe tomatoes
3 cups/ 1½ lb/ 750 g sugar
3 tablespoons/ 45 ml lemon juice
1 small cinnamon stick

Cut the tomatoes in pieces and simmer them very gently until soft. Strain through a jelly or cheesecloth bag. Heat the juice with the lemon juice and cinnamon stick and stir in the sugar until dissolved. Boil hard to setting point. Remove the cinnamon stick and pour into small hot jars. This can be eaten as a spread, with ham or poultry, or with cream cheese.

Tomato Sauce (for storage)

4 lb/ 2 kg red tomatoes
4 large onions
2 cups/ 1 lb/ 500 g brown sugar
2 tablespoons/ 1 oz/ 25 g salt
⅓ cup/ 2 oz/ 50 g black peppercorns
1 tablespoon/ ½ oz/ 15 g whole cloves
2 teaspoons/ 10 ml cayenne pepper
2⅔ cups/ 1 pint/ 500 ml vinegar

Wipe the tomatoes and slice them without peeling. Mix with the chopped onions and all the remaining ingredients in a thick saucepan. Simmer gently for 2 hours, stirring occasionally. Put through a fine sieve, leaving only the spices, seeds and skin in the sieve. Put the pulp into a clean saucepan and bring to the boil. Boil for 5 minutes. Pour into clean bottles and screw on lids, then release one half-turn. Stand the bottles in a pan on a thick pad of newspaper, and pour in hot water to cover the bottles. Bring to simmering point 65°C/150°F and keep this temperature for 30 minutes. Take out the bottles and screw the tops on tightly immediately.

Turban Squash

see Squash

Turnip, White

Turnip is the generic word used for a thick, fleshy, edible root. There are two distinct varieties. The white one is known as the *Brassica campestris rapa*, which is not to be confused with its cousin *Brassica campestris napaprassica*, which is yellow, larger and sweeter. The latter is known as rutabaga in the United States and swede in Britain.

Turnips need careful choosing and cooking to be appreciated. They should be small and young, when their refreshing flavor can be enjoyed in stews and with duck, pork, goose, ham and sausages in particular. Older turnips have a very strong flavor which can be improved by preliminary blanching in salted water before they are incorporated in a recipe. The turnip absorbs a great deal of liquid and should be very well drained if cooked in water – this absorbency is an advantage in dishes made with rich meats when the vegetable will take up the flavorsome juices. Butter is the best fat for dressing turnips, and cooking fat, bacon fat and margarine should be avoided when preparing them. Turnips make a pleasant vegetable if mashed to a purée with butter, plenty of seasoning and a little thick cream. In the East, the turnip is much appreciated as a stir-fried vegetable, or thinly sliced and eaten raw in a soy-flavored sauce.

Although the turnip is chiefly eaten for its root, the young green tops may be boiled and eaten, and can be used in the same way as kale.

White Turnip Soup

6 medium white turnips
Salt and pepper
2 tablespoons/ 1 oz/ 25 g butter
1 egg yolk
Pinch of chopped marjoram

Peel the turnips, cut them in pieces and cook in enough boiling salted water to cover. When they are tender, rub through a sieve with the cooking liquid, or liquidize in an electric blender. Reheat and season with salt and pepper. Stir in the butter and then add the egg yolk mixed with a little of the liquid. Serve at once with a sprinkling of marjoram.

Roast Duck with White Turnips

4½ lb/ 2 kg duck
2 tablespoons/ 30 ml honey
1 teaspoon/ 5 g thyme
10 small white turnips
10 button onions
2–3 tablespoons/ 25 g brown sugar
Salt and pepper
⅔ cup/ ¼ pint/ 125 ml red wine
⅔ cup/ ¼ pint/ 125 ml cream
2 tablespoons/ ½ oz/ 15 g cornstarch

Wipe the duck inside and out and brown it in a heavy pan in a little butter. Drain off any fat. Mix the honey and thyme and spread over the duck skin, and put the duck into a roasting tin. Peel the turnips and onions and brown them in some butter mixed with the brown sugar. Arrange around the duck and season with salt and pepper. Add the red wine, cover and cook at 170°C/325°F/Gas Mark 3 for 1½ hours. Put the duck and the vegetables on to a serving dish and keep them warm. Heat the pan juices to reduce them to 1 cup/ ½ pint/ 250 ml. Mix the cream and cornstarch, and stir gently into the pan juices. Simmer until creamy and serve separately.

Glazed White Turnips

6 medium white turnips
2 tablespoons/ 1 oz/ 25 g butter
2 tablespoons/ 1 oz/ 25 g soft brown sugar
Pinch of ground nutmeg

Peel the turnips and cut them into neat dice. Boil for 10 minutes in salted water and drain thoroughly. Melt the butter in an ovenware dish and stir in the turnips. Sprinkle with sugar and nutmeg and cover tightly. Cover and cook at 200°C/400°F/Gas Mark 6 for 30 minutes, stirring occasionally. Serve hot with beef dishes.

Stir-Fried White Turnips

1 lb/ 500 g small young white turnips
3 cups/ 1 lb/ 500 g small white onions
2 medium green peppers
½ cup/ 4 oz/ 100 g butter
Salt and pepper

Peel the turnips and onions. Remove seeds and membranes from the peppers. Cut all the vegetables into very thin strips. Melt the butter and stir-fry the vegetables until they are just tender but still slightly crisp. Season well and serve at once.

White Turnip Salad

8 small young white turnips
1 small onion
3–4 tablespoons/ 45 ml olive oil
1 tablespoon/ 15 ml white wine vinegar
Salt and pepper
1 tablespoon/ 15 g chopped parsley
1 teaspoon/ 5 g mixed fresh herbs

Peel the turnips and slice them very thinly. Put into a serving dish with the very finely chopped onion. Mix the oil and vinegar, season well and pour over the turnips. Sprinkle with parsley and chopped herbs.

Chinese White Turnip Salad*

1 lb/ 500 g small young white turnips
1 tablespoon/ 15 ml sesame oil
1 teaspoon/ 5 g sugar
Pinch of ground ginger
1 tablespoon/ 15 ml soy sauce
1 tablespoon/ 15 ml cider vinegar

Peel the turnips and cut into very small thin slices. Mix the oil, sugar, ginger, soy sauce and vinegar and pour over the turnips. Leave for 4 hours before serving.

White Turnip and Pork Pie

3 cups/ 1 lb/ 500 g white turnips
2 slices of bacon
4 cups/ 1½ lb/ 750 g lean pork
⅓ cup/ 2 oz/ 50 g onion
⅓ cup/ 2 oz/ 50 g celery
1 garlic clove
4 tablespoons/ 1 oz/ 25 g flour
1¼ cup/ ½ pint/ 250 ml beef stock
Salt
1 bay leaf
1 sprig of parsley
Pinch of mace
3 cups/ 12 oz/ 350 g pastry (see page 12)

Cut the turnips into small cubes. Cut the bacon into small pieces and brown them lightly in a large thick pan. Cut the pork in cubes and chop the onion and celery. Add these to the bacon together with the crushed garlic, and cook until the meat is lightly browned. Add stock, salt, crumbled bay leaf, chopped parsley and a pinch of mace. Cover and simmer for 30 minutes. Leave to cool for 10 minutes. Roll out the pastry and use half to line a pie plate. Put in the pork mixture and cover with the remaining pastry. Seal the edges and brush the pastry with a beaten egg or a little melted butter. Bake at 220°C/425°F/Gas Mark 7 for 15 minutes, then at 180°C/350°F/Gas Mark 4 for 25 minutes. Serve very hot.

Chinese
White Turnip Salad

see page 151

small white turnips
sesame oil
sugar
ground ginger
soy sauce
cider vinegar

Inset : White turnips

Turnip, Yellow

The yellow turnip, also known as rutabaga, swede (Swedish turnip), Russian turnip or turnip-rooted cabbage, may be cooked in the same way as white turnips. The yellow-orange flesh has a sweet flavor and goes particularly well with beef and poultry. They are most commonly served as a purée, mashed with plenty of butter and seasoning, and the purée can be lightened with mashed potatoes. The yellow turnip is one of the vegetables which tastes just as good if left-over and reheated.

Oven-Baked Yellow Turnips

4 cups/ 1½ lb/ 750 g yellow turnips
¼ cup/ 2 oz/ 50 g butter
1⅓ cup/ ½ pint/ 250 ml chicken stock
Salt and pepper
1 tablespoon/ ½ oz/ 15 g sugar

Peel the turnips and cut into matchstick-sized pieces. Heat butter, stock, salt, pepper and half the sugar until boiling, and pour over turnips. Cook for 10 minutes, then put into a casserole and sprinkle with sugar. Bake at 180°C/375°F/Gas Mark 5 for 45 minutes.

Yellow Turnip with Cheese

1 lb/ 500 g yellow turnips
½ lb/ 8 oz/ 225 g potatoes
2 cups/ ¾ pint/ 375 ml beef stock
Salt and pepper
2 teaspoons/ 10 g sugar
½ cup/ 4 oz/ 100 g grated cheese
1 tablespoon/ 15 g minced onion

Peel and cut the turnips and potatoes into pieces. Put into a pan with the stock, salt and sugar, and bring to boiling point. Boil for 3 minutes, then cover and boil for 12 minutes until the vegetables are tender. Mash them with the pepper, cheese and onion and beat until light and fluffy. Serve very hot with a garnish of chopped parsley with cold meat or ham.

Yellow Turnip in Cider Sauce

2 cups/ 12 oz/ 350 g carrots
2 cups/ 12 oz/ 350 g yellow turnips
2 tablespoons/ 1 oz/ 25 g butter
⅔ cup/ ¼ pint/ 125 ml creamy milk
2 tablespoons/ ½ oz/ 15 g cornstarch
5–6 tablespoons/ 75 ml cider
1 teaspoon/ 5 g sugar
Salt and pepper

Scrape and slice the carrots. Peel the turnip and cut into dice. Cook together in boiling salted water for 15 minutes until tender but unbroken. In a separate saucepan, melt the butter and add the milk. Blend the cornstarch with half the cider and then add to the milk together with the remaining cider. Bring to the boil, stirring well. Add the sugar, salt and pepper, and simmer for 3 minutes. Drain the vegetables well and mix with the sauce. Serve hot with bacon or ham.

Upland Cress

see Cress

Vegetable Oyster

see Salsify

Water Chestnut

The Chinese water chestnut is a roundish flat-based tuber of a type of rush. The tubers have a dull or glossy brown or black skin and firm white flesh. They are rarely found fresh in the West, but can be bought in cans, packed in water, and are an essential ingredient of many Eastern dishes. After draining and peeling, the water chestnuts should be either quartered, diced or cut in wafer-thin slices. They may be used raw in salads or added to clear soup towards the end of cooking, or quickly cooked by stir-frying in a variety of dishes so that they retain their crispness and nutty flavour.

Below: Waterchestnut (left) and watercress.

Polynesian Rumaki

1 small can water chestnuts
1 cup/ 8 oz/ 225 g chicken livers
8 slices of bacon
1⅓ cups/ ½ pint/ 225 ml milk

Drain the water chestnuts and cut them into halves. Rinse the chicken livers and cut each one in half. Cut each strip of bacon in half lengthwise. Take a piece of water chestnut and a piece of chicken liver and wrap them together in a piece of bacon. Secure with a cocktail stick or toothpick. Put the bacon rolls into a shallow pan and cover with the milk. Leave in the refrigerator for 3 hours. Drain well and cook under a hot grill until the bacon is crisp. Serve very hot. Pieces of fresh pineapple may be substituted for the chicken livers, and then the Rumaki should *not* be marinated in milk.

Watercress

Watercress is traditionally used as garnish for meat, poultry or fish, but this versatile vegetable has many other delicious uses. A colorful bunch of watercress makes healthy eating too, packed with Vitamin A which is essential for growth in children and invaluable for good eyesight and a clear complexion in adults. Watercress has riboflavin to keep skin supple, iron to combat anemia, Vitamin C, calcium, phosphorous and other essential ingredients, but only two calories to the tablespoon (15 g) so it makes a useful slimming aid.

Always use watercress that is fresh, and rinse the bunch thoroughly in cold water. Use an airtight plastic bag or container and put the bunch into a refrigerator. Eat it while it is still fresh, and use the stalks as well as the leaves. Watercress sandwiches seasoned with sea salt and made with brown bread are always popular.

Watercress and Orange Cocktail

2 bunches watercress
4 oranges
Salt and pepper
Celery salt

Pick the leaves from the watercress. Squeeze the juice from the oranges. Blend the juice and leaves together in an electric blender and season with salt, pepper and celery salt. Pour into glasses over ice cubes.

Watercress Omelette

2 bunches watercress
1 medium onion
⅔ cup/ 4 oz/ 100 g bean sprouts
⅓ cup/ 2 oz/ 50 g mushrooms
½ cup/ 4 oz/ 100 g butter
2 eggs
Salt and pepper

Chop the watercress, onion and mushrooms. Melt half the butter, and stir in the watercress, onion, mushrooms and bean sprouts, and season with salt and pepper. Cook for 3 minutes. Beat the eggs lightly and season with salt and pepper. Melt the remaining butter in an omelette pan and stir in the eggs. Cook and stir until just setting. Put on the vegetable mixture, fold over the omelette and serve at once.

Watercress Mayonnaise

2 bunches watercress
2 garlic cloves
1⅓ cups/ ½ pint/ 250 ml mayonnaise
2 teaspoons/ 10 ml lemon juice

Chop the watercress roughly and crush the garlic. Put into an electric blender with the mayonnaise and blend until creamy. Stir in lemon juice and check seasoning. Serve with salmon, avocado pears or salad.

Cream of Watercress Soup

2 bunches watercress
3 cups/ 1 lb/ 500 g potatoes
1 small onion
¼ cup/ 2 oz/ 50 g butter
4 cups/ 1½ pints/ 750 ml water
1⅓ cup/ ½ pint/ 250 ml cream
Salt and pepper

Chop the watercress, reserving a few leaves for garnish. Peel and cube the potatoes. Peel and slice the onion. Melt the butter in a thick saucepan and add the onion and chopped watercress. Season with salt and pepper, and cook with a lid on over low heat for 3 minutes. Add the potatoes, stir and cook with a lid on over very low heat for 15 minutes without browning. Pour on hot water, stir and bring to the boil, and then simmer for 20 minutes. Strain the soup or liquidize in an electric blender. Return to the saucepan, check the seasoning, and reheat. Just before serving, stir in the cream and reserved watercress leaves. Serve hot or cold. If desired, chicken stock may be used instead of water.

Watercress is normally considered to be an aquatic plant but it can be grown successfully without running water. If you have a dank, shady area in your garden, then you can grow watercress.

Inset : Yellow turnip, rutabaga or swede tends to be larger and sweeter than the white turnip, and it stores well.

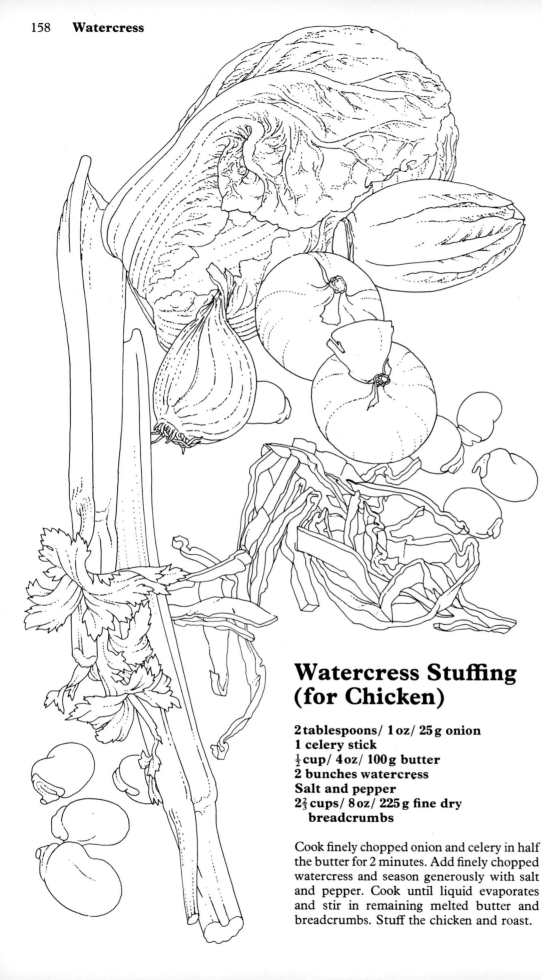

Welsh Onion
see Onions, Welsh

White Cabbage
see Cabbage

White Leaf-Beet
see Chard

Wild Mercury or Spinach
see Good King Henry

Windsor Beans
see Beans, Broad

Winged Peas
see Peas, Asparagus

Winter Cabbage
see Cabbage

Witloof
see Chicory, English

Wong Boksee Cabbage
see Cabbage, Chinese

Watercress Stuffing (for Chicken)

2 tablespoons/ 1 oz/ 25 g onion
1 celery stick
½ cup/ 4 oz/ 100 g butter
2 bunches watercress
Salt and pepper
2⅔ cups/ 8 oz/ 225 g fine dry
   breadcrumbs

Cook finely chopped onion and celery in half the butter for 2 minutes. Add finely chopped watercress and season generously with salt and pepper. Cook until liquid evaporates and stir in remaining melted butter and breadcrumbs. Stuff the chicken and roast.

Yam

Although commonly known as Indian potato, the yam should not be confused with the sweet potato. There are many varieties of yams, the oblong tubers ranging from a few inches in length and a weight of about 1 lb (500 g) right up to giant types which can weigh 100 lb (45 kg) and measure more than 8 ft (2.5 m) long. These giant or white yams are somewhat inferior in texture and flavor to the smaller types. The Oriental or Chinese yam, sometimes known as Chinese potato or Cinnamon Vine, is a medium-sized yam with gray or blackish skin, an inner purple skin, moist white flesh, and has a very good flavor. In India, the winged-stalked yam grows to an enormous size, and the dark purple or malacca yam with its dark purple stems and tubers is considered superior. The West African yellow yam is also grown in the West Indies and is also known as the prickly-stemmed yam or Guinea yam or afou, but this does not have the quality of the Chinese and Indian varieties.

Yams may be used for any potato recipe, and they are equally good boiled, steamed, roasted, baked or fried, but the smaller yams with a mealy texture and nutty flavor are worth special treatment.

Name Buñuelos

3 cups/ 1 lb/ 500 g small yams
¼ cup/ 2 oz/ 50 g butter
1 tablespoon/ 15 ml cream
½ cup/ 2 oz/ 50 g flour
1 egg
Pinch of salt
1 teaspoon/ 5 g sugar
Lard for frying
Icing sugar
Honey or guava jelly

Peel the yams, cut them into small pieces and boil in salted water with a lid on until tender. Drain well and push through a coarse sieve or break up with a fork. Mix in softened butter, cream, flour, egg, salt and sugar. Mix very well and leave to stand for 15 minutes. Fry tablespoonsful in hot lard until golden brown. Drain well and dust with icing sugar. Serve hot with honey or melted guava jelly.

Yam Chips

Small yams
Oil for frying
Sea salt

Peel the yams and slice them wafer-thin. Put into cold salted water and leave to soak for 2 hours. Drain well and dry with paper towels. Fry a few at a time in deep hot oil until golden, drain well and sprinkle with salt while hot.

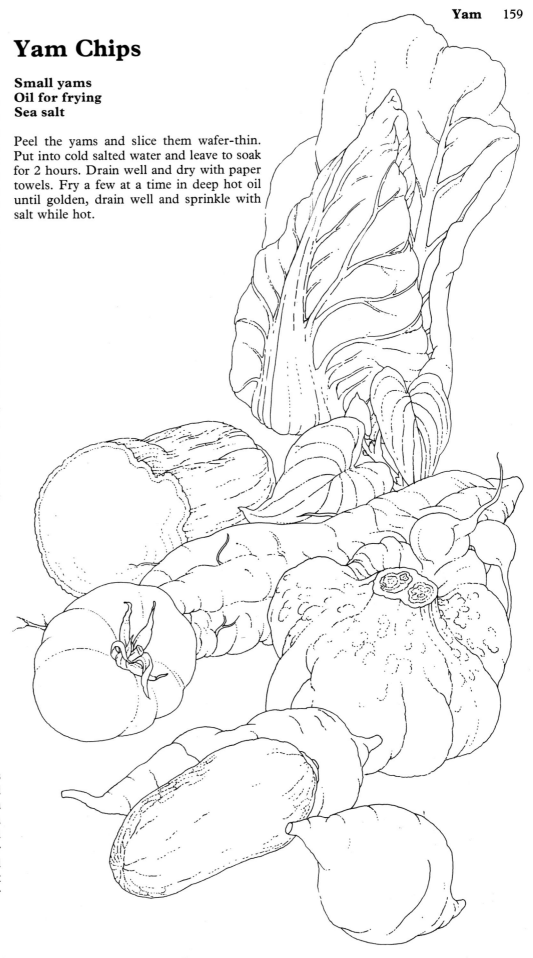

Zucchini is the Italian name for this type of marrow and this name has been adopted in the USA. The French name, courgette, is the name the British have chosen to use. Generally, all marrows are fairly easy to grow, unless the weather is very wet and cold, and if properly and regularly cropped they will be very prolific.

Zucchini (Courgette)

These small vegetables are miniature vegetable marrows or squashes, which should be used when young and slim and no more than 3–4 in (7.5–10 cm) long. They do not need peeling, but should only be wiped and the stems trimmed off, then cut in lengths or in rounds. Like all members of the squash family, they are best kept away from excessive water, and respond best to being partly cooked in oil before any liquid is introduced. Zucchini pairs well with tomatoes, eggplant (aubergines) and peppers to make tasty hot-weather dishes, and can take plenty of seasoning, herbs and strong cheese, as their natural flavour is somewhat bland.

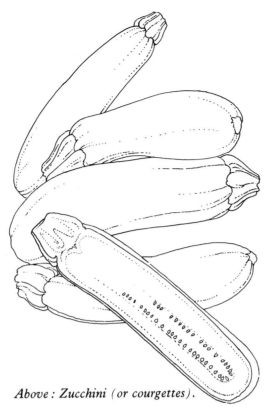

Above : Zucchini (or courgettes).

Braised Zucchini

1½ lb/ 750 g zucchini
4 tablespoons/ 60 ml water
¼ cup/ 4 oz/ 100 g butter
Salt and pepper
1 tablespoon/ 15 g chopped parsley
Squeeze of lemon juice

Use small zucchini for this recipe and wash them well. Trim off stems, but do not peel. Put into a heavy saucepan with the water, butter, salt and pepper. Cover and cook gently, shaking the pan occasionally, until the zucchini are tender. Put into a serving dish and sprinkle with parsley and lemon juice.

Zucchini and Cheese Bake

1½ lb/ 750 g zucchini
¼ cup/ 2 oz/ 50 g butter
1 tablespoon/ 15 g chopped basil
1 teaspoon/ 5 ml lemon juice
Salt and pepper
¾ cup/ 6 oz/ 150 g Mozzarella cheese
½ cup/ 2 oz/ 50 g dry breadcrumbs

Wipe the zucchini but do not peel them. Cut across in thick slices. Melt half the butter and cook the zucchini slices for about 10 minutes until just tender. Take off the heat and stir in the basil, lemon juice, salt and pepper. Arrange half the zucchini in a greased ovenware dish. Cut the cheese in thin slices and put half on top of the zucchini. Put in remaining zucchini, then cheese. Melt the remaining butter and fry the breadcrumbs until golden. Spread on the cheese and bake at 180°C/350°F/Gas Mark 4 for 35 minutes until crisp and golden. If Mozzarella cheese is not obtainable, any other soft cheese may be used.

Zucchini in Tomato Sauce

1½ lb/ 750 g zucchini
1 medium onion
2 garlic cloves
4 tablespoons/ 60 ml oil
Salt and pepper
1 lb/ 500 g tomatoes
2 teaspoons/ 10 g chopped marjoram

Wash the zucchini and trim off stems, but do not peel. Cut into 1-in (2.5 cm) lengths. Peel and slice the onion and chop the garlic. Put the zucchini, onion and garlic into a heavy saucepan with the oil, salt and pepper. Cover and simmer for 10 minutes, stirring occasionally. Take off the lid and raise the heat, and cook until the vegetables are golden. Peel the tomatoes and remove the seeds. Chop the flesh coarsely and add to the other vegetables. Simmer for 10 minutes and add more seasoning if necessary. Serve sprinkled with marjoram. This may be eaten hot or cold with meat or fish.

Sweet and Sour Zucchini

1 lb/ 500 g zucchini
¼ cup/ 2 oz/ 50 g butter
1 small onion
½ teaspoon/ 2.5 g paprika
2 teaspoons/ 5 g flour
3–4 tablespoons/ 45 ml cider vinegar
⅔ cup/ ¼ pint/ 125 ml water
¼ teaspoon/ 2.5 g dill seed
¼ teaspoon/ 2.5 g sugar
Pinch of salt

Use small zucchini and wash them well. Trim off stems but do not peel, and cut into strips about the size of French fries. Melt the butter and cook the finely chopped onion until soft and golden. Add the zucchini strips and paprika and stir over high heat for 2 minutes. Stir in the flour and then add the remaining ingredients. Cover and simmer until the zucchini strips are just tender but still slightly crisp.

Zucchini in Soured Cream

1 lb/ 500 g zucchini
2–3 tablespoons/ 30 ml olive oil
1 small onion
1 garlic clove
½ teaspoon/ 2.5 g salt
¼ teaspoon/ 1.25 g pepper
1⅓ cup/ ½ pint/ 250 ml soured cream
1 teaspoon/ 5 g chopped chives

Use small zucchini and wash them well. Trim off stems but do not peel, and cut into very thin crosswise slices. Heat the oil and cook the finely chopped onion and crushed garlic until soft and golden. Add the zucchini slices and stir over high heat until golden. Add salt and pepper, cover and cook on low heat for 5 minutes so that the zucchini slices retain their shape. Leave to cool. When at room temperature, stir in the soured cream. Chill and sprinkle with the chopped chives.

PULSES

Dried Beans, Lentils and Peas

Dried beans, lentils and peas are known as pulses and are a staple protein food for many people all over the world. In addition to protein, they contain calcium and vitamin B, and in many countries have been eaten instead of meat for centuries. There is an enormous variety of these pulses and it is worth keeping a few different ones in store. They should be kept dry, preferably in a tightly sealed moisture-proof storage jar or container. They are best kept in a cool place at a constant temperature, and will keep in good condition for a year.

Pulses
1 split peas, 2 black-eyed beans, 3 pearl beans, 4 lentils, 5 chick peas, 6 dried peas, 7 red kidney beans, 8 flageolets, 9 white haricot beans.

Dried Beans

Beans should be soaked in cold water before use. It is generally recommended that they should be soaked overnight, but some experts say that after 3–6 hours the beans may start to ferment and become slightly toxic. To speed up cooking, cover unsoaked beans with cold water, bring to the boil, then simmer for 5 minutes. Remove from the heat and leave to stand for an hour, then continue cooking. Since beans take a long time to cook, it may be necessary to add more seasoning, spices and herbs at the end of cooking time to boost the flavor. It is very important not to salt beans during cooking or they will become hard. They go particularly well with olive oil, pork fat or rich poultry fat and are a good accompaniment to fat meats and salt meats. All dried beans make a good vegetable dish with a simple dressing of butter, seasoning and herbs, while chilled beans make an excellent salad with French dressing.

Boriotti Beans may be brown or white and are tender, cooking to a floury, creamy consistency. They are the ones to use for Italian recipes, and so are Saluggia beans which are similar but smaller.

Soya Beans are very nutritious and are often used as a meat substitute. They may also be sprouted as Mung beans.

Butter Beans are large white beans with a floury texture, usually cooked and served with roast meat. They are rather insipid in flavor and are improved by being served with tomato sauce.

Brown Dutch Beans are a type of haricot bean, rich brown in color and full of flavor, and they may be used in place of white haricot beans.

Haricot Beans see Brown Dutch Beans, White Haricot Beans, Pearl Beans and Flageolets.

White Haricot Beans are useful all-purpose beans to use in soups and salads, and to serve as a vegetable with roasts. They are good creamed and flavored with a little garlic and rosemary.

Red Kidney Beans are bright and shiny and much used for soups and highly spiced dishes, and particularly favored in Spain and Mexico.

Black Beans are much favored in Caribbean cooking and combine well with hot spicy sauces. They are also used in China.

Lima Beans are white or very pale green and like a small butter bean. They are particularly used in American cookery and may be substituted for haricot beans.

Black-eyed Beans are small white beans with a distinctive black mark and a strong flavor. They go well with other strongly-flavored food such as garlic, spinach and ham.

Adzuki Beans are a great favorite in Chinese cookery. They are small, round and red with a sweetish flavor. They may also be sprouted like Mung beans.

Pearl (and Navy) Beans are haricots, good for long slow cooking in such dishes as Boston Baked Beans.

Broad Beans which are usually eaten fresh, are dried and can be bought ready-skinned for use in Greek dishes. They need long soaking and cooking, and make a good cold salad.

Egyptian Brown Beans are small, round and brown and are greatly enjoyed in the Middle East, particularly cooked and seasoned with oil, lemon juice, garlic and parsley as a salad.

Flageolets are small green haricot beans with a very delicate flavor. They go particularly well as a vegetable or as a purée with lamb, or can be mixed with other beans in salad.

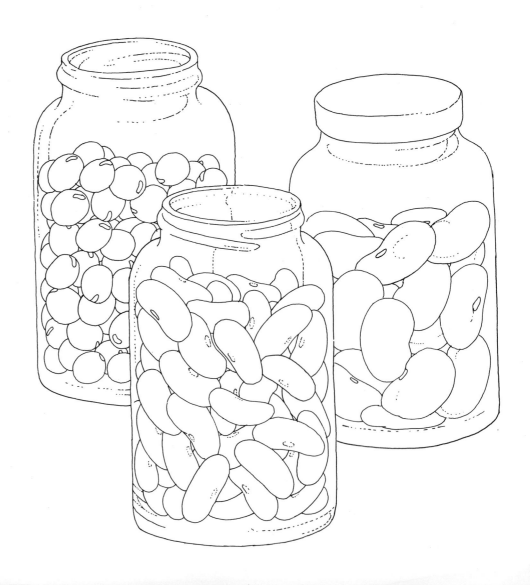

Navy Soup

¾ cup/ 6 oz/ 150 g dried haricot beans
2 carrots
1 celery stick
1 cup/ 8 oz/ 225 g concentrated tomato
  purée
1 medium onion
3 garlic cloves
2 tablespoons/ 30 g chopped parsley
4 tablespoons/ 60 ml oil
Salt and pepper
1 teaspoon/ 5 ml lemon juice
Toasted bread cubes

Soak the beans in cold water overnight. Drain well and cook in fresh water for 30 minutes. Chop the carrots and celery and add to the beans. Stir in the tomato purée and chopped onion, with crushed garlic, parsley and oil. Cover and simmer for 1½ hours, adding a little more water if necessary. Take off the heat and leave to stand for 30 minutes. Reheat to boiling point and add salt, pepper and lemon juice. Serve very hot with a garnish of toasted bread cubes.

Below, left to right : Egyptian brown beans, haricot beans, butter beans and flageolets. Dried beans keep for a long time if stored properly in air-tight containers such as the screw-top jars shown below.

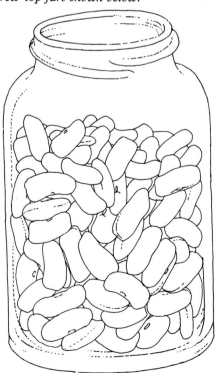

Creamed Haricot Beans

2 cups/ 1 lb/ 500 g dried haricot beans
½ cup/ 4 oz/ 100 g butter
1⅓ cup/ ¼ pint/ 125 ml cream
Salt and pepper
Pinch of ground nutmeg

Soak the beans overnight in cold water. Drain well, cover with fresh water and bring slowly to the boil. Boil for 1½ hours until tender and add a little salt at the end of cooking. Drain very thoroughly. Put the beans through a sieve or put them in an electric blender. Stir in flakes of butter and heat gently. Stir in the cream and seasoning and heat through. This is very good served with roast lamb.

Greek Bean Salad*

1 cup/ 8 oz/ 225 g dried haricot beans
⅔ cup/ ¼ pint/ 125 ml olive oil
1 medium onion
2 garlic cloves
1 bay leaf
Pinch of thyme
2 teaspoons/ 10 ml concentrated
  tomato purée
Salt and pepper
Juice of 1 lemon
2 tablespoons/ 30 g chopped parsley

Cover the beans with cold water and leave to soak overnight. Heat the oil in a thick pan and add the finely chopped onion. Cook until soft and golden. Add the beans, crushed garlic, bay leaf, thyme and tomato purée. Simmer gently for 10 minutes. Add enough boiling water to cover the beans and simmer for 2 hours until the beans are tender and the water has just been absorbed. Season with salt and pepper and stir in the lemon juice. Cool and stir in the parsley. If liked, add a few thin raw onion rings. For a complete meal, seal some small pieces of lean lamb in the oil with the onion, and cook them with the beans.

Hot Bean Salad

2 cups/ 1 lb/ 500 g dried haricot beans
3 medium onions
3–4 tablespoons/ 35 ml olive oil
6 anchovy fillets
Salt and pepper
Pinch of ground nutmeg
Juice of 1 lemon
1 tablespoon/ 15 g chopped parsley

Soak the beans overnight in cold water. Drain well, cover with fresh water and bring slowly to the boil. Boil for 1½ hours until tender and add a little salt at the end of cooking. Drain and reserve the liquid. Slice the onions and cook them in the oil until soft and golden. Add the chopped anchovies, salt, pepper, nutmeg and lemon juice and 6–8 tablespoons/ 90 ml cooking liquid. Simmer for 5 minutes and mix with the beans. Serve very hot sprinkled with parsley.

Boston Baked Beans

2 cups/ 1 lb/ 500 g dried haricot beans
2 teaspoons/ 10 g mustard powder
1 teaspoon/ 5 g salt
1 teaspoon/ 5 g black pepper
¼ cup/ 2 oz/ 50 g concentrated tomato
  purée
2 tablespoons/ 30 ml molasses
¼ cup/ 2 oz/ 50 g dark soft brown sugar
2 large onions
½ lb/ 8 oz/ 225 g salt belly pork
1 tablespoon/ 15 ml oil

Soak the beans overnight and then drain. Mix the mustard, salt and pepper and stir into the beans. Put the beans into a casserole, cover with water and stir in the tomato purée, molasses and sugar. Cut the onions in quarters and add to the casserole. Cover and cook at 140°C/275°F/Gas Mark 1 for 8 hours, adding a little water if necessary so the beans do not become dry. Meanwhile, soak the pork in cold water. When the beans have been cooking for 6 hours, drain the meat and cut it into cubes. Brown quickly on all sides in the oil and stir into the casserole to cook for the remaining 2 hours.

Greek Bean Salad

see page 165

dried haricot beans
olive oil
onion
garlic cloves
bay leaf
thyme
tomato purée
salt and pepper
lemon
parsley

Kidney Bean Salad

see page 168

red kidney beans
garlic clove
wine vinegar
olive oil
mustard powder
tarragon
salt and pepper
onion
tomatoes

Pork and Bean Casserole

1½ cups/ 12 oz/ 50 g dried haricot beans
2 large onions
2 carrots
Salt and pepper
1 tablespoon/ 15 ml oil
½ lb/ 8 oz/ 225 g lean pork
2 tablespoons/ 1 oz/ 25 g molasses
6 slices of bacon
6 pork sausages
½ lb/ 8 oz/ 225 g garlic sausage
⅔ cup/ ¼ pint/ 125 ml red wine

Soak the beans for 3 hours in enough water to cover. Do not drain but put into a large pan with the diced onions and carrots, cloves, salt and pepper, and 3 cups/ 1¼ pints/ 625 ml water. Cover and simmer for 1½ hours. Meanwhile cut the pork in pieces and brown on all sides in the oil. Put the oil into the bottom of a large casserole and put on half the beans, then the pork and the remaining beans. Add the molasses and top with bacon. Cover and bake at 150°C/300°F/ Gas Mark 2 for 4 hours. Cook sausages, cut into pieces and stir in the beans, with the garlic sausage cut in chunks and the wine. Cover and continue cooking for 30 minutes.

Kidney Bean Salad*

2 cups/ 1 lb/ 500 g red kidney beans
1 garlic clove
1 tablespoon/ 15 ml wine vinegar
3–4 tablespoons/ 45 ml olive oil
Pinch of mustard powder
Pinch of tarragon
Salt and pepper
1 small onion
3 medium tomatoes

Rinse the beans. Put them into cold water, bring to the boil, and boil for 2 minutes. Remove from the heat and leave to stand in the cooking water for 1 hour. Bring back to the boil and simmer for 1 hour until tender but not broken. Drain the beans well. Crush the garlic and mix with the vinegar, oil, mustard, tarragon, salt and pepper. Pour this mixture over the hot beans and leave them to cool. Chop the onion very finely. Dip the tomatoes into boiling water to loosen the skins. Peel them and remove the pips. Chop the tomato flesh, and mix with the onions. Stir the onion mixture into the beans, chill and serve. This salad may be made with drained canned beans.

Chili Con Carne

1 cup/ 8 oz/ 225 g red kidney beans
1 large onion
1 garlic clove
¼ cup/ 2 oz/ 50 g butter
1 lb/ 500 g raw ground beef
1 teaspoon/ 5 g chili powder
1 teaspoon/ 5 ml wine vinegar
1 teaspoon/ 5 g sugar
2 tablespoons/ 1 oz/ 25 g concentrated
   tomato purée
2 cups/ 1 lb/ 500 g canned tomatoes

Soak the beans overnight and drain them well. Cover with fresh water and cook for about 1 hour until tender but not broken. Drain the beans well. Chop the onion and crush the garlic, and cook in the butter until soft and golden. Stir in the meat and cook until well-browned and the pieces of meat are separated and not lumpy. Stir in the chili powder, vinegar, sugar, tomato purée and canned tomatoes with their juice. Stir well, cover and simmer for about 30 minutes until the mixture is creamy. Serve very hot.

Lamb and Bean Casserole

½ cup/ 4 oz/ 100 g red kidney beans
3–4 tablespoons/ 45 ml oil
3½ cups/ 1½ lb/ 750 g shoulder lamb
   (cubed)
2 leeks
1 tablespoon/ 15 g chopped parsley
Juice of 1 lemon
1 teaspoon/ 5 g dill leaves
2 teaspoons/ 10 g turmeric
1 teaspoon/ 5 g chopped mint
Salt and pepper

Soak the beans overnight and drain them well. Cover with fresh water and boil for 1 hour. Drain and reserve the cooking liquid. Heat the oil and cook the cubed lamb until lightly brown on all sides. Drain the lamb and put into a heavy pan. Cut the leeks in thin slices and fry in the oil until golden. Drain and add to the lamb with the parsley, lemon juice, dill, turmeric and mint. Season with salt and pepper and add 2⅔ cup/ 1 pint/ 500 ml of the bean cooking liquid. Cover and cook gently for 1 hour. Add the beans and continue cooking for 20 minutes. Serve hot, garnished with a little more chopped mint.

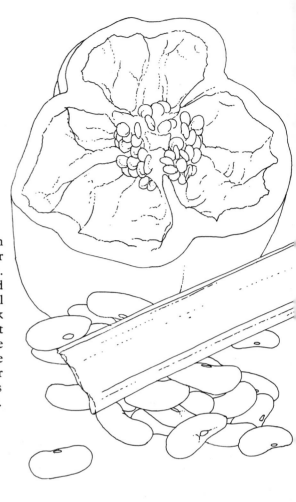

Soya Bean Loaf

1 cup/ 8 oz/ 225 g soya beans
1 chicken stock cube
Pinch of sage
1 small onion
Salt and pepper
1 teaspoon/ 5 ml Worcestershire sauce
⅔ cup/ ¼ pint/ 125 ml tomato juice
1 celery stick
1 small green pepper
1 medium carrot

Soak the beans overnight and then drain. Cook in fresh water for 1 hour. Drain and cool. Put into an electric blender with the stock cube, sage, onion, salt, pepper, Worcestershire sauce and tomato juice. Blend until smooth. Chop the celery, pepper and carrot finely and mix with the bean purée. Put into a casserole or loaf tin and bake at 200°C/400°F/Gas Mark 6 for 45 minutes. Serve hot or cold with tomato sauce.

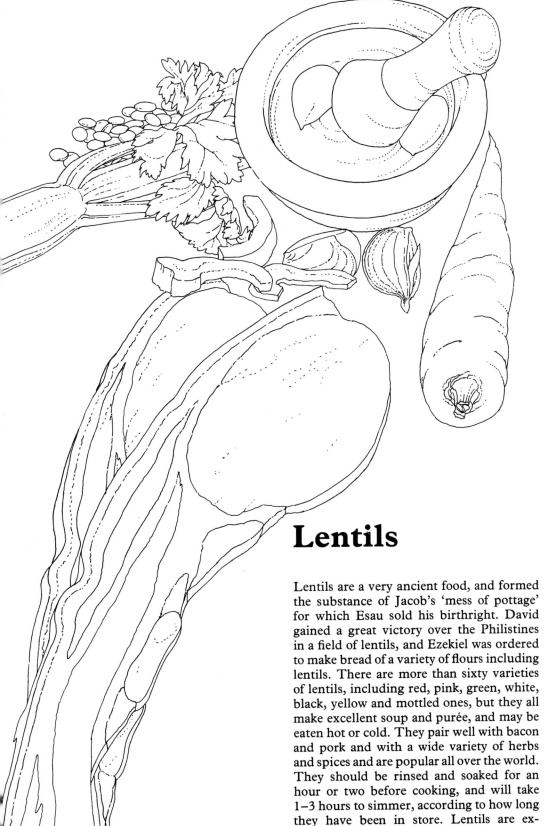

Lentil and Bacon Soup

1 onion
2 slices of bacon
2 carrots
Fat for frying
½ cup/ 4 oz/ 100 g lentils
Salt and pepper
4 cups/ 1½ pints/ 750 ml water
1 meat stock cube
2 tablespoons/ ½ oz/ 15 g cornstarch
⅔ cup/ ¼ pint/ 125 ml milk

Peel and chop the onion, chop the bacon and slice carrots. Heat the fat in a saucepan and fry onion, bacon and carrots for a few minutes. Add lentils, salt and pepper, water and stock cube. Bring to the boil and simmer for 45 minutes. Put the soup through a sieve, pressing as much of the vegetables and lentils through as possible. Return to the pan, reheat and stir in the cornstarch blended with the milk.

Syrian Lentil Soup

1 cup/ 8 oz/ 225 g red lentils
1 lamb bone
10 cups/ 4 pints/ 2.25 liters water
3–4 tablespoons/ 45 ml olive oil
2 large onions
1 large green pepper
1 lb/ 500 g tomatoes
¼ teaspoon/ 1.25 g marjoram
Salt and pepper

Rinse the lentils and soak them in cold water for 4 hours. Use a raw lamb bone or one left over after roasting, but preferably with some meat on it. Put into a large pan with the water and bring to the boil. Skim well. Add the drained lentils, cover and simmer. Heat the oil and cook the chopped onion and green pepper until soft and golden, stirring them often. Peel the tomatoes, remove the seeds and cut the flesh in pieces. Add to the onions and green pepper mixture and season with marjoram, salt and pepper. Simmer for 15 minutes. Add this mixture to the lentils, stir well and simmer until the lentils are very tender. Take out the lamb bone and cut off any pieces of meat. Chop them finely and add to the soup just before serving.

Lentils

Lentils are a very ancient food, and formed the substance of Jacob's 'mess of pottage' for which Esau sold his birthright. David gained a great victory over the Philistines in a field of lentils, and Ezekiel was ordered to make bread of a variety of flours including lentils. There are more than sixty varieties of lentils, including red, pink, green, white, black, yellow and mottled ones, but they all make excellent soup and purée, and may be eaten hot or cold. They pair well with bacon and pork and with a wide variety of herbs and spices and are popular all over the world. They should be rinsed and soaked for an hour or two before cooking, and will take 1–3 hours to simmer, according to how long they have been in store. Lentils are extremely nutritious, containing about 25 percent protein, and make a filling meal with only bread if necessary.

Stuffed Marrow

see page 86

large marrow
cooked beef or lamb
bacon or ham
onion
flour
pepper
fresh breadcrumbs
parsley
tomatoes
cooking fat

Creamed Lentils

2 cups/ 1 lb/ 500 g lentils
⅜ cup/ 3 fl oz/ 75 ml whipping cream
Salt and pepper

Soak the lentils overnight in cold water. Drain them and put into boiling water. Simmer for 3 hours and drain off any liquid which remains. Season well with salt and pepper and whip in the cream. Heat very gently for 5 minutes and serve hot with pork or bacon.

Savory Lentils

2 cups/ 1 lb/ 500 g lentils
4 slices of bacon
1 garlic clove
1 carrot
1 onion
1 bay leaf
1 sprig of thyme

Soak the lentils overnight in cold water. Drain and put into a pan with the chopped bacon, crushed garlic, finely chopped carrot and onion, and add the herbs. Just cover with water and bring slowly to the boil. Reduce the heat and simmer until the lentils are completely soft, adding a little water if necessary. When the lentils are soft and the liquid has been absorbed, season with salt and pepper and serve hot with ham, pork or bacon.

Roman Lentils

2 cups/ 1 lb/ 500 g lentils
2 medium onions
2 garlic cloves
⅔ cup/ ¼ pint/ 125 ml olive oil
12 medium tomatoes
Salt and pepper

Soak the lentils overnight. Drain well and just cover with fresh water. Bring to the boil and then simmer for 30 minutes. In another pan, cook the finely chopped onions and garlic in the oil until soft and golden. Peel the tomatoes, remove the seeds, and chop the flesh coarsely. Add to the onions and cook gently for 5 minutes, stirring well. Add the lentils and cooking liquid, and season well with salt and pepper. Continue simmering and stirring until the lentils are soft,

adding a little more water if necessary so that the lentils do not become dry. This is very good with lamb dishes.

Austrian Lentil Salad

2 cups/ 1 lb/ 500 g lentils
8 cups/ 3 pints/ 1.5 liters water
2 bay leaves
1 large onion
4 cloves
1 teaspoon/ 5 g salt
¼ teaspoon/ 1.25 g pepper
½ teaspoon/ 2.5 g mustard powder
½ teaspoon/ 2.5 g paprika
6 scallions
⅔ cup/ 4 oz/ 100 g dill-pickled
    cucumbers
3–4 tablespoons/ 45 ml wine vinegar
4–5 tablespoons/ 60 ml oil
4 medium potatoes
1 large lettuce
2–3 tablespoons/ 30 g chopped parsley
1 teaspoon/ 5 g chopped chervil

Rinse the lentils and leave them to soak in cold water for 4 hours. Put into a pan with the water, bay leaves, onion, cloves and salt. Cover and bring to the boil. Take off the heat and leave to stand for 1 hour. Cook for about 5 minutes until the lentils are just tender. Drain well, and discard bay leaves, onion and cloves. Mix the pepper, mustard, paprika, finely chopped scallions, finely chopped pickled cucumbers, vinegar, oil and a pinch of salt. Shred the lettuce and arrange on individual plates. Boil the potatoes and slice them thinly. Arrange on the lettuce and top with the lentils. Pour on the dressing and sprinkle with parsley and chervil.

Dhal

2 cups/ 1 lb/ 500 g lentils
4 cups/ 1½ pints/ 750 ml water
¼ teaspoon/ 1.25 g chili powder
1 teaspoon/ 5 g salt
¼ teaspoon/ 1.25 g turmeric
¼ cup/ 2 oz/ 50 g butter
1 large onion
1 garlic clove

Rinse the lentils and leave them to soak in cold water for 4 hours. Drain and put into the water with chili powder, salt and turmeric. Cover and simmer until the lentils are soft and the water is almost absorbed. Melt the butter in a small pan and cook the chopped onion and crushed garlic until soft and golden, stirring occasionally. Drain the lentils and put into a serving dish. Pour on the garlic and onion mixture and serve hot or chilled with curry, or with beef or lamb. The fat should be *ghee* (clarified butter), but ordinary butter will do if no clarified butter is available.

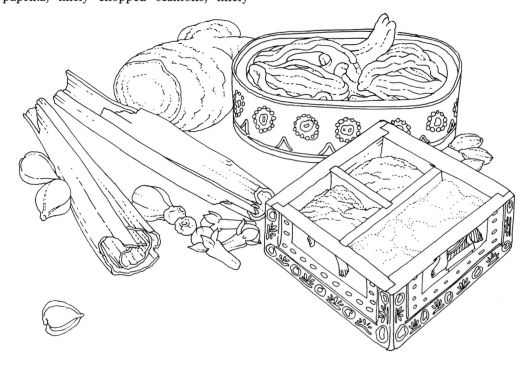

Dried Peas

Dried peas fall into four groups (a) whole green peas (b) split green peas (c) split yellow peas (d) chick peas. They are all full of flavor and go particularly well with bacon and pork. Whole green peas can be cooked to a purée with butter and seasoning to accompany fried fish or boiled bacon. Split green peas are peas which have been skinned and split and are the best to use for soup and pease pudding, and for a purée to serve with roast or grilled meat. Split yellow peas are much used in India for making small fried patties, and are the main ingredient of Swedish pea soup. Like other pulses, dried peas should be rinsed and soaked in cold water before use. Chick peas are small and very hard and may need soaking for at least 24 hours, followed by 3 hours cooking to make them palatable.

Dried spices and herbs and fresh ginger and garlic added to dried peas, beans and lentils can lead to gourmet meals which will whet the appetite of the entire family.

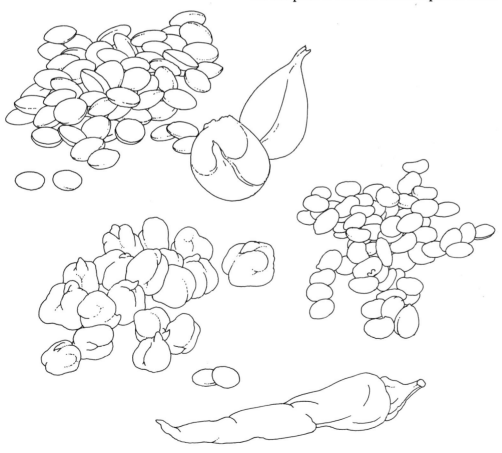

Baked Pease Pudding

2 cups/ 1 lb/ 500 g split peas
Salt and pepper
¼ cup/ 2 oz/ 50 g dripping(s)
1 medium onion

Soak the peas overnight in water. Drain well, cover with clean water and bring to the boil. Simmer for 2 hours until the peas are tender. Drain and mash well with salt and pepper and the dripping(s). Add very finely chopped onion and put into a greased baking pan. Bake at 180°C/350°F/Gas Mark 4 for 30 minutes until golden brown on top. Serve with hot or cold meat and pickled beets.

Pease Pudding

2 cups/ 1 lb/ 500 g split peas
Salt and pepper
¼ cup/ 2 oz/ 50 g butter
2 eggs

Soak the peas overnight in water. Tie them loosely in a clean cloth so that there is room for the peas to swell. Put into a pan of water and boil for 2 hours until the peas are tender. Drain and strain the peas. Mash them with salt and pepper, butter and the beaten eggs. Tie into a clean piece of cloth lightly dusted with flour, and boil again for 1 hour. Serve with boiled ham or pork, boiled beef or roast pork.

Garbanzos

2 cups/ 1 lb/ 500 g chick peas
Pinch of salt
Butter
Pinch of pepper
Pinch of paprika

Soak the peas overnight with a pinch of salt in cold water. Drain and put into a pan of boiling water. Boil for 10 minutes, then simmer for 3 hours. Drain and serve hot with salt, pepper and paprika and a piece of butter stirred in. If left until cold, dress the peas with an oil and vinegar dressing. The *garbanzo* is a chick pea which may be white, black or red and is a staple item of food in Asia, Mexico, South America and some Mediterranean countries. This recipe is from Spain. In Arab countries, the *garbanzo* is known as *hommos* or *hummus*. If the above recipe is made up with plenty of garlic and a dressing of oil and lemon juice with a liberal dressing of chopped parsley, it is very good accompanied with pieces of Greek or Arab bread.

Dutch Pea Soup

2 cups/ 1 lb/ 500 g whole or split dried peas
1 pig's knuckle
1 medium onion
3 sticks celery
1 potato
12 cups/ 5 pints/ 3 liters water
Pepper
Fried bread or toast cubes

Soak the peas overnight in cold water. Soak the pig's knuckle in another bowl of cold water overnight. Drain the peas and the bacon and put into a pan with the chopped onion, celery and potato. Cover with the water and bring to the boil. Cover and simmer for 3 hours. Remove the meat bone, discard fat and bone and chop the meat. Stir into the soup and season with pepper. Reheat and serve hot with a garnish of fried or toasted bread cubes.

CULINARY HERBS

A wide variety of fresh herbs can be grown in a small piece of ground, or even in pots or window-boxes on a patio or balcony, while one or two will actually grow in pots on a kitchen windowsill. Plants can be grown from seeds or from the division of older plants, and most of them take up little room as they grow in neat clumps. The ground round them (or the earth in the pot) should be kept clean and forked regularly to keep it light, and the plants only need a little trimming to keep in shape. The trimmings can be dried or frozen for cold-weather use. Try some of the following to give savor to vegetable dishes. Fresh herbs have a delightful fragrance and flavor which is missing from the dried variety.

Top row, left to right: variegated sage, thyme, marjoram, parsley.
Bottom row, left to right: dill, bay, sage, rosemary and fennel.

Basil

The sweet clove flavor of basil goes well with tomatoes, sausages and liver. Basil is a tender plant which hates cold, and the seeds should be sown in gentle heat and then the seedlings planted in rich warm soil or pots.

Bay

A bay tree can grow very large, but a small one is decorative in a large pot or tub. A leaf should be included in *bouquet garni*. Bay leaves give a distinctive flavor to beef, fish and milk puddings. The flavor is very strong and a single leaf, or even half a leaf, will be enough.

Caraway

The seeds should be sown one year for harvesting the next. The delicate foliage may be used to give a slight caraway flavor, but the seeds are mainly used for cabbage dishes and to flavor cakes, sweets and biscuits.

Chervil

This herb looks like parsley but has a more delicate flavor and is used for salads, egg and fish dishes. Chervil does not dry or freeze well, so it is best to sow a succession of seeds in the warmer weather keeping them well watered.

Chives

This member of the onion family grows in a cluster of small bulbs, but it is the green tops which are used to give a light onion flavor, and the finely chopped bright green tops make an attractive garnish. Chives are mainly used for salads, egg dishes, cream cheese and soup.

Coriander

This plant looks similar to caraway with feathery leaves and large seed heads, and it has a delicious scent of orange and curry. Use the seeds in sweets and curries, and the leaves in soups and stews.

Dill

A highly aromatic herb with feathery leaves and a large seed head. The herb has digestive and sedative qualities and is used a great deal in Scandinavia and central Europe. There is flavor in both the leaves and seeds which can be used with new potatoes, fish and cucumber, and in pickles.

Fennel

A highly aromatic herb with a scent of aniseed. The feathery leaves are good with fish, salads, and pickles.

Lovage

This plant has leaves like celery, and they have a hot spicy celery-like flavor when used in soups and stews.

Marjoram/Oregano

Marjoram is a highly aromatic herb with tender leaves used in stuffings, soups and stews.
Oregano is a member of the same family but grows in warm countries and has a hotter, more pungent flavor.

Mint

There are dozens of varieties of mint and the plant spreads so rapidly it should be placed away from other plants or it will smother them. Try lamb mint, apple mint, pineapple mint and spearmint for variety, and use the leaves in sauce with lamb, or chop them to garnish vegetables and salads or to use in fruit salads. A sprig of mint in the cooking water gives a subtle flavor to peas and new potatoes.

Parsley

Parsley is a most useful flavoring and garnishing herb and will flourish well in open ground or in a pot, although the seeds take a long time to germinate. Use for garnishing vegetable dishes and salads, and for flavoring fish, ham and chicken. Parsley is an essential herb in *bouquet garni*.

Below: Rosemary.

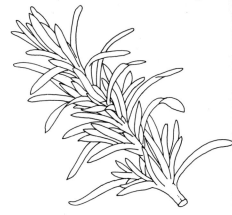

Rosemary

An aromatic shrub which needs to be grown in a sheltered place. Use for beef, duck, lamb, pork, and mushroom dishes.

Sage

There are many different varieties of this broad-leaved shrub, but all help the digestion and are reputed to ensure long life. Use with rich meat such as duck, goose, pork and sausages.

Savory

Winter savory is a perennial plant but summer savory is raised from seed, and has a more subtle flavor. Savory is known as 'the bean herb' as it is commonly used with broad beans.

Tarragon

French tarragon is the more pleasant variety; Russian tarragon is coarser in flavor. The thin leaves are an essential ingredient for classic sauces, and for chicken and fish dishes. Tarragon vinegar is particularly prized for salad dressings.

Thyme

There are many varieties of thyme, including the subtle lemon thyme. Use the tiny leaves in forcemeats and stuffings, and in salads.

Cauliflower
Polonaise

see page 50

**cauliflower
butter
white breadcrumbs
hard-boiled egg
bacon
parsley**

HERBS

Cooking with Herbs

Herb flavoring should complement the basic dish, and not overshadow it – the correct herb helps to bring out flavor and many foods have a special affinity with individual herbs.

Basic food	Complementary herbs
Beef	marjoram, rosemary, savory, thyme
Cheese	basil, marjoram, tarragon, thyme
Cream cheese	basil, caraway, chives, dill, mint, sage
Eggs	basil, chervil, chives, marjoram, tarragon, thyme
Fish	basil, chervil, chives, dill, fennel, mint, parsley, sage, thyme
Fruit	mint, rosemary
Lamb	dill, marjoram, mint, rosemary, savory
Pickles	dill, tarragon
Pork	sage, rosemary
Poultry	marjoram, parsley, sage, savory, tarragon, thyme
Salads	basil, chervil, chives, dill, fennel, mint, parsley, savory, tarragon
Veal	rosemary, sage, savory, thyme
Vegetables	basil, chives, fennel, mint, parsley, rosemary, savory, tarragon

There are a few herb mixtures which are frequently used in recipes and it is worth making up batches of these for quick use. Dried herbs are stronger in flavor than fresh ones ($\frac{1}{2}$ teaspoon/ 2.5g dried herbs equals 2 teaspoons/ 10g fresh ones), but dried or fresh mixtures can be prepared in advance and used in different proportions as needed.

Bouquet garni is a mixture of a sprig of parsley, a sprig of thyme and a bay leaf to which a sprig of marjoram may be added. Bunches of these fresh herbs may be made up and frozen in twists of foil or polythene bags. Dried powdered mixtures can be prepared and stored in small cheesecloth bags which can be put into dishes while cooking and removed before serving.

Fines herbes consist of chopped parsley, chervil, chives and tarragon.

Mixed herbs are more strongly flavored, being a mixture of chopped sage, parsley, marjoram and thyme.

Below, left to right : thyme, basil, chives, tarragon, fennel seed, marjoram, dill, sage, rosemary, bay and winter savory.

Freezing Herbs

Tender-leaved herbs which are best for freezing include tarragon, mint, parsley, chives and basil. Either pack them in small bunches in foil or polythene, or chop the herbs finely and freeze in ice-cube trays with a little water. The herb cubes can be wrapped in foil and then in polythene bags for storage. Whole herbs can be crumbled and used straight from the freezer, but will be too limp for garnishes. The herb cubes may be added to dishes while still frozen, or they can be thawed and strained before use.

Drying Herbs

Sage, thyme, marjoram, tarragon, mint, rosemary and bay all dry well, but the shrubby ones can be picked right through the year, so it may be unnecessary to dry them unless you are away from a regular supply. Gather them early in the day when the dew has just dried, and before they flower. Hang in a dry place covered lightly with muslin, cheesecloth or thin paper where the air can circulate. Crush the herbs with a rolling pin and pack in airtight tins or jars, but leave bay leaves whole. Parsley should not be dried in this way or it loses color and flavor. Wash parsley sprigs well in cold water, shake well and remove the leaves from the stems. Spread on a wire rack and dry at 190°C/375°F/Gas Mark 5 for 4 minutes exactly. Cool, crush the leaves and store in an airtight tin or jar. Dried herbs should be packed in dark glass for preference and stored away from light or they quickly lose color and flavor.

Sweet Herb Seasoning

4 tablespoons/ 2 oz/ 50 g dried parsley
4 tablespoons/ 2 oz/ 50 g dried
   marjoram
4 tablespoons/ 2 oz/ 50 g dried chervil
2 tablespoons/ 1 oz/ 25 g dried thyme
2 tablespoons/ 1 oz/ 25 g dried lemon
   thyme
2 tablespoons/ 1 oz/ 25 g dried basil
2 tablespoons/ 1 oz/ 25 g dried savory
1 tablespoon/ ½ oz/ 15 g dried tarragon

Mix all the herbs and rub them to a coarse powder or put them in an electric blender. Store in a screwtop jar and use a little when mixed herbs are required for a recipe.

Five-Herb Butter

1 teaspoon/ 5 g chopped fresh parsley
½ teaspoon/ 2.5 g chopped fresh mint
½ teaspoon/ 2.5 g chopped fresh chives
½ teaspoon/ 2.5 g chopped fresh
   tarragon
½ teaspoon/ 2.5 g chopped fresh
   marjoram
1 tablespoon/ 15 ml lemon juice
½ cup/ 4 oz/ 100 g butter

Chop the herbs very finely by hand or in an electric blender. Mix them with the lemon juice. Cream the butter until light and soft and work in the herb and lemon juice mixture. Leave to stand at room temperature for 2 hours. Pack into a screwtop jar and store in the refrigerator. Use on vegetables, fish or broiled or grilled meat.

Herb Cheese

1 cup/ 8 oz/ 225 g grated Cheddar
   cheese
1 tablespoon/ ½ oz/ 15 g chopped
   parsley
1 tablespoon/ ½ oz/ 15 g chopped
   chives
1 tablespoon/ ½ oz/ 15 g chopped thyme
1 tablespoon/ ½ oz/ 15 g chopped sage
1 tablespoon/ ½ oz/ 15 g chopped
   summer savory
2 tablespoons/ 30 ml whipping cream
4 tablespoons/ 60 ml dry sherry

The cheese should be grated very finely. Stir together the cheese and herbs and work to a paste with the cream and sherry. Press into a pot, cover and chill. Use as a topping for vegetables, or to spread on small crackers or biscuits. This makes a good filling for pieces of uncooked celery.

Cream Cheese with Herbs

½ cup/ 4 oz/ 100 g cream cheese
1 garlic clove
1 tablespoon/ ½ oz/ 15 g chopped
   parsley
1 tablespoon/ ½ oz/ 15 g chopped thyme
1 tablespoon/ ½ oz/ 15 g chopped chives
Salt and pepper

Cream the cheese with a fork and add the crushed garlic and herbs. Season with salt and pepper and form into a ball. Chill and serve with salads, or as a dressing for vegetables.

Herb Vinegar

Cider vinegar or white wine vinegar
Fresh herbs

Use herb leaves which are freshly picked before the plants flower. Put them into a wide-mouthed screwtop jar, bruising them slightly with a wooden spoon. Put the vinegar into a pan and bring just to the boil. Pour over the herbs and cover tightly. Leave in a warm place for 10 days, shaking the jar occasionally. Drain off the vinegar and fill bottles, filtering the vinegar through cheese-cloth or filter paper. For a very strong flavor, pour the unfiltered vinegar over a second batch of herbs and leave for 10 days before straining and bottling.

Tarragon, fennel, mint, marjoram, basil and dill make very good herb vinegars. To measure the herb leaves, press them down lightly in a measuring cup – 1⅓ cups/ ½ pint/ 250 ml herbs will flavor 2⅔ cups/ 1 pint/ 500 ml vinegar. These vinegars are excellent for salad dressing and mayonnaise.

Mixed Herb Stuffing

¼ cup/ 2 oz/ 50 g butter
1 small onion
1 cup/ 3 oz/ 75 g fresh white breadcrumbs
1 lemon
Salt and pepper
3–4 tablespoons/ 45 g fresh herbs
   (variety)
1 egg

Melt the butter and cook the finely chopped onion until soft and golden. Take off the heat and stir in the breadcrumbs, grated lemon rind and juice, salt and pepper. Use a variety of herbs and chop them finely. Stir them into the mixture with the egg and leave the mixture crumbly, not solid. If liked, add a little chopped bacon or ham. This stuffing may be used for poultry, but is very good for stuffing tomatoes, zucchini, peppers and eggplant.

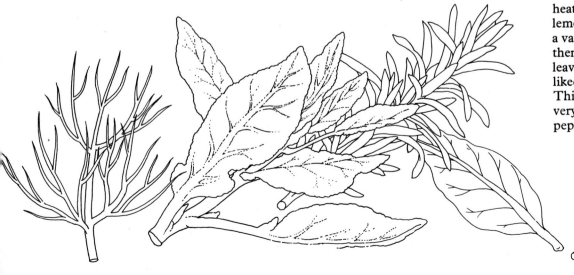

Beets in
Soured Cream

see page 30

cooked beets
soured cream
chives
lettuce leaves

HOW TO FREEZE VEGETABLES

Freezing is the best way of preserving vegetables because it keeps their flavor, color, texture and nutritive value better than any other method. Freeze only young tender vegetables immediately after harvesting, and harvest regularly, freezing the produce at once rather than waiting until a large batch is ready, by which time some vegetables will be tough and stringy.

It is recommended that no more than 3 lb (1.5 kg) of fresh food should be frozen for each cubic foot (30 liters) of freezer space at any one time. It takes about 6 hours to freeze garden produce completely, so it is possible to deal with two batches during one day.

Preparation for Freezing

Prepare vegetables just before freezing. Make plenty of extra ice and store it in the freezer during the peak freezing season, as a lot will be used during preparation. Switch to fast-freeze 2–3 hours before freezing. Wash all vegetables thoroughly in cold water, grade by size or cut as necessary. It is possible to freeze unblanched vegetables for storage for up to 3 months, but they will quickly lose color, flavor and nutritive value after that.

Blanching

Use a blanching basket or wire salad basket and a lidded saucepan which will hold at least 20 cups/ 8 pints/ 4.5 liters water, a large bowl, a colander, a stop watch or minute timer and a bucketful of ice. Blanching must be timed accurately: over-blanching results in flabby, colorless vegetables, and under-blanching means a color change and loss of nutritive value. Put 20 cups/ 8 pints/ 4.5 liters water into the saucepan with the wire basket. Bring to the boil and add the vege-

tables (not more than 1 lb/ 500 g). Put on the lid, and bring the water quickly back to the boil. Start timing as soon as it boils, and when the time is up, remove the wire basket. Tip the vegetables into the colander in a bowl of water chilled with ice cubes; running water from a tap is not cold enough. The vegetables should be chilled for the same length of time as they were blanched. Drain thoroughly and open-freeze or pack at once. Put bags in single layers in the fast-freeze compartment, or in an older freezer, see that each bag touches a side or the base of the cabinet.

Open-freezing

Many vegetables can be open-frozen before packing so that they remain separate and will pour freely. Use a baking sheet, or tray, a polythene box lid, or a special fast freeze tray with a foil lining. Spread the vegetables

Above : A head of broccoli

out in a single layer and freeze till hard. Pack in bags or rigid containers. Peas and beans are particularly suitable for open-freezing.

Packaging

Polythene bags in a range of sizes are extremely useful, but must be made of heavy-gauge material to withstand very low temperatures. They are most easily sealed with a twist-tie. Rigid containers are best for delicate produce which could be broken or damaged during storage, such as asparagus or broccoli; these are made of aluminum foil or a rigid plastic. All packages should be labeled with the date of freezing and the weight of produce, and a record kept to ensure a regular turnover of stocks. It is important to exclude air from packages in the freezer. It can be pushed out with the hands, extracted with a drinking straw or with a special pump. When a rigid container is used, allow $\frac{1}{2}$ in (1.25 cm) free space above the contents to allow for their expansion which can push off a lid.

Cooking

Vegetables are partly cooked by blanching, and need only a little additional cooking before serving. Broccoli and spinach are better partly thawed before cooking and corn-on-the-cob must be completely thawed to allow the heat to penetrate. Use the minimum of water for cooking vegetables, steam them or cook them without water in a casserole in the oven with a knob of butter.

Storage times

Most vegetables will keep well for 12 months in the freezer, but 9 months or so is about the maximum time before fresh produce is in season again.

Non-freezables

Salad vegetables which contain a lot of water, for example lettuce and radishes, are not suitable for freezing. Some crops such as celery, English chicory and tomatoes can be frozen, but are only useful for cooking and cannot be eaten raw after thawing.

Freezables

Asparagus Wash well and remove woody stems and small scales. Cut asparagus into 6-in (15 cm) lengths, and grade according to thickness. Do not tie in bundles, but blanch each size separately. Blanch 2 minutes (thin stems) 3 minutes (medium stems), 4 minutes (thick stems). Cool and drain thoroughly and pack according to size in rigid containers, alternating the heads.

Beets Use small young beets no more than 3-in (7.5 cm) in diameter. Cook completely, cool quickly and rub off skins. Pack either whole, sliced or diced. Do not freeze uncooked.

Broad beans (Lima) Use small young beans with tender skins. Remove them from the pods and blanch for 1½ minutes. Open-freeze and pack in bags.

Broccoli and Calabrese Use compact heads with tender stalks not more than 1-in (2.5 cm) thick. Trim off woody stems and outer leaves. Wash well in salted water for 30 minutes, and rinse in clean water. Blanch for 3 minutes (thin stems), 4 minutes (medium stems), or 5 minutes (thick stems). Cool and pack in rigid containers, alternating the heads. ↓

Brussels sprouts ↑ Use small compact sprouts and remove discolored leaves. Grade for size and blanch for 3 minutes (small), 4 minutes (medium). Cool, open-freeze and pack in bags.

Cabbage Shred finely and blanch for 1½ minutes. Pack in rigid containers.

Carrots Use young carrots, remove tops, wash and scrape well. Leave the small ones whole, but slice the larger ones. Blanch for 3 minutes (whole) or 2 minutes (sliced), cool, drain and pack in bags.

Cauliflower Use firm heads with close white curds. Freeze very small heads whole, or break into sprigs. Wash thoroughly. Add the juice of 1 lemon to the water and blanch for 3 minutes.

Celeriac (Celery Root) Cut into slices, add the juice of 1 lemon to the water and blanch for 3 minutes. Cool and pack in bags. Celeriac can be cooked in a little water and frozen as a purée. It cannot be used in salads after freezing.

Celery Use crisp stalks and remove strings. Wash well, cut into 1-in (2.5 cm) lengths and blanch for 3 minutes. Cool, drain and pack dry in bags. Pack some of the blanching liquid to use for cooking later. Leave ½ in (1.25 cm) headspace in rigid containers. Celery cannot be eaten raw after freezing, but is useful to serve as a vegetable, or to add to stews and soups.

Chicory, English (American Endive) Use compact heads with yellow tips. Trim stalks and remove any bruised outside leaves. Add the juice of 1 lemon to the water, and blanch for 2 minutes. Cool and drain thoroughly before packing in rigid containers. Chicory cannot be used for salads after freezing. ↓

Dwarf beans (French or String) Use young tender beans about the thickness of a shoelace. Top and tail. Freeze small beans whole, or cut into 1-in (2.5 cm) pieces. Blanch for 3 minutes (whole) or 2 minutes (cut). Cool and pack in bags.

Eggplant (Aubergines) Use tender, mature, medium-sized eggplants. Do not peel but cut into 1-in (2.5 cm) slices. Blanch for 4 minutes, cool, drain and pack in rigid containers in layers separated by plastic or freezer paper.

Parsley grows well anywhere in any climate and will seed itself.
Inset left : A bulb of garlic
Inset right : Top center – Chick Peas
Left – brown lentils
Bottom center – red lentils
Right – Soya beans

Globe artichokes ↑ Trim outer leaves and stalks and wash thoroughly removing hairy 'chokes.' Blanch for 7 minutes with 1 tablespoon (15 ml) lemon juice in the water. Cool, drain well and pack in rigid containers. Alternatively, remove all the leaves and blanch the hearts for 5 minutes. Pack in bags or rigid containers.

Herbs Pick soft-leaved herbs (basil, chervil, chives, mint, parsley, tarragon) when young. Wash the sprigs and pack them in bags. Alternatively chop the herbs finely and put them into ice-cube trays with a spoonful of water. Freeze and transfer the frozen cubes to bags for storage. This method is particularly useful for mint and parsley. Frozen herbs become limp when thawed and are not then suitable for garnishing.

Jerusalem artichokes Peel and cut into pieces. Soften slightly in hot butter and cook in chicken stock. Blend and freeze as purée in rigid containers.

Kale Use young, tender, tightly curled kale, and discard any discolored or tough leaves. Wash well and separate leaves from stems. Blanch for 1 minute and drain thoroughly after cooling. Leaves can be chopped for easier packing in bags, but do this after blanching.

Leeks Use young even-sized leeks, remove coarse outer leaves and trim off green tops. Wash in cold running water. Cut larger leeks into ½-in (1.25 cm) thick rings, but leave the small ones whole. Blanch for 3 minutes (whole) 2 minutes (sliced). Cool, drain and pack in rigid containers or in bags, but overwrap bags as leeks smell strongly.

Marrows and Zucchini Large older marrows are best cooked and frozen as purée. Cut tender young courgettes, or very small marrows into ¼-in slices without peeling. Blanch for 1 minute, or toss in hot butter until tender. Open-freeze blanched slices and pack in bags, pack the fried slices in rigid containers.

Mushrooms ↑ Grade mushrooms for size, wipe but do not peel them. Pack in bags. Small button mushrooms can be cooked in butter (⅓ cup/ 3 oz/75 g butter to 1 lb/ 500 g mushrooms) for 5 minutes and then packed in rigid containers for freezing.

Onions ↑ Peel small onions and leave them whole, but peel and chop larger ones. Blanch for 3 minutes (whole), 2 minutes (chopped). Cool, drain and pack in rigid containers or in bags, but overwrap bags as onions smell strongly.

Parsnips Old parsnips are best cooked and frozen as purée. Young parsnips should be peeled and cut into thin strips or small dice. Blanch for 2 minutes. Cool, drain and pack in bags.

Peas Use young, tender sweet peas. Blanch for 1 minute. Cool, drain and pack in bags. Peas may be open-frozen before packing. Sugar peas (edible-pod peas) should be frozen while the pods are still flat. Top, tail and string them and blanch for 2 minutes. Cool, drain and pack in bags.

Peppers Use firm, plump, glossy peppers. Wash and dry them, cut off the stems, and remove the seeds and membranes. Cut into halves, slices or dice. Blanch for 3 minutes (halves) 2 minutes (slices or dice). Cool, drain and pack in bags.

press out excess moisture. Pack in bags or rigid containers. Do not add any water during reheating.

Squashes and Pumpkins

Cook the flesh of squashes and pumpkins in very little water until soft. Mash well and freeze as purée in rigid containers.

Tomatoes

Tomatoes cannot be used for salads after freezing but they are very useful for cooking. Wipe whole tomatoes, grade them for size and freeze in bags (the skins will drop off when thawed). Alternatively cut tomatoes into halves and open-freeze before packing (these halves are useful for grilling or frying). Tomatoes may also be skinned and simmered in their own juice before mashing and freezing as purée.

Turnips, Yellow and White

Peel, dice and blanch for 2½ minutes. Cool, drain and pack in bags. These roots can be cooked completely, mashed and frozen as purée.

Potatoes

Do not freeze potatoes blanched in water, or plainly boiled old potatoes. Cooked jacket potatoes, roast, creamed, duchesse and potato croquettes can all be frozen. Chips must not be frozen raw nor boiled in water, but fried in clean fat until soft (not coloured). Drain, cool and pack in bags. New potatoes should be scraped, graded for size, and slightly undercooked. Drain, toss them in butter and pack in boil-in bags (for serving, put the whole bag in boiling water, remove from heat and leave 10 minutes).

Runner beans (Green beans)

Use young beans, no longer than 7 in (17.5 cm). Do not shred finely, but string the beans and slice them thickly. Blanch for 2 minutes, cool and pack in bags.

Spinach

Use young tender leaves without heavy ribs. Strip leaves from stems, and remove any that are bruised or discolored. Wash well and blanch for 2 minutes, shaking the wire basket occasionally so the leaves do not mat together. Cool quickly and

GLOSSARY

American	British
bacon	streaky bacon
baking soda	bicarbonate of soda
basic pastry	shortcrust pastry
batter	cake mixture
beat/whip	whisk
blender	liquidiser
broil	grill
broth	stock
can	tin
celery root	celeriac
cheesecloth	muslin
chicory	endive
cornstarch	cornflour
cream – whipping	double cream
– table	single cream
double boiler	double saucepan
eggplant	aubergine
endive	chicory
ground meat	mince
ham	ham/some bacon joints
legumes	pulses
mixer/blender	mixer/liquidiser
paper towel	kitchen towel
pie shell	flan case
raisins	sultanas and raisins
rutabaga	swede or yellow turnip
scallions	spring onions
sherbet	sorbet
skillet	frying pan
stoned (olives)	pitted
strainer	sieve
tomato paste	tomato purée
turnip	swede and white turnip
wax paper	greaseproof paper

A Note on Conversions

Comparing conversion units between recipes is not to be encouraged. Each recipe in this book has been individually tested so that the dish will turn out properly. Thus in some recipes 4 fl oz will be 100 ml and in another, 120 ml; however the other measurements of ingredients within the recipe have been adjusted accordingly. Similarly 8 oz of breadcrumbs is $2\frac{1}{4}$ cups; 8 oz of butter or sugar is 1 cup; 8 oz of flour is 2 cups.

Confusing? Pick the type of measurement you like, the one which best suits your kitchen and your utensils, AND STICK TO IT. If your utensils are metric, use the metric units. If you have measuring cups, then use the relevant quantities. Try to be consistent within each recipe and you will produce delicious, appetizing and attractive dishes.

Acknowledgments

Line drawings by Ann Winterbotham
Photographs by Derek Whitty

Index

Index